TWO MOONS IN AFRICA

Two Moons in Africa

Barbara and Brent Swan's
Story of Terrorism

To: Dale Lewis,
Thank you for Being there
for Jeff, A Long time friend
And carrying him of the
past years
Brent Swan

Patricia Camburn Behnke

To order additional copies of this book, contact:
Xlibris Corporation
1-888-795-4274
www.Xlibris.com
Orders@Xlibris.com
63073

CONTENTS

To all victims of crime who have been forced to endure the judicial system.

ACKNOWLEDGMENTS

From the Swans:

We want to thank so many people who have helped us come to this point in our lives. Words cannot express all the appreciation we feel in our hearts. Many thanks to coworkers, friends and family;
Ed, newly appointed to PHI's human resources in 1990, whose first task was, taking care of Barbara;
Gary and Scott for their help;
Rita, for her continuous support to help us understand the legal system;
Patricia, for taking on this overwhelming project; and
Joyce, for just being there.

From Barbara:

To my loving mother, who was by my side through all the ups and downs of this life-altering event. I wish she was here to see this book become a reality.
And to Brent, my soulmate.

From Brent:

I dedicate this book to my wife for her patience, understanding, and generous support. Without her, I have serious doubts that this book or I would exist.

From Patricia:

I wish to thank the Swans for allowing me into their lives and giving me the opportunity to write this book. I also want to thank those who supported me through this effort—Linda Turner, who gave me a place to write; Karen Powers, who read the book and cried; and Kevin McCarthy, for taking the time to comment on the manuscript. I also thank all of you who supported and encouraged me during this sometimes heartwarming, often arduous journey. And finally, to my dear friend Jack Hunter, who always told me to write from the heart.

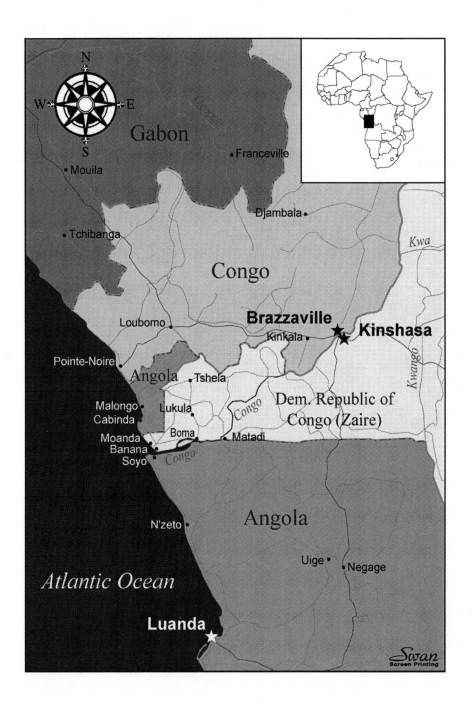

PROLOGUE

The television and the movies conclude terrorist tales when the traumatic situation ends. The survivor hugs loved ones, grins for the cameras, and skips away into the sunset. If only that scene played out in real life. No, in reality, beneath the relief, at the end of the physical terror lies the horror of the psychological terror that lasts beyond the final scene in the movie.

Barbara and Brent Swan have lived with that type of terrorism since 1990. The retreat into post-traumatic stress symptoms occurs with any trigger that takes them back to the memory of Brent's capture by rebel forces in Angola on October 19, 1990.

When I first met Barbara and Brent Swan in 2004, I knew nothing about that. Brent saw an advertisement for my writing services, so one day he decided to call me. "My wife and I might be in need of a writer," he said.

Several days later, we met for almost two hours in the back room of a sandwich shop in Alachua, Florida. As the three of us munched on salads, I sensed that their story, whatever it was, brought them considerable pain. So I spent the majority of the time filling the empty spaces left by their lack of disclosure. I talked about the publishing business, I talked about my life as a reporter, and I touched on the tragedies in my life. Only then did I sense a bond forming. I assured them I understood grief because I knew they suffered from a deep wound. After my bout of verbal diarrhea, I still didn't know why they wanted to see me.

"I think I've got a story to share," Brent finally said.

And then he told me enough for me to realize the man was absolutely right.

We walked out to the Swans' car. Brent pulled out an album with pictures of him in the jungle surrounded by men holding AK-47s.

"How did you get these photos?" I asked as the sun beat down on us in the parking lot on that sunny, spring day.

"They gave them to me when they released me," Brent said.

A story to tell, indeed.

I went home and began searching the Internet for "Brent Swan." Brent went home and promptly put all the books and albums back into the Angola box and took the box back to the basement.

Then I didn't hear from Brent again until January 2005.

"We came home and decided to forget about writing the book," Brent told me later. "We told you we'd think about it, but instead we packed everything back into the box."

But that didn't mean Brent had forgotten about it.

"The box sat there like a sore thumb with a festering wound," he said.

"How many times can you open the box and then put it away?" Barbara asked. "It's still going to be there."

The rest of 2004 brought no resolution for the Swans. In the fall, their therapist suggested they call that writer and write the book so the whole thing could be purged from Brent's brain and hopefully from Barbara's as well.

Brent considered the suggestion. On New Year's Day 2005, he made a resolution to do something about the box. He no longer wanted the box to have any power over him. It loomed as large as their comfortable home. He took things out of the box and then put them back in again.

"I thought about burning it, destroying it," Brent said. "But does it go away when you do that? Probably not. Did it go away when I put it in the basement?"

When Barbara found him in the basement one day, fiddling with the items in the box, she said, "We've got Pat's number. Let's make the call wherever it might take us."

Brent called me the second time on January 21, 2005.

"I'm ready to take the next step," he said. "And I'd like you to help me."

His voice had changed. Before where there had been tentativeness, I now heard determination. Where there had been fear, I now sensed courage. And where there had been doubt, I now knew he was sure.

We met again four days after his call, in the same back room.

"I hope first impressions really stick," he said when we greeted one another. "I'm not doing as well as I was back in March."

He wore a green military hat, and his beard looked heavier than it had the last time we met. I soon discovered that Brent let his beard grow beginning every October 19, the anniversary of his capture.

"I thought you sounded much stronger when you called Friday," I said.

Brent showed me his hat during our second meeting. He had worn it during his sixty-one days of captivity. A pin with the acronym FLEC rested next to a small hole that had been patched.

"That's a bullet hole," he said. "It's a hat they forced me to wear with that hole over the forehead."

Brent refers to it as "the dead man's hat."

"It doesn't bother you to wear it?" I asked.

"He wore it for you today," Barbara said.

I realized this would be more than a job. I had been given a sacred trust and a gargantuan responsibility.

"When you interview me about being in the jungle, you need to do one other thing," Brent said. "If you bring me into the jungle, you need to bring me back out again."

When Brent wore his "dead man's" hat that day, it meant he had opened the box fully and felt ready to bring things out into the daylight. In addition, donning the hat was an act of defiance and an act of control. He could decide when the hat went on his head and when it came off.

Both Barbara and Brent seemed anxious to begin the project, so we talked about logistics and legalities during this meeting. We also discussed economics. They decided to hire me to write a book proposal, which would include the first three chapters of *Two Moons in Africa*, an outline for the rest of the book, and the market plan. Brent was concerned about ownership of the story, and I was concerned about authorship. Barbara and Brent agreed that my name should be listed as the writer of the book, but I needed to investigate copyright.

I drew up a contract, but Brent was not comfortable signing it because he was afraid he was turning over his story. At the time I remember wondering how we could complete anything, but soon I began to understand that he feared losing control of what rightfully belonged to him. We finally signed the contract on February 8, 2005—the day of the new moon—at their home in Chiefland.

We began meeting regularly a few weeks later in the upstairs spare bedroom that I called *Two Moons* Central the first time I saw it. I was apprehensive because I knew I had been given a large responsibility, which on the surface seems to be rather simple. I turn on the tape recorder, I listen and watch as Brent and Barbara talk, and I take little notes here and there.

From the beginning it was obvious the sessions with Brent would be unlike any other interview I had conducted. I would come with a plan for the day's questions, but Brent always starred as the director of these sessions. I felt frustrated at first because it was so different from what I was accustomed to as a journalist. But in hindsight, and with all the research I have done on post-traumatic stress disorder, I see now that the only way Brent could tell the story to me would be if he maintained total control of how he told it. And as I let go of the hold I had as the interviewer, I sensed Brent began to trust me.

We met from 10:00 a.m. to 2:30 p.m. on that first day. I wanted background information about their lives. But probably more important, I wasn't ready to take him into the jungle. I wanted to be sure I knew how to bring him out of the jungle before that happened.

> Pat's Notes – Day One
>
> *They [Brent and Barbara] had been busy since we last talked. The spare bedroom in the upstairs of their home had been turned into Two Moons Central. They had spread out materials on one double bed and had purchased a fax/copier. We began talking. Brent seemed eager to share, but I was careful we did not go "into the jungle" today. I wanted to know how they met and get background information, which I did. I asked Brent why he asked Barbara to marry him after four years of living together. He perked up and a glint appeared in his eyes. "Because I loved her," he said. A boyish grin emerged from the beard. I have much to sift through in the next few days.*

We met again several weeks later, and at the beginning of the second session, Brent put on his "dead man's hat."

"I'm going into the jungle today," he said.

Pat's Notes – Day Two

Tough day going over day of capture. Two hours of taping Brent's account. Fifteen minutes with Barbara. The journey into the jungle wore me down, but Brent appeared buoyed and somewhat lighter. Although that seems to be his external face, he tells me internally that the diarrhea has begun again, and the rash on his rear begins to bother him within days of my visit. Today (March 17) when I arrive, Barbara has taken her mother to the doctor. Brent tells me that Barbara has had a bad time since my last visit. She had to give a deposition for a lawsuit at her job, and the memory of giving a deposition so soon after the ones given for Brent's kidnappers brings everything to the front for her.

When she returns today, she's rattled, but soon settles into a routine as we make it to base camp."

I conducted seven interview sessions with the Swans, each lasting four to five hours. We established a routine where we would work for two hours and then break for lunch, finishing up by three o'clock. There were days when I sensed Brent wanted to continue, but mentally, physically, and emotionally, I couldn't do any more. The sessions exhausted me, and sometimes my eyelids drooped and my mind refused to accept any further information. I felt a huge responsibility to end each session in a way that would leave Brent in as good a place as possible, and when I was not with the Swans, I was reading and researching and transcribing those tapes, which took hours. It was an exhausting process.

If I can feel such a heavy burden in just hearing the story, then I can only imagine how it must be for the Swans to have lived it every day for nearly twenty years.

I received a call from Brent on June 24, 2005, two days after I turned over the seventeen-chapter outline and proposal. He left a message on my cell phone. His voice scared me when I heard it. He spoke in a monotone. He sounded dead.

"I guess you got chapter 18 now," he said. "They just arrested terrorist number two."

Fifteen years after his kidnapping and the case was opened all over again, but this time Brent and Barbara resolved to not be the victims any longer.

Even though our professional relationship only covered the writing of the proposal, I wanted to finish this story and write more than just the first three chapters. Beginning in July 2005, I began writing the entire book and indeed discovered I had a chapter 18.

Two Moons in Africa became more than a job. I felt a deep desire to tell this story in its entirety. Barbara and Brent have been victims for nearly twenty years, and very few people seem to understand. When no one listens, the whole of the individual human experience becomes discounted, as if it does not matter. For too long, Barbara and Brent have been pawns on a chessboard filled with oil rigs and dollar signs. Angola, FLEC, and the U.S. government do not care that Barbara sleeps very little or that Brent cannot work any longer. They only care if Brent can testify in court or attest to FLEC's cause in an interview. The troubles of one family in Chiefland, Florida, matter little in the political and economic maneuverings of countries, factions, and big business.

And so I joined the journey of Barbara and Brent Swan as they struggled to become whole once again. It has been my pleasure to listen to their story and my honor to bring the story alive in the pages of this book.

Two Moons in Africa brings Brent out of the jungle with Barbara at his side. It is the story of Brent's literal journey into a dark and dank jungle at the hands of rebels. It is the story of Barbara's journey as well as she awaited first his release and then his recovery. It is the story of the love between two people who suffered and survived. Bringing both Barbara and Brent out of that jungle begins with the telling of their story of ordinary people put in extraordinary circumstances.

Chapter 1

Just Another New Moon in Africa

Reuters—Chevron Corporate Communications

LUANDA, Angola (Oct. 19, 1990)—Angola said Friday UNITA rebels had kidnapped an American working in the oil-rich Cabinda enclave.

Official sources said the kidnap victim, named as Brent Swan, is a helicopter mechanic working for the U.S. firm Chevron in the Cabinda oil fields. He has worked in Angola since 1983.

Angolan sources said Swan's family was told of his kidnap by the rebels through the Angolan legation at the United Nations in New York.

A statement issued in the Angolan broadcast media said the kidnap could be a reprisal by National Union for the Total Independence of Angola rebels for a vote by the U.S. House of Representatives to suspend lethal aid to UNITA.

The Capture

Brent Swan stared down the barrel of an AK-47 assault rifle after halting his truck on the road to Cabinda City, Angola. A movement at the passenger window caused him to turn his head to the right, only to find a grenade launcher that resembled a cannon.

Minutes earlier, he had been cruising south down a road that paralleled the Atlantic Ocean, having left Malongo, the Chevron oil compound, at six o'clock on Friday morning, October 19, 1990. The fog lay heavy around his new company pickup as he drove to the airport in Cabinda City, and the ever-present odor from the flares burning off excess natural gas at Malongo permeated the air.

He needed to be at the Cabinda airport to inspect the oxygen masks on the King Air before the plane took off for Luanda, the capital of Angola. Cabinda, one of Angola's eighteen provinces, does not border any part of Angola, but is separated from its governing body by the Democratic Republic of Congo, known in 1990 as Zaire.

As Brent drove toward the airport, the sky lightened, but the day remained overcast. The Atlantic Ocean pounded the coastline to his right and before him lay a tropical savannah in the coastal lowlands of the country. Farther inland, the rainforests of Cabinda ruled the terrain.

Brent passed six Angolan policemen on the left side of the road. They wore the red berets of the military or FAPLA, the People's Armed Forces for the Liberation of Angola. The communist government of Angola had formed FAPLA to keep the country's insurgents under control, and by 1988 it represented "one of the largest and most heavily armed militaries in Africa," according to the Library of Congress. Its force of one hundred thousand included fifty thousand Cuban troops. Training and weapons came from the Soviet Union, which had adopted the AK-47 in 1949 for its motorized infantry.

No matter how well armed and how strong the military might have been, the sight of these soldiers did not alarm Brent. He slowed the vehicle because a bus was parked in the middle of the lane. He had only driven his truck twice, both times under dry conditions. Uncertain how it would react on this road, wet and slippery from the previous night's rain, he slowed down sooner than he normally would have.

As he approached the bus, three men rushed out of the tall grass. One fired an AK-47 at the bus.

Brent simultaneously heard the shots and saw flames coming from the gun. The AK-47 shooter strode over to the truck and aimed it at Brent.

In one swift motion, the man opened the door and pushed Brent out of the driver's seat. Brent tried to keep his foot on the brake—to no avail. The man at the passenger side window held the grenade launcher pointed at Brent. When the truck began to roll, the soldier banged the weapon against the window until Brent understood. He leaned over and pulled up the lock.

Brent Swan began his twenty-eight-day stint as an aircraft mechanic at Malongo on October 17, 1990, having left his home and wife Barbara in Chiefland, Florida, on Monday, October 15. He arrived in Angola on Wednesday afternoon. The first two days after his arrival in Cabinda followed the same routine he had established six years earlier when he received the overseas assignment. His "opposite," the mechanic who had completed his twenty-eight-day stint, and Brent went over the mechanical details on the Beechcraft King Air, a twin-engine turboprop used by the managers and executives of Chevron, Halliburton, and other oil companies and contract companies such as Petroleum Helicopters Inc., Brent's employer.

As usual, Brent wrote to Barbara during his flight to Africa. Once in Angola, he gave the letter to the mechanic he replaced, who mailed it when he arrived in the States on Thursday. Barbara received that letter the day after she learned of her husband's disappearance.

Brent had worked the 28/28 schedule since 1984, but hoped to increase his overtime hours so he could earn additional pay to go toward the building of their home on the secluded pine-laden seventeen-acres in rural north Florida. He wrote to Barbara about his hopes and dreams for the future.

October 17, 1990
Hi Sweetheart,

> *Hope you had a good birthday—wish I could have been there to enjoy it with you.*
> *I've got some good news / bad news, however you want to look at it. Dad always told me if you want something, then you've got to work for it. And he made me earn every penny for that ten-speed out in the barn. Next time I'll be home for three weeks, leaving one week early on December 3, one week of work-over, then normal four weeks. Mike Carriere don't know it yet, but I might put in another week of work-over so maybe it's three, work six, off three. It sure will help buying the land in the middle of building house. I guess if you want it, you've got to earn it. The bad note is I'll be away for a whole six weeks.*

My plane just came in.

Oh, Mike Carriere's dad died. He was only here three days,
went home, then came back for two weeks.

I love you,
Brent

The drive to Cabinda City at the beginning of the hitch was routine until Brent reached the third village. Even though he'd slept well the night before, the effects of jet lag had left him groggy.

Brent began writing a journal on November 13, 1990, his twenty-sixth day of captivity.

"I have no idea why I chose to write this, except that it will occupy time. It seems I'll have a lot of it. I'd much rather be looking back on all this than being in the middle of it. But just in case somewhere along the line somebody wants to know every detail about what happened, it'll be here, at least all that I can recall. It's been almost four weeks since day one."

On that first day of writing, using scraps of paper and a pen from his carry bag, he wrote about the first half of day one in captivity. By the time he began chronicling his stay, he thought in terms of the number of days in captivity.

Day One—October 19, 1990

In Malongo, I woke to the sound of rain on October 19, the first day of rain onshore. I had just arrived two days ago on Wednesday. Still in jet lag stage, I hoped to sleep well that night. We had an oxygen mask inspection scheduled for 6:30 a.m., so I hustled about after waking.

I met Joe Kettles [area manager of PHI] at the mess hall and asked him if the rain would delay the inspection. He said, "Ask the pilots. If one wants to go with you, no problem." [The pilots could receive clearance easily, if needed.] I talked to BJ, and thank God, BJ and Bill [pilots] decided to go by helicopter. However, as I write this, I selfishly think I could sure use some company right now.

I departed Malongo at 6:00 a.m. sharp. I was glad it was raining because it would knock down the dust, and hence, airborne disease. I knew this hitch would go by fast. I just had six weeks off and scheduled maintenance on the King Air was good. There would be enough to do—maybe I'd bust ass here and there, but overall it would be a good hitch, I thought that morning. Was I ever wrong about that.

I had just passed through the third village en route to the airport. I might have been three-fourth of a mile past when I saw a bus stopped in the middle of the road on the crest of the next hill. I passed half a dozen military and slowed before going around the bus, but I never got around the bus.

Just before I got to it, all hell broke loose with military coming out of the grass all around me. Automatics were rapping out a cadence, and in the blink of an eye, I was surrounded, looking down two AK-47s in front and a grenade launcher at the passenger window.

I realized my hands were up by my head, and I wasn't dead yet, so I must be doing something right. One AK jumped in the driver's side, and the grenade launcher jumped in the passenger side along with another AK, and I was shoved in the middle. And then I noticed this asshole outside the truck taking pictures.

Brent's truck was stopped in the middle of the road as he drove to work. His abductors are inside the truck with Brent in the middle of the front seat when this photo was taken by an asshole.

The driver turned us around and went back about two hundred feet and took a right off the main road, and pulled a piece of paper from his pocket, which had four names on it. "Schumacher, Carriere, Swan, Bouillion." [The names of the four PHI employees allowed to leave base.] He verified I was Swan and punched it. We drove due east, inland, at about sixty miles per hour. I'm asking all the questions I can think of, and all I got was, "No problema."

I grabbed the radio mike and got heliport King Air maintenance. I meant to say "Mayday" but the mike disappeared and the radio got ripped out of the rack. I know I transmitted but was on "A" channel. I heard no response. We got inland I guess about three to five miles, and they stripped the truck and headed south. About twenty minutes later the rest of the troops caught up making a total of eighteen, with one captured Angolan Police.

When the truck was stripped, so was I. My pockets were emptied and my watch taken, so time is estimated here. We walked an hour south-southeast, mostly across open field scattered with six—to seven-foot-high bushes and then into trees maybe one hundred yards. The carpet from the truck was laid on the ground, and I could sit down.

A cup of water was provided, but yuck. I drank it anyway. Here I was told, "Don't be afraid." After all that, don't be afraid. I'm surrounded now by twenty-five combat soldiers, destination unknown, but don't be afraid. Shit.

"We are not FAPLA, we are FLEC. Don't be afraid. We only want you for your government."

Brent is followed by the Angolan policeman who also had been captured on the same day by members of FLEC. The FLEC rebels are leading the men away from the road at 7:30 a.m. on October 19, 1990.

Brent tried that first day in captivity to remember everything. He noticed the abandoned aboveground pipeline that snaked all around Cabinda before it went offshore to the oil fields. That pipeline had been blown up several times by rebel forces. Chevron had to quit using it because of the rebels. This fact represented the extent of Brent's knowledge of rebel groups in Cabinda until his capture by FLEC.

He knew when they said they were not FAPLA he was in trouble because Angola's police force always treated the workers from Malongo with respect. He did not know of any other groups except those that blew up things. The name FLEC meant nothing to him except that they were not the Angolan police.

Brent had enjoyed an easy relationship with the locals during his previous hitches in Cabinda. He brought items from the United States for the workers at the airport and traded it for local art. His home in rural Florida contained woodcarvings and paintings traded for items not available in Angola, such as cosmetics, cameras, and watches.

Brent helped Bunda, one of Brent's assistants at the airport, build his home. When the King Air left the airport for the day, Bunda and Brent hopped in the truck and traveled around the city, either trading items or dealing with the red tape of Bunda's life.

Brent spent at least two weeks during one of his hitches with Bunda trying to secure gas for his home so that his family had fuel with which to cook. They never did get the task accomplished.

"Malongo has such an overabundance of natural gas that they burn those flares 24/7," Brent said. "But between the red tape and fees to get the tanks filled for the locals, it ends up costing more than the gas.

"Chevron is just there for the oil," he said. "There is no way to economically transport natural gas, and they won't build a pipeline for the locals because Chevron can't make money."

And so just miles from a wealth of petroleum, the poor of Cabinda often go without. The contrasts in this temperate climate did not escape Brent's sense of irony.

"Here's these rich oil deposits and the most beautiful sunsets I have ever seen," he said, "amidst the poorest people I have ever seen."

Back in the United States, the *New York Times* ran a story on October 19, 1990, about Americans increasing dissatisfaction with the U.S. government as the November elections drew near. Many interviewed for the article felt that everyone in Washington should be voted out.

Also in the news that day is as follows: "In Lebanon, 750 were killed in the defeat of that country's General Michel Aoun. Just before the deadly fight, American and British hostages in Beirut were moved to a small village in eastern Lebanon."

Elsewhere, rock star Madonna released a video in which she wore an American flag urging young people to vote.

One American citizen taken hostage in Angola did not even make the news in the big papers back in the United States, even though Chevron sent out a press release.

The Folks at Home

In Chiefland, Florida, Barbara Swan slept unaware that her husband had been abducted on his way to a routine day of work. When she woke, she went to the kitchen and began poaching eggs for her breakfast. She still wore her pajamas when Gary Weber, Petroleum Helicopter Inc.'s vice president of the Foreign Relations Department, called.

Barbara knew as soon Gary Weber identified himself that something was wrong.

He told her there had been an accident in Cabinda, and Brent had been abducted. He could provide no details on the event except that it probably happened around 6:00 a.m., Angolan time. By the time Gary called Barbara, Brent had been missing for almost nine hours.

In 2002, Barbara wrote about her husband's abduction.

It's amazing how the mind works—the details you remember after so long and the major things you forget. I'm having a difficult time putting this on paper, but I'll try.

I can even remember what I had for breakfast that morning, but don't ask me what I had yesterday for breakfast. I had eaten poached eggs and was getting ready for work. I was still in my pajamas when Gary called. I knew something was wrong when I heard his voice, just because Brent had just started his hitch. Why else would Gary be calling unless something was terribly wrong? Gary has a very deep, serious sounding voice, and it was hard to comprehend what he was telling me. I remember asking him "What do you mean abducted?" It was not a word in my vocabulary. He had very little details, just that his truck was found abandoned by the side of the road and everything was gone, including Brent. No notes, no sign, or no indication of who might have done this. He told me he would be in touch as soon as he had more information.

After he hung up, I leaned against the wall in the kitchen, and my back followed the wall to the floor. I was crying so hard that I could not think, and when I finally could, I did not know who to call first or what to do. It was such a feeling of fear and complete helplessness. I tried to call my mother first, but there was no answer. I called Brent's mother, Denise, and she was home. When I told her, she began crying immediately and said, "I never knew it would

come to this." Somehow we finished the conversation, and I called
my mother in New Hampshire. She couldn't understand me—I was
incoherent—she thought someone had died.
I was in shock, disbelief, denial, and so alone.

Not knowing what to do, Barbara went to her job at Wal-Mart. She remembers Gary asking her what she wanted to do next. "Go to work," she said. Gary probably meant in the whole scheme of things, but Barbara could not think beyond the immediate. She also wondered how she could call her supervisor and say, "I can't come into work today because my husband has disappeared into the jungles of Africa." She did not think anyone would believe her.

So she went to work. A few hours later, her uncle Arthur came into the store. She saw him walk down the main aisle toward her. He wrapped her in his arms, giving her a bear hug. They stood that way for a few moments. Barbara suspected Arthur fought to gain control over his emotions during the time they hugged. When he finally spoke, Barbara heard his voice crack.

"Barbie, we have no idea what this can mean."

Until then, Barbara functioned by rote, in a state of shock where the enormity of the situation did not penetrate her consciousness. Standing there with her uncle, watching him fight the tears in the middle of Wal-Mart, the reality hit her, and it hit her hard. Her husband had been abducted. With the effects of shock no longer protecting her, she put her hands to her face and cried.

Barbara agreed to go home, to await the unknown. Her mind refusing to accept that Brent might have been hurt, she concentrated on the practical matters.

"He always wore his glasses on the plane," Barbara said. "And then when he got to Malongo, he would put in his contacts, so I'm thinking, 'What if something happens and he loses a contact or he has to take one out because he gets dirt in it.' He can't see without them.

"I wasn't worrying about him being dead at this time," she said. "It wasn't until a few days later that I started thinking about other possibilities."

Brent's sister Melanie, a teacher living in Maine near Brent's parents, began jotting down notes almost immediately after she heard her brother had been taken hostage. At first, her notes just contained facts to be kept near the phone.

October 19, 1990
Brent A. Swan, age 31
Resides: Chiefland, FL
Married: Barbara Tilton Swan (originally from NH)
Parents: Hugh and Denise Swan, Maine
Employed by: PHI, Petroleum Helicopters, Inc., as an aircraft
mechanic for the aircraft that Chevron Oil leases from PHI
The Chevron compound is in Cabinda, Angola
The compound is protected by Cuban troops
Angola is in Civil War
State Department contact has called Barb to let her know they
were working on it
Mom and Dad have decided to try to keep the press out of it. They
do not want the group to know how to contact them
There is no embassy in Angola, but there is one in Zaire
Surrounding countries have been notified

"Everything was so confusing and happening so fast," Melanie said.
"People were contacting Mom and Dad, and we had no idea who they
were. I thought it would help to begin organizing names and numbers and
facts—to help keep track of everything," Melanie said. "Later it became
my job, something I could do to help. We all felt so helpless."

The first reports came from Gary Weber, who had been assigned to help
Barbara and the family. He called Barbara three times on that first day. The
family clung to anything to give them hope in those first few hours. Melanie
wrote down the facts as they came to the Swans. However, they soon learned
that not all the news accounts coming out of Angola were accurate.

Melanie continued documenting the facts as they were reported to
the family.

> *Brent was abducted at gunpoint in the early morning. He*
> *had been driving to work at the airport hangar from the Chevron*
> *compound. They found his pickup truck. The radio was gone, but*
> *the tools were left there. There were two local people who witnessed*
> *it. A police officer had also been taken and released about the same*
> *time. Possibly taken by FLEC, a political group, which has taken*
> *hostages before. They may also have some Portuguese hostages. This*
> *group normally doesn't release demands or information for a few*

days after abduction. Brent may have been moved to Zaire. Chevron Oil may be the target. They said to be clear in any press releases that Brent works for PHI, not Chevron. Brent knows several local people and has good relations with them. The area has been very quiet lately, no gunfire or fighting in this area.

The Trouble with Angola

Malongo sits on the coast of Cabinda, the 2,807-square-mile Angolan enclave, as a fortress to the abundant oil reserves offshore. Malongo, often referred to as Cardboard City because of its hastily constructed buildings that housed workers for the American companies, which had been contracted by Sonangol, Angola's state-owned oil company, to bring that oil up out of the ground and export it abroad. Despite Malongo's presence in Cabinda, barbed wire and a well-guarded gate kept its expatriate workers inside or offshore. Brent Swan was only one of a handful of foreigners in 1990 who could leave the compound, but only between the hours of 6:00 a.m. and 8:00 p.m.

Even though Angola claims Cabinda as their own, many Cabindans desire independence as a separate country. Cabinda provided two-thirds of Angola's oil production in 1990, according to a report by the Center for Strategic and International Studies in Washington DC. They estimated that Angola's total oil revenues provided 95 percent of the government's earnings, yet the government directed only 1 percent of that amount back into Cabinda itself. The vast amount of oil under the ground, both onshore and offshore, result in approximately one million barrels of crude oil being produced in this enclave daily.

In 1990, Angola's communist government depended upon the military support of Cuba and Russia to protect its resources. Malongo, managed by Chevron and other American oil companies, contracted with PHI to keep its helicopters running back and forth to the offshore oil rigs. The King Air also needed expert maintenance to stay in tip-top shape for all the VIPs who traveled back and forth to the Angolan capital of Luanda.

Angolan troops had installed three barbed fences around Malongo, spaced thirty to fifty feet apart, running parallel to each other all around the camp. Brent said it was common knowledge that the troops had placed land mines between the outer fencing and the middle one. Other sources confirm that land mines existed in and around the multilayered barbed wire surrounding the compound.

On the outside of the fence surrounding Cardboard City, Cuban soldiers guarded Malongo in 1990, although the Cuban presence in Cabinda began lessening by 1990 as communism began losing its control in Angola. This political shift may have caused fighters for Cabindan independence to believe the time was perfect to pressure United States and European companies operating in Cabinda for support. After all, for years the United States had been funding UNITA, another Angolan rebel group, intent on overthrowing the communist government of Angola.

Despite being in a communist country, as a U.S. citizen, Brent never had trouble with the Cuban and Angolan military guards.

"It was a unique situation," he said. "It was something you wouldn't see anywhere else in the world.

"Their position was to protect the Americans and to see that nobody got hurt. They wanted to let the Americans do what they needed to do because we were getting the oil out of the ground for them, which was making money for them," Brent said.

The checkpoints could be annoying, but Brent enjoyed more freedom than others because he could actually leave Malongo, and he was seldom detained in his travels. Brent's work took him to the airport and only three other PHI employees were allowed the luxury of leaving Cardboard City without a special permit to travel.

Some of the executives lived in Luanda in Angola proper, several hundred miles south of Cabinda. They flew on the King Air to and from the airport in Cabinda City and, from the airport, took helicopters the seventeen miles north to Malongo and back again. Brent's assignment allowed him to work his days at the airport, leaving Cardboard City and driving to Cabinda City. The drive generally took him thirty-five minutes on a good day.

When Angola achieved its independence from Portugal in 1975, civil war broke out among three liberation movements within the country. One of them, UNITA, became the first suspect in the disappearance of Brent, but within hours of his capture, the focus had turned elsewhere.

As the civil war in Angola proper seemed to be ending in 1990 with the coming of elections, eyes turned to the 2,807-square-mile enclave of Cabinda located along the Atlantic Ocean and separated by the other provinces of Angola by twenty-five miles of Zaire.

—

Those living in Cabinda did not want to be a part of Angola nor did they want to be recognized as Angolans. They considered themselves Cabindans. Many Cabindans did not see the benefits of the rich natural resources as most of Cabinda's people remained illiterate and without the means to pull themselves out of the poverty that existed there.

FLEC, or the Front for the Liberation of the Cabinda Enclave, formed even before Angola's independence from Portugal. Several Cabindan nationalist groups came together in 1963 in the Congo and formed FLEC, and in 1967, this group created a government in exile and continued to fight for Cabindan independence throughout the 1970s and '80s, quietly and ineffectually.

A month before Brent's kidnapping, on September 20, 1990, FLEC claimed responsibility for the kidnapping of Portuguese workers in Cabinda, and some, such as Gerald J. Bender, PhD, professor at the University of Southern California and Angolan scholar, raised the possibility that FLEC might present a threat to the area. In July of 1990, he wrote in an article on FLEC, "In terms of motivation, then, FLEC may be positioning itself to have a piece of any future nation-wide political settlement."

Members of FLEC blamed the Angolan government for the situation in Cabinda and called Angola's treatment of the Cabindans a form of genocide, just one of their many claims against Angola. FLEC hoped that Chevron and the United States would be benevolent and open to their cause.

And Brent Swan became FLEC's pawn in a quest to achieve recognition and funds to become their own small nation.

CHAPTER 2

A Hammock in the Jungle

Associated Press

LUANDA, Angola (Oct. 19, 1990)—A U.S. helicopter mechanic for a company contracted by Chevron Corp. was kidnapped in northern Angola, the Portuguese news agency reported Friday.

Angolan officials declined to confirm the report, and it was not immediately possible to contact Cabinda Gulf, which contracts with Chevron in the southwest African nation.

Bonnie Chaikind, a spokeswoman at Chevron headquarters in San Francisco, had no further information about the report.

The LUSA news agency identified the kidnapped man as Brent Swan. It did not give his hometown.

According to the LUSA report, Swan was kidnapped early Friday in the province of Cabinda, an oil-rich enclave surrounded by Zaire.

No group claimed responsibility for the kidnapping by late Friday, LUSA said.

Chevron operates a joint venture with the Angolan state oil company to operate platforms in the Atlantic Ocean.

Last month, two Portuguese aid workers were kidnapped by a Cabinda separatist group linked to U.S.-backed rebels fighting Angola's Marxist government.

The Portuguese government said the Front for the Liberation of Cabinda Enclave was holding the two in Zaire.

The front is linked to the National Union for the Total Independence of Angola, or UNITA, which has been fighting the Soviet-backed government since Angola gained independence from Portugal in 1975.

Under a 1988 peace agreement, about 12,000 Cuban troops remaining in Angola are due to withdraw by mid-1991.

Sleeping with Guards

The men walking alongside Brent carried either an automatic weapon or a grenade launcher. Some of them had grenades clipped to their vests. Brent assumed the arms came from the same place as the red berets that caused Brent to make his earlier false assumption. As they walked through the open field with knee-high grass and scattered trees, more FLEC soldiers met them.

The new soldiers brought another captive, and Brent recognized his uniform as that of an Angolan policeman. He wore the simple olive drab outfit adorned by a pin with a medallion and ribbons. At one point, the man was taken away from Brent and brought back blindfolded. They continued walking for another hour until they came to the edge of the grasslands and entered a wooded area.

They pulled the truck's carpet out of one of the backpacks and laid it on the ground for Brent. As he sat there waiting for something to eat, the FLEC soldiers dragged the policeman down the trail toward Brent.

"He didn't want to come with them," Brent said. "He was fighting all the way, but they brought him in front of me, and they took his blindfold off."

Then the soldiers began pointing at Brent, talking in their native dialect tinged with Portuguese.

"It was obvious to me that they wanted that policeman to see me," Brent said.

They turned the policeman around and took him back down the same trail. The men followed a curve in the path, and soon Brent could not see them any longer, but he could hear the shouts and arguing. He heard gunfire.

Then silence.

—

"I have trouble believing that the policeman was not killed," Brent said.

Someone claiming to be that policeman ended up near Malongo later in the day, bringing word that Brent's captors were treating him kindly. Reports differ as to whether the man actually made it to the gates of Malongo or if he was found wandering on the road where Brent had driven just hours earlier.

Andre, one of Brent's captors and the one taking all the photographs, told Brent in English to not be afraid. Until Brent reached the base camp five days later, Andre would be his only source of communication. Before they began the walk again, the Catholic soldiers bowed their heads and prayed for a safe passage for all of them.

Despite all the political intrigue and civil unrest in Angola, the workers at Malongo were kept safe behind the fences and land mines.

"I never feared for my life while working there," Brent said. "Everyone was friendly. You were their best buddy—all you had to do was shake their hand."

Brent's attitude changed upon his capture. From the very first moment when he looked into the gaping hole of the grenade launcher, he began to fear for his life. His fear intensified with Andre's proclamation that they wanted him for "his government."

> Brent's Diary—Day One—October 19, 1990
>
> *Oh, boy, everybody wants the U.S. government. So what's new? All the stuff from the truck was packed into soldiers' packs. They prayed and off we went into the jungle south-southeast. About an hour and a half later we broke out into another open field and stopped on the crest of a hill. The soldiers took off their shoes and socks, and we walked down the hill to a road running east and west. We stopped by a grassy embankment maybe fifteen-feet high. The soldiers dropped their pants, and I was told to remove my shirt, shoes, and socks. My brain went into overdrive, and I was whirling. I thought "Shit, these guys are going to gangbang my white ass and leave me here dead and steal my clothes and money."*
>
> *I suddenly realized that the embankment was tall grass, fifteen-feet high. Now barefoot, we followed a wet path, and I was given two eight-foot long sticks, one for each hand.*

Marching through the marsh with his bare feet, Brent uses long poles to maneuver through the leech-infested water.

We walked on poles laid on the ground, and at first it wasn't so bad, but the farther we went, the worse it got. Water up to the ankles. That's when I realized I had a cut on my ankle, and it smarts a little. The water is up to the knees and then to the crotch.

When we finally hit solid ground, we hit their temporary camp. They gave me a bar of soap, and I cleaned myself in the swamp water. Then they gave me long pants and a long-sleeved shirt, and they gave me back my watch. It was 11:43 a.m.

Before they entered the marsh, Brent heard the sounds of a village nearby. Voices and children crying let him know that the everyday life of the Cabindans continued. Brent kept track of the direction by the sun that had now made its way through the cloud cover of the morning. They had been traveling parallel to the main road that ran along the coast, north and south. Now Brent knew they turned inland. When they began the trek through the marsh, Brent imagined insects and snakes in the dark mud waiting to grab his ankles and pull him under. He concentrated on walking, trying to not let his imagination rule.

They laid large trees end to end, forming a type of balance beam over the swamp. As long as Brent managed to stay on the poles, using the long sticks to balance, the water never went much over his knees. He walked slower than the men in front of him, and at one point, he reached the end of a pole and could not find the footing for the next one and down he went, chin deep in the murky water.

They emerged from the marsh and entered a temporary camp where Brent received camouflage garments and a hat with a bullet hole positioned right in the center of the forehead.

"I don't know if that hat came from a dead man," Brent said, "but I think it was a scare tactic so I didn't get cocky on them."

They gave Brent strips of rubber cut from inner tubes to tie around the bottom on his pant's legs to keep out the spiders and insects they might encounter along the way.

One of the soldiers handed Brent the lunch he had picked up that morning in the cafeteria at Malongo. The prime rib leftover from Thursday night's dinner fulfilled Brent and would be one of the last good meals he would eat for a long time. He even offered his captors some of this meal later in the day.

"At this point, I was more concerned with keeping the ice and water in the igloo fresh. I didn't want to contaminate it with spoiled food," Brent said. "And I hoped that if I shared my lunch with them, they would share their lunch with me."

After the meal, they wiped away all traces of the camp before beginning the afternoon's trek, which took them east around the marsh. Brent suddenly realized why they had come through the marsh. No one would be able to track them through the muddy water, and if they did manage to figure it out, once out of the water there would be no sign of them. As they raked the leaves to hide their luncheon spot, Brent finished a cigarette and, without detection from the soldiers, left the butt in the crotch of the tree. If someone was tracking him, he wanted to make sure some sign of his presence was noticed.

—

Brent's Diary—Day One—October 19, 1990

We left the temporary camp at 2:00 p.m. and made our way east then north around the marsh this time. Much better, but hilly terrain, and jungle all the way. We stopped for supper at 5:45 p.m. In the middle of a prime rib sandwich, I heard a 212 [helicopter] approaching Malongo. It landed and the throttles rolled off. I figured we were two to three miles from Malongo. After supper, the soldiers are removing their shoes again. I ask, "More agua? Not another marsh?" I got a laugh out of them. "No, no agua."

At 6:35 p.m., we stepped out of the woods, in the dark, and what do I see due west, but Malongo. Now there's a sight. I could see the lights of the control tower, and I had never seen it from this angle. We humped up this road for an hour with Malongo to our backs, leaving FAPLA territory.

Brent soon understood the reason for the removal of the shoes. The soldiers hurried him along and walked as quietly as possible, instructing Brent to walk on the light parts, not on the dark clumps or on the foot-high termite hills. The black areas were clumps of burned grass left from the annual uncontrolled burns. Stepping on these clumps of burned grasses created a loud crunching noise. Brent realized they were in a very vulnerable position as they walked quickly through FAPLA territory. He worried that the military might start shooting, and he imagined hitting the ground if shots rang out.

"They kept telling me to hurry, and that played on my mind," Brent said. "They were afraid too."

They rested once they left the open area. When they resumed their walk at a slower pace, Brent got into the rhythm of the march. He noticed he was losing sight of Malongo, and his thoughts turned morose as he thought about never seeing Cardboard City again.

Even before the soldiers announced themselves as FLEC, Brent tried to change his thinking.

"Today you're not an aircraft mechanic," he told himself that morning as they walked through the prairie grass. "Your job today is just to stay alive."

As Malongo disappeared from view, Brent's tiredness sank deep into his brain, and the depression began. Tears poured down his cheeks as he watched his old life disappear as quickly as the lights from the control tower.

Workers at PHI knew something was wrong when Brent did not appear at the airport by 6:30 a.m. because Brent always came to work on time. They knew he had been captured fairly soon afterward because an Angolan worker at Malongo had been following close behind Brent that morning as he passed through the third village. The man saw the soldiers take over Brent's truck. He turned around immediately and brought the first word back to Malongo that Brent had been kidnapped. Later in the day, the Angolan policeman was released and somehow made his way to Malongo where he told his story of Brent's treatment.

On Brent's first day of captivity, they marched until 10:00 p.m. when they came to the edge of the woods where the trees grow thickest and are nurtured by the sun. Just one hundred feet into the woods, they stopped and set up camp for the night. Using flashlights, the soldiers strung a hammock between two trees for Brent. The constant itching in Brent's rear quarters began on this night and did not abate for nearly two months. But that first day would turn out to be better than others in captivity—the diarrhea had not yet started.

The tropical setting filled with banana and palm trees reminded Brent of home in Florida. The trees even reminded him of his native state of Maine at times, except in Africa, the trees grow much taller.

"All day I had been using the sun to see which direction we were going and where they were taking me," Brent said. "I wanted to know where I was going in case I got away from them and could find my way out.

"Then when it turned dark, I used Malongo as my guide knowing which direction it was until it disappeared, but then the road went pretty straight so I didn't pay attention to the stars, and the moon—the new moon—was nonexistent."

Brent's Diary—Day One—October 19, 1990

Hunched down we tiptoed north and hit a road and headed northeast "Avancar Rapido" or quick advance. Single file we humped up this road for an hour. Malongo at our backs, getting out of FAPLA territory. Rest twenty minutes. Since supper, the only thing on my mind was where to dive if I saw a muzzle flash. Hit the dirt, find a tree, find a termite hill, find a low spot, anything, just get down and stay flat. But nothing—we got by totally undetected.

A hill on the left side—Malongo radio tower slipped out of sight. By this time my brain had settled down some. I realized that might be the last I'll ever see of Malongo. With that thought, emotion set in—depression—or "weak moral fiber" my supervisor would say. Tears flowed.

At 10:00 p.m. we hit trees again. Camp. One hammock in the trees, and the American is tucked in. Lights out at 10:10 p.m.

I was tired. I slept, but not good.

The Home Front

Information trickled slowly out of Malongo, and Gary Weber told Barbara he waited before calling her with the news. He hesitated telling her with no family members present. When he finally called at 9:00 a.m., Brent would have been eating his Malongo prime rib leftovers and sharing with his captors by the time Barbara received the news.

Barbara does not remember if she slept the night of October 19 or not. If she did go to bed at all, she only tossed and turned. She remembers the constant ringing of the phone.

Despite Brent's lack of fear for his life while working in Cabinda, Barbara always had her reservations about her husband's choice of job.

"I was worried about his safety because I knew he traveled off by himself out of the secure area," Barbara said. "But he would always tell me, 'I know these people, it's OK.'"

While Brent called his routine in Malongo a "gravy job," Barbara developed her own routine back in Chiefland. She began working at the local Wal-Mart in 1989, and she tried to get more time off when Brent was home. She joined a bowling league and had a set of friends, but when Brent came home, he often did not want to leave their homestead. Barbara might get him to take a canoe trip down the nearby Suwannee River, but for the most part, he wanted to plant trees and work on the new house.

It annoyed Barbara when Brent began bringing home African Grey parrots since by her own admission she was "not a bird person." But by the time Brent had been captured, the birds had become a part of the Swan family. These shy, yet talkative, birds are thought to have an intelligence equal to a three-year-old child. Before long, Barbara referred to the birds as "my African Greys," despite the teasing she received from her husband.

Once Brent began working in Cabinda in 1984, the need to remain near PHI's headquarters in Louisiana lessened. They had moved to Lafayette, Louisiana, several years earlier from New Hampshire. But with Brent working overseas, he and Barbara could live anywhere as long as he was in close proximity to an airport. When members of Barbara's family began settling in the north Florida area in Levy County, twenty miles from the Gulf of Mexico, Brent and Barbara found themselves drawn to the area.

"We didn't much like the landscape in Louisiana," Brent said. "It didn't make much difference where we lived, and we liked the warmer climates of the South.

"With me being gone so much, moving here meant that Barbara would have some family close by."

Barbara's aunt Beth lived next door to the original five acres near Chiefland purchased by the Swans in 1985. Eventually, they purchased property from neighbors, including Barbara's uncle Arthur. They moved their mobile home from Louisiana to the property with hopes of building their dream home in a few years. By 1990, with house plans developed, permits in place, and holes dug, the Swans poured the basement foundation.

Brent grew up in Maine, the oldest child of Denise and Hugh Swan. He enjoyed outdoor activities and took his Boy Scouting seriously. Some of those lessons learned in the woods of Maine would help him in the jungles of Africa—or at least help keep his mind active as he charted the flow of rivers and the position of the constellations and the direction of the flights of bats.

Brent loved working on the King Air owned by PHI and used to transport Chevron VIPs to and from Luanda and Cabinda City.

"Best job a mechanic could ever have. It was one aircraft," he said. "I was pretty much my own boss."

His love of aviation literally hit him over the head when he was a young boy.

"I was watching jets going over the house," he remembered. "I was so taken with what I saw that I didn't notice an old washtub in the yard. I tripped and hit my eye, blood was dripping down my face, and I had to have stitches.

"And that was beginning of me wanting to get into aviation."

He originally wanted to be a pilot, but his fascination with mechanics led him to learn how those planes flew before he ventured to fly one.

After high school, he went to school for one year to earn his aircraft technician's license.

His first job took him to New Hampshire where he and his coworkers frequented Papa Gino's, a New England pizza chain. One of the waitresses began to take notice of the handsome young mechanic, so one of her friends invited Brent and his buddies to the pizza restaurant's Christmas party on December 18, 1979. Whatever interest the waitress had in Brent was instantly returned to her that night. Barbara, the waitress, and Brent became inseparable from that point.

Brent tired of working in the cold New Hampshire winters, and a year later, he put in an application with Petroleum Helicopters Inc. based in Lafayette, Louisiana. Barbara eventually moved to Louisiana, and the two set up housekeeping, but did not marry.

"She wasn't ready," Brent said. "She says it was me, but I don't think she was ready."

"I would have," Barbara responded.

Brent advanced at PHI and by 1984 became one of their few mechanics of fixed-wing aircraft. When Chevron, then Gulf Oil, decided they needed an airplane to go back and forth between Malongo and Luanda in Angola, they also needed the mechanics. Brent put in for duty in Angola.

And Barbara, upset by his decision, moved back to New Hampshire.

After Brent's first hitch in Cabinda, he flew home via Maine and then he went to New Hampshire and asked Barbara to marry him.

"I'd been in love with her for five years, but I guess traveling overseas kind of opened my eyes to everything that is out there in the world," Brent said. "I wanted to settle down, and I cared about her."

They married in 1985 in the backyard of Barbara's family farmhouse in New Hampshire in an informal ceremony. Brent dressed up for the ceremony but stripped down to his cutoffs that he had under his dress pants as soon as they were pronounced husband and wife.

"Open that keg of beer," he commanded.

Angola's Wars

The soldiers' prayers for safe passage as they marched Brent through the jungle were quite appropriate. Safe passage in Angola in

1990 required many prayers. Years of civil war brought its own form of terror to this country. UNICEF estimates that Angolan provinces contain approximately ten million land mines planted by Cuban soldiers, FAPLA, UNITA, and any other rebel forces hoping to create a ring of protection around their territories. Many of these had been planted prior to 1990, and it is estimated that land mines can remain active for at least fifty years.

As a result of these mines, Angola—a country long plagued with poverty and poor medical conditions—has a total seventy thousand amputees according to the United Nations. As the insurgencies continued in Angola, education of the young was neglected, as noted by the Library of Congress. In 1987, Angola had a literacy rate of 20 percent with 46 percent of the population under the age of fifteen.

Brent noticed almost immediately that the soldiers surrounding him could hardly be called men. In a country where life expectancy for men was forty-one, some of those guarding Brent would be approaching their middle age.

"They hadn't reached full maturity yet," he said. "They were just following the leaders, attempting to follow in their footsteps.

"They don't know any other life except living in the jungle—they were born in the jungle, and they were fighting for their freedom, and they don't know anything different."

And they were fighting for their life. As Brent marched along on that first day with his captors, they strode single file. A dozen soldiers, with grenades on their bodies and assault weaponry slung over their shoulders, marched ahead of the American prisoner, not knowing if their next step might be their last step in terrain loaded with land mines not made in Angola. Most land mines are manufactured in the United States, Italy, Germany, France, and fifteen other countries. Angola was not a source for weapons, only a depository.

Even though the United States did not enjoy diplomatic relations with Angola in 1990, the U.S. government was well aware of the importance of this African nation. With the election of Ronald Reagan as U.S. president in 1980, UNITA—one of the groups trying to remove the communist regime from power—received great monetary support from the U.S. government because, according to Reagan's ambassador to the United Nations, Jeanne Kirkpatrick, the president "cared a very great deal about freedom. He detested tyranny. He detested imperialism and colonialism, and he detested communism because it stood for these things."

That policy of friendly relations with the group trying to oust MPLA—the recognized government—continued until the election of Bill Clinton in 1992, when the relationship with Angola began to change drastically, with communism banished and the first democratic elections held.

Portugal ruled Angola from the fifteenth century until 1975. When the Portuguese explorer Diogo Cao entered the area now known as Cabinda through the Congo River in 1483, the king of the Kongo ruled the Angolan monarchy. This king enjoyed an easy trade relationship with Portugal until the slave trade drove a wedge between the two countries and between the different tribes in Angola. Cabinda became a large trading area for the slave traffic, which continued until the mid-nineteenth century, providing slaves for Brazilian plantations. It is estimated that three million Angolans made the voyage to the New World during the three centuries of slavery.

Tribal wars and uprisings continued into the twentieth century, resulting in two separate wars for independence in 1961. Several guerrilla groups formed political parties during the sixties and continued to plague the Portuguese for another decade. The most prominent of these groups, the National Front for the Liberation of Angola (FNLA), the Popular Movement for the Liberation of Angola (MPLA) and the National Union for the Total Independence of Angola (UNITA) signed the Alvor Accords with Portugal in 1975, which granted Angola its freedom and provided for a provisional government where the three parties would share power. By mid-1975, this government collapsed, and civil war had broken out all over the country.

Outside forces funneled money into these groups. MPLA received support from the Soviets and Cubans, and UNITA and FNLA received support from the United States and other European nations. MPLA eventually became the ruling party, with the help of Soviet weaponry and the Cuban military presence.

Nobody paid much attention to another rebel group, which formed in 1963. FLEC originated to not only break away from Portugal, but to also break its connections with Angola. FLEC created its own government in exile in 1967, and Cabindan nationalism grew in direct proportion to the fortunes of the oil industry after 1968 when it became apparent that Angola would not share its fortune with its source, Cabinda.

Gerald J. Bender's report in July of 1990 concluded that FLEC regarded the move from a communist form of government to a republic as an opportunity.

Bender states, "Cabinda nationalists may nonetheless perceive this as a 'now or never' chance to establish legitimacy and to stake their claim."

On the first day, Brent is marched down the road that runs east/west through Cabinda Province. He is surrounded by members of FLEC who all carry AK-47s.

CHAPTER 3

The Walk to Nowhere

Lafayette Daily Advertiser

LUANDA, Angola (AP) (Oct. 20, 1990)—A Petroleum Helicopter Inc. mechanic was kidnapped by armed guerrillas in northern Angola on Friday, a government official said.

According to the official, mechanic Brent Swan and an Angolan colleague were abducted as they drove to a helicopter in Cabinda, an oil-rich province where rebels have staged anti-government operations.

But no group had claimed responsibility for the kidnapping by late Friday.

Gary Weber, a spokesman for Petroleum Helicopter Inc. in Lafayette, confirmed Swan is an employee, but declined to discuss the incident "at this time." PHI is contracted by Chevron Corp. in Angola.

The Angolan official, who spoke on condition of anonymity, did not give Swan's age or hometown.

Marching to Base Camp

Brent did not sleep well in his hammock in the jungle that night. He remained in his clothes, covered with a space blanket, but any time he shifted his body in any way, the blanket crinkled and woke him. At least it kept the night chill off because even in the warm jungles of Cabinda, the dampness can chill to the bone without the sun.

He slept for several hours out of sheer exhaustion. By the time they roused him at 5:30 a.m., the fog created a mist that drizzled on him for most of the morning. Hungry and still tired when he woke, he also suffered from an itching rear end that plagued him.

Brent's Diary—Day Two—October 20

It was not a good night's sleep at all. I was told we would walk a short ways before breakfast. Continuing on course, north-northeast, we went downhill into a valley. I did not see any water, if there was any. We took a right and continued uphill, up the valley then back on course uphill. I was told there was a small village here of Cabinda people, and I heard women talking. We went around the village undetected and broke out on a road and went downhill a long ways northeast. It flattened out, and we picked up an east direction.

We stopped for breakfast in a banana patch at 9:00 a.m. Breakfast? Bananas and sardines and water from the Igloo. As fast as the ice was melting, I was drinking.

I was told I'd meet their leader on Tuesday when we got to base camp. I settled on the fact that I would at least live another three days.

Here in the banana patch I found out the cameraman—the one who could speak some English—was Senhor Andre. Well, Senhor Andre, Mother Nature is knocking on my back door, and I grabbed a handful of banana leaves and said, "bathroom." That didn't work so how about "toilet?" Comprehension. Someone pulled out a roll of toilet paper so I dropped the leaves. Then they realized what I had picked the leaves for, and they were still laughing when I came back out of the woods.

Andre must have been one of the few educated Cabindans and perhaps selected for his assignment as Brent's personal guard because of this education. The march, the violence, the kidnapping—this represented the way of life for anyone living in Angola in the twentieth century. Certainly the entire country of Angola had known only strife, war, famine, and violence for nearly five hundred years when the Portuguese discovered the rich assets of this African nation, which had a fairly sophisticated culture by the 1400s.

A peace existed between the European country and its African tribal monarchy in those early years, until the Portuguese engaged Angolans in exporting not only diamonds and gold, but also Angolans themselves to the more popular Portuguese colonial holding in Brazil.

So Andre had knowledge of English, but that did not make him suited for his job, and Brent pointed that out to him soon after breakfast on that second day. When Brent emerged from the woods with his armed guards and roll of toilet paper, they began getting their packs together. Andre had leaned his rifle against a tree while cleaning up the breakfast camp. When they started marching again, Andre fell in behind Brent without his AK-47, which Brent took great pleasure in pointing out to Senhor Andre.

"If he had left his rifle there it wouldn't have made any difference," Brent noted. "There were still too many rifles for me to overpower the group and get away from them—still too much firepower. So one rifle wasn't going to make a difference.

"But by telling him he had forgotten his rifle, I put him down in front of his peers, but I also showed him that I wanted them to realize they could trust me so I could get closer to them."

Brent imagined establishing the trust so the young soldiers would let down their guard just enough to allow Brent to break away and escape.

Andre grabbed his assault weapon, and they began marching again. Soon they came to a grouping of plantain trees in the valley. Brent loved the taste of these bananas fried in just a little oil as it represented one of the few food treats allowed on this journey.

After cutting down some of the plantains, they continued walking until they came to a cone-shaped hill, forty to fifty feet high. Brent remembered the grassy hill as a unique feature of the savanna they had traversed. While they marched, Brent always tried to keep track of how many men were guarding him, but it was difficult to count without drawing attention to himself. Often some would slip away into the woods only to be replaced by several others. His best estimates put his guards at twenty to twenty-five during most of the days on the trail. Once they reached this hill, sixteen soldiers went off in sixteen different directions looking for a place to camp with water. After thirty minutes, they all returned and one of them had found the perfect place, with a clear-running stream.

—

"One of the things you learn in Boy Scouts is running water isn't stagnant," Brent said. "I only hoped it wasn't running out of a stagnant swamp."

But he saw them fill their own canteens and containers, and he knew it probably was the best water they had found so far on the trip. They spent the rest of the day and night in this spot, and if not for the assault weapons bearing down on him, Brent would have thought himself on a camping trip or safari. Since he had clean water in which to bath and wash his clothes, he asked for his carry bag he had seen in one of the packs. They gave it to him and he searched it until he found his wedding ring, which he had removed when he arrived in Malongo. He could not work on the planes with the ring on his finger in case it became entangled during routine maintenance.

"I wasn't sure how they were going to react about taking things out of the carry bag," Brent said. "But I took my wedding band out and put it on and thought to myself, 'They're not getting this back. I'll go fighting.'"

As Brent wondered what might be happening to him and as his family waited for word, oil fell to its lowest price per barrel in over a month as talks of a war with Iraq abated somewhat. However, the U.S. embassy in Iraq received daily protests on the U.S. occupancy of Kuwait. The *New York Times* reported on October 19, 1990, "A token Iraqi Army presence [remains] outside the Baghdad mission, usually two soldiers with AK-47 rifles maintaining a seemingly friendly vigilance."

While Brent might not have described his captors with the same "friendly vigilance," he wanted them to view him as trustworthy as he registered everything around him. When they made camp in the peaceful setting next to the babbling brook, Brent ate a lunch of sardines and bread. He knew the bread had come from Malongo made by NCCC, the company who provided food and housekeeping at the compound.

"They made a very distinctive round bread roll," Brent said. "The locals made a longer French-type, like a baguette.

Brent knew some of the locals who worked at Malongo could take leftovers home from the dining area. They piled extra food on their plates just so they would have some to take with them. As he ate his sardine sandwich, he thought about someone taking extra bread rolls from camp and smuggling them to members of FLEC. How and why the connections were made, Brent did not know, but he knew they were there.

"Once we made our way to base camp, I was just guessing the freshest ones were a couple of days old, and the oldest ones were moldy," he said. "I didn't eat those."

The afternoon brought fresh breezes and sunny skies. Brent felt clean and his clothes received a good washing with ample time to dry. When it became dark, he could not see the lights of the tower at Malongo any longer, but he did hear the helicopter come in for its final run.

He fell asleep early only to be woken at 9:00 p.m. by the sounds of gunfire.

Brent's Diary—Day Two—October 20
I woke with a start. Gunfire. I rolled the hammock and hit the dirt flat. Nothing. Quiet. I was told, "No problema," and climbed back into the hammock. All tucked in by 9:00 p.m. The hammock they have is a two-foot by eight-foot piece of rubberized canvas overlapped and sewn at each end. A stick through one end and a rope attached at shoulder width. The foot end has just a rope attached with a plastic fly to keep out the rain. At night, I had a space blanket for warmth. Yes, it gets quite chilly at night in the jungle. I slept fully clothed.

The next morning, Brent did not have to wait long to learn why he had heard the gunfire from the night before. He woke at 5:30 a.m., and before long, breakfast was served, and it wasn't sardines. On this morning, he was treated to *porco-espinho,* or porcupine that had been boiled. The hunters from the night before had only snagged one for the twenty-five or so soldiers plus Brent, who was given the hindquarters.

"They gave me the best portion of the porcupine," he said. "They always fed me better than themselves."

The rest of the porcupine became a stew for the others. Brent knew he ate better than the soldiers. If they killed a deer, Brent received the steak from the animal.

"It was encouraging to see they were trying to take care of me better than their troops," he said. "Made me realize I was their special little pawn.

"I was close enough to the troops to know that one of them wasn't going to shoot me. It would be their president or someone on the outside negotiating team who would say, 'We don't need you anymore,'" he imagined.

By the third day, Brent felt secure enough to begin asking questions. Before they began marching again, he asked what they were saying as they stood together in a circle before leaving. Andre told him they were all praying for "safe passage" through the jungle for all of the troops and Brent. They prayed there would be "no problema."

Brent, third from the right, stands with his abductors in a prayer circle on the beginning of his third day of captivity. The prayer was for "safe passage" through the jungle although Brent wasn't sure his passage would be safe at all.

As they began walking, Brent continued diligently recording all that he saw in his memory. They moved into a canopy of trees, and Brent noticed how tall these trees in the tropical setting of Cabinda grew. Parts of Cabinda contain a small rainforest, and Brent and his captors traveled in and around this damp woodland. When they came to an open area where Cubans had felled trees, Brent saw logs lying there rotting. The waste made him angry.

"We would see the logs they would keep," he said. "These eighteen-wheel trucks would travel the same road I traveled to the airport, and they would be loaded with one log, eight-feet across the length of the truck.

"We would meet these trucks on the road from time to time, and we'd have to get off onto the shoulder. They would get rolling, and they didn't know how to stop. It was such a shame to see these trees lying here in the woods."

Before he could dwell on the rotting logs further, several African Greys flew into one of the nearby trees still left standing. Brent enjoyed the sight of the birds in their natural habitat, and briefly he thought about the beauty of being a free bird.

Brent's Diary—Day Three—October 21

We followed a trail in the bottom of the river valley for an hour and then stopped. We would rest until dark. We camped out the afternoon beside a twenty-foot wide river. I slept well after a bath despite the intimidation. Try this sometime: stand buck naked in the middle of a twenty-foot wide stream with water halfway up to your knees, taking a bath. Twenty fully equipped combat soldiers stand on both banks four feet above you. Would you be intimidated?

Lunch and dinner consisted of the same thing: sardines and rock-hard biscuits. At 6:35 p.m. we crossed the river and picked up a trail east-northeast. At 8:00 p.m., we stopped. We were on a side of a knoll. The lights of Malongo shown like a beacon. On the other side of the knoll was a village of "Cabinda people," I was told.

There was a hell of a party going on with people singing and drums a-beating. And the same thing was going on off to the northwest at another village. Tonight's Party Night!

Scouts went ahead to the village, and we sat until 9:00 p.m. We left the trail and went across a soccer field through some backyards, into the village, and stopped beside a house and waited. We continued into a grassy field and waited to reassemble the troops. Here I was given back my mini-Maglite. At 10:00 p.m., we crossed a road running north/south. We were going east. Then we went crazy, zigzagging back and forth. I was tired, and I got confused, but generally we were going north to see a big man with a sword in his belt and his sisters. The lights of Malongo were gone.

A great exodus for the cities of Angola began after independence in 1975. Shantytowns sprouted up on the outskirts of Luanda and became known as the *musseque* where people built simple shacks of tin and palm fronds. Life within the *musseque* imitated the closeness of the small rural villages dotting the countryside, despite the harsh conditions of city life with low-paying jobs, if any at all.

In the rural areas of Cabinda, folks spent their evenings gathered together around a fire, telling stories about those who had ventured most recently into the larger cities. The elders of the village might share traditional stories as women cooked stews over their individual fires outside their homes. The marimba drumbeat out its cadence as the background music for all within miles to hear.

Brent heard the drums on his march that night, and after he and his captors crossed a soccer field, he stepped into someone's pot of stew. After that, the soldiers gave him back his Maglite so he could see where he stepped. The drums beat out their marching cadence as the rebels took Brent on a zigzagged course throughout the night.

As they lost the light of the fires, Brent and the other soldiers periodically turned on their flashlights to show the path ahead, and with no light in the woods, Brent began looking to the constellations and recognized the "big man with sword with seven sisters."

"I knew these were in the north in the northern hemisphere, but they could still be seen in the northeast," he said. "And then we came to the ants."

Brent's Diary—Day Three—October 21

We crossed roads, we followed trails, we followed roads, and we made our own trails. Along one of these roads we hit a very large fire ant hill in the stump of a log in the water. The log was surrounded by water—really just a mud hole one-eighth of a mile long and eighteen inches deep. Everyone ran through the fire ants out onto this log. My mini-Maglite became a lifesaver as I could easily have been bitten to death. One of the soldiers, a fifteen-year-old, switched his fifty-pound pack to his front and carried me piggyback through the knee-deep water and mud. Ants were biting the hell out of us. We hit solid ground, stripped naked, and picked ants off of each other. At 12:30 a.m., the troops started complaining. We were in an orchard of some kind—maybe cashew trees. The only way I could tell the troops were complaining was the tone of voice spoken in their own dialect, not Portuguese. At 1:30 a.m., we went downhill fast, steep, and at the bottom was a camp shelter similar to the ones at base camp with a palm frond roof. This is deepest,

*darkest Africa. Lights went out at 1:45 a.m. From 10:00 p.m.
to 1:30 a.m., we only stopped long enough for water and to rid
ourselves of ants. Let me tell you about African fire ants. They are
not like the little fire ants we have in Florida. They are the size of
carpenter ants and leave a half-inch wide red welt with a pimple
in the middle of it. When you squeeze it, it pops just like a pimple,
but a lot more stuff comes out.*

Ant bites and all, I slept well.

"Americano Brent Swan," the radio blared at 5:45 a.m. on October 22, waking Brent from his hammock bed. His situation became more real than ever, and fear began to form as he heard "FLEC" and "Cabinda" interspersed with the Portuguese. Red welts appeared everywhere on his body from the ant bites of the night before, and the only water left to drink came from two fish ponds at the bottom of a ravine in this camp. This water tasted like waste matter. Fish—which they ate later in the day—swam around in the murky pond. The bony fish contained little meat, but with rice and baked bread, Brent ate greedily.

And then the diarrhea began.

"I was miserable because my stomach was upset, and I was having diarrhea," Brent said. "Three or four trips out to the woods, and that's enough to make you miserable right there.

"The ant bites stung and itched, and they were all over my legs."

When Brent raced to the woods to relieve himself, three or four of the soldiers ran alongside him and stood guard as he squatted on the ground with cramping stomach and uncontrollable bowels. The AK-47s dangling from the shoulders of these young men did not improve his condition.

Many of the FLEC rebels are young men still in their teens. Brent sometimes thinks of the experience as being with the Boy Scouts as a way to keep his fear at bay.

A priest entered camp as they rested, and Brent watched as he conducted a service. The soldiers stood in a circle, singing or listening to the priest speak as he waved his arms. Brent lay in his hammock, watching in between his trips to the woods.

As night settled over the jungle, they began to march again on a small trail leading away from the cashew groves. They followed the road south for four hours under the slight light given off by the sliver of a moon waxing. As they came into a village, Brent looked around and realized they were marching through the same village as the night before where bonfires had lit the night sky. He saw the soccer field and remembered a white fence around one of the houses. Afterward they came up on a hill, and he once again could see the lights of Malongo.

As they walked down the road, away from Malongo, Brent saw a large bonfire burning at the end of the road. They stopped on a bank two or three feet above the road and rested. Brent stared up at the sky looking at the stars.

"It was the blackest sky I'd ever seen," he said. "I could look deep into space there."

They tried to leave, but Brent asked to stay just a little while longer. His captors agreed.

"I just sat there staring into space and trying to enjoy the moment as much as I could," Brent said.

They began to march again, and they crossed a rickety bridge in a valley. At one point, the soldiers shined their flashlights into the woods and brought Brent close to see one of the strangest catlike animals Brent had ever seen. He never found out what it was, and he has never seen one since. At midnight, they made camp, and Brent settled once more into his hammock in the trees. The next day was Tuesday, the day Brent had been told he would meet their leaders.

October 22, his fourth day in captivity, marked Brent's sixth anniversary working in Cabinda.

Waiting at Home

Barbara's Notes

I guess at this point I was really thinking about what Brent might have with him. I knew enough of his routine to know that after a day at camp, he takes his carry bag to the airport with him. I was hoping that he had it that day. If he didn't, I was worried about things like whether or not he had his glasses with him. I couldn't even think of him out there having to take out his contacts and not being able to see—that was my biggest concern. He was in scary enough a situation without that added to it. It wasn't until many days later that we found out he had his bag with him. Thank God, he had glasses and a toothbrush! Small comfort, but some was better than none.

Melanie's entry for October 20 in her diary read, "No Entry. Waiting."

Barbara received a note from Joe Kettles, the PHI area supervisor in Cabinda, written on October 21. He informed her about the rumors floating around among the local natives. Speculation suggested Brent was being taken into Zaire by FLEC, a group in the Cabinda province asking for recognition of a new government. Joe told Barbara that Angolan officials assured his people that Brent would not be harmed.

Melanie's Notes—Day Four—October 22

5:00 p.m. Stuart Hatcher called.

FLEC stands for Front for the Liberation of the Enclave of Cabinda.

They are a group of five hundred to one thousand people with organizational groups in Zaire, the Congo, and Paris. They have had Portuguese hostages for a month. The State Department has notified all countries around Cabinda that Brent is to be released immediately.

At 5:30 p.m., Barb called with news from Gary Weber. They interviewed the police officer who was captured with Brent. He and Brent were driven around blindfolded. The captors tore the patches off from the officer's uniform. They had a cot and blankets. They were packed heavily. They put down a poncho for Brent to sit on while they regrouped. There were eight or nine black men, speaking the local dialect. They left the police officer behind, took off on foot. They yelled back when it was OK for him to go. He didn't know which direction to go in, that's why he was found wandering. It was raining when he was captured.

UNITA has nothing to do with this. They are trying to help him out.

Ross [Brent's and Melanie's brother] *found an article in the* Portland Press Herald *on Saturday. We fear Brent may have been taken to Zaire.*

REACTION: It was great news today that the men had laid down a poncho for Brent to sit on. Maybe he will be taken care of. It's sounding more like an organized group. If FLEC has him, they expect a week to go by before they acknowledge it.

Dealing with Terrorists

Brent's situation remained a complicated one simply by the nature of politics in 1990. Angola and the U.S. government did not enjoy diplomatic relations. The United States had a strict policy regarding the treatment of terrorists, and it did not include negotiations. Therefore, at the same time Chevron and PHI tried to contain the situation while working toward the safe return of Brent, the FBI tracked the movement of the negotiators to see if U.S. policy was being violated.

In Africa, the nearest embassy to Angola—in Kinshasa, Zaire—became the center of operations for dealing with FLEC and Brent's kidnapping. The U.S. Department of State's Bureau of Consular Affairs had very clear guidelines regarding its relationship with hostage takers and their demands in 1990. The policy, outlined in the brochure, "Crisis Abroad—What the State Department Does," states "The U.S. Government will make no concessions to terrorists holding official or private U.S. citizens hostage. It will not pay ransom, release prisoners, change its policies, or agree to other acts that might encourage additional terrorism. At the same time, the United States will use every available resource to gain the safe return of American citizens who are held hostage by terrorists."

The brochure further justifies the government's position by stating all attempts are made by the United States to protect its employees and those in the service of the private sector by maintaining diplomatic relations with other countries. However, it does not address what happens when those diplomatic relations are no longer active, such as those between the United States and Angola at the time.

In bold, italicized print, set off from the rest of the text, the brochure states, "The U.S. Government will make no concessions to terrorists holding official or private U.S. citizens hostage."

However, the government will make every effort to communicate with the representatives of the captors to release the hostage. The policy further "urges American companies and private citizens not to pay terrorist ransom demands. It believes that good security practices, relatively modest security expenditures, and continual close cooperation with embassy and local authorities can lower the risk to Americans living in high-threat environments."

Once again the policy does not address what happens when the U.S. government directly opposes the government of a country in which an American citizen has been taken hostage. The United States had been funneling funds to the opposition party UNITA since 1985. In fact, that support may have created the atmosphere in which FLEC believed it could also gain the support of the United States. FLEC hoped by taking an American hostage, an employee of one of the United States' largest corporations—Chevron—the U.S. government would take notice of them and be sympathetic to their plight.

The MIPT Terrorism Knowledge Base Web site states FLEC received its funds "through the kidnapping of foreign oil companies' employees who are working in Cabinda." The two Portuguese aid workers who had been kidnapped by FLEC on September 20, 1990, were released on November 15 after the Zaire and Portuguese governments intervened. Earlier in 1990, twenty-three employees of the ELF oil company—thirteen French nationals and ten Congolese—were kidnapped by a faction of FLEC. Most of them were released within hours and the rest within ten days of their capture. The earliest account on the Web site occurred in 1977 when three French technicians were captured by FLEC and released two weeks later with no payment of a ransom.

Gerald Bender, an Angolan scholar and professor, remembers being surprised when he learned Chevron was possibly negotiating with FLEC.

"It seemed that would make Chevron too vulnerable to future demands," he said.

CHAPTER 4

Take Me to Your Leader

The News (Meredith, New Hampshire)

MOULTONBORO, New Hampshire (Oct. 24, 1990)—"Moultonboro Woman Following Angolan Uprising Closely"

Dot Tilton's son-in-law Brent Swan was taken hostage on Friday in Angola. Brent was a helicopter mechanic and they believe he was taken mistakenly by the rebels, thinking he was Cuban. Hopefully he will be released shortly.

Dot's daughter, Barbara, lives in Chiefland, Fla., and Dot will be there in support of her daughter. Her sister Beth Rodgers is facing surgery there this week.

Meeting the Heads of FLEC

Brent woke at 5:30 a.m. on day five, October 23. This time, when the soldiers broke camp, they did so haphazardly, not trying to hide their tracks anymore. One of the young men flung Brent's hammock over his shoulders, and after prayers, they began to march at five forty-five. Brent discovered they were only fifteen minutes from the base camp.

As Brent and his captors marched into the camp, the soldiers sang Cabinda's national anthem. Two of FLEC's leaders awaited their arrival. Lt. Col. Alfredo Nhumba, vice president, and Lt. Col. Francisco Rodrigues, chief of staff, did not greet Brent, which only added to his anxiety.

He imagined the words "Take me to your leader" but he was not at all sure that he really wanted to meet these leaders. He feared what the leaders might direct the young soldiers to do. Brent had become accustomed to walking the trails and sensed the soldiers would not harm him, but now he knew the situation had changed. These men could give orders that would be followed. He had developed a rapport with the troops. Brent knew he had convinced them he wanted to be their friend.

When Rodrigues and Alfredo did not come forward to greet him, Brent's fear became pronounced. The troops presented themselves, the flag was raised, and they sang the national anthem once again. "Viva la Cabinda" reverberated through the camp as Brent wondered about "Viva la Brent Swan."

After breakfast, Brent finally met the two leaders. Afterward one of the soldiers asked Brent to write a letter to his government.

The presentation of the hostage by the members of FLEC occurs on the day they arrive at the first base camp.

Brent's Diary—Day Five—October 23

    Between 8:30 and 9:00 a.m., I wrote the hardest letter of my life, to the U.S. Embassy/Cabinda Gulf/PHI.

    The first letter of "help, get me out of here," was sent October 23, 1990. Reply on the thirty-first—care package. We'll see you home soon????

"It was proof of life," he said. "I don't know what they expected me to write. I said it was the hardest letter of my life to write because I didn't know what to say.

"I tried to give clues," he said. "I wanted them to know I could walk out of there if necessary. I knew whatever I wrote down they [FLEC] would read, and they would translate 'fed well,' but those on the outside would say, 'Oh my God.'"

The Letter—Written October 23

Greetings Gentlemen,

I have finally arrived at FLEC base camp; it has been a long hike. I am in fair health, insect bites, scratches, bruises, typical jungle rash. My feet are tired, but I could go another day, and I'd still be in good shape. I am told I am not in Angola, but in the country of Cabinda.

So far I have been fed well from barbecued banana to sardine soup, and the porcupine is mighty tasty. We have rested well during the day and hiked mostly at night, three-four hours, last night was south six hours, until then it was northeast more than four. I know where the bat shits in the woods.

Though it may not seem it, my mind is almost at ease; I look at this as one hell of a camping trip. I am free to do as I please within, of course, camp. One scratch with infection has been looked at by camp Medical Officer, treated with oxygen water. I take as hydrogen peroxide and an ointment. Basically, I am being treated as could be expected. I know the meaning of severe depression.

God willing and the creek don't rise, the sun will set and rise tomorrow. I certainly hope that an agreement can be reached soon, I fear that this could be a long hitch. New Hampshire has a pretty license plate, and I hope my options stay favorable.

I guess I have been "lucky." My travel bag has made the trip as well as the rest that's missing from the truck. I assume you found it, five miles out on the left. I take it communication may be slow as I understand this will go through Kinshasa. I'm sure my wife is in contact. Please tell her I Love her and will be home soon? I only hope.

—

Wish I could have written neater or more, but we just arrived one hour ago, hunger and tiredness is sloppiness. Hope to hear from you soon.

Having a "great time"
Wishing you were here,
K-Air M ENE
Brent A. Swan

Somehow, despite guards standing over him with assault weapons, Brent managed to send a message in almost every line.

The fruit bats lived in the trees at Malongo. Brent described them as having huge bodies the size of a rat and with a wingspan of at least fourteen inches. They eat nothing but fruit, earning their name. Every night when the sun goes down, they leave the trees and fly northeast; and every morning by the time the sun comes back up, they are back in the trees at Malongo, sleeping. Brent assumed when the bats flew, they "shit in the woods," hence giving the clue that he was also north-northeast of Malongo.

His reference to not being in Angola came directly from his captors.

"They had specifically told me, 'You're not in Angola, you're in Cabinda, and it's our country,'" Brent said. "I wasn't going to argue with them."

His reference to "God willing and the creek don't rise" was a favorite saying of one of the pilots of PHI, who had served in the armed services in a department in charge of navigational directions for troops.

"I was trying to tell them to get this guy to read the letter, and he'd understand," Brent said. "I don't know if they ever did."

The day the embassy received the letter—day eight— Brent's captors moved him to another camp, an hour and a half walk away. Brent suspected they knew he had sent directional signals via the letter; however, he enjoyed the walk to the next base camp, which went through the valley. They marched at a slow pace.

"I liked walking in the woods," Brent said. "At least it was better than what we were about to do, which was sit around and things got a little boring."

The FLEC rebels prepare to march their hostage
to the second base camp.

And then two days later, on day ten, the diarrhea took a turn for
the worse, and every two hours, Brent had to squat in the woods over a
hole, placing his feet on the boards placed on either side of the hole. His
discomfort from the diarrhea did not allow him to consider the assault
weaponry leveled at him every time he went into the woods.

"There was one time I couldn't get out there fast enough," he said.
"After that they built a latrine closer to the sleeping quarters.

"I had to get up, and whoever was on watch would get up, and they would
get the rest of them up, and they'd all get their guns, then we'd all go out.

"There was one night when I got out of the hut to take a pee without
anyone. I'd finished and walked about five feet back toward camp, and
I just kind of stopped, and there was no movement going on, and then
all of a sudden everybody started moving. Somebody had woken up and
realized I wasn't in my bunk.

"I got reprimanded. 'Don't ever go to the bathroom unless someone's awake and knows you're leaving,' they said. I thought, 'Yeah, right, if I get out of here again, I might not ever come back.'"

Communicating to the Outside World

Barbara's memories of this time come and go. Sometimes she remembers nothing of incidents others remember. Other times, she has a great amount of clarity of certain defining moments.

One such moment occurred when Gary Weber called her on October 26, to tell her they had received the letter from Brent.

> Taped Interview with Barbara
>
> *I don't remember much about that weekend, but I remember the letter vividly. I was at work that day. I was getting ready to go to lunch with a friend who worked in the sporting goods department, and I was there waiting for her. I was behind the counter, and as you can imagine, in our neck of the woods, was very active. The phone was behind the counter. They said I had a phone call, and it was Gary.*
>
> *He said, "We got a letter from Brent. Let me read it to you." I was behind the counter, and so I sat on the floor trying to listen. As he was reading it, I guess the biggest thing for me was "New Hampshire has a pretty license plate." I said, "Oh my God." And Gary said, "What does that mean?" I told him the slogan on the license plate was "Live free or die." I knew about the bats because Brent had told me about them. I told Gary that means he could be out there wherever the fruit bats go. "He's probably trying to tell you where he is," I said, and Gary agreed.*
>
> *To our knowledge, the State Department issued a statement asking all the countries to let him go. They [State Department] just said they were doing what they could. We didn't know if they were tracking Brent, and they would not tell us.*
>
> *I told Gary he was trying to get a message to us. But here's Gary in Louisiana and the FBI telling him not to get involved. That afternoon, after he read it to me, he faxed the original letter to the bank in town. They wanted me to verify that it was really*

Brent's handwriting. And of course immediately I knew that it was. But I also knew that day when I hung up the phone that I did not need to be there at work trying to absorb all this. So right afterward, I told my supervisors that I could probably only work a few hours a week, and the store manager told me to do whatever I felt I could do.

The letter sounded like Brent, Barbara told Gary. Barbara knew he was trying to send directions on his whereabouts through the reference to the bats because he had often described their habits to her. But the mention of severe depression scared her. Barbara remembers hearing that Chevron did not want any connection to the kidnapping at first, but FLEC only wanted to negotiate with Chevron. Along with the letter from Brent, Barbara also received a list of FLEC's demands sent to Chevron. FLEC wanted Chevron's help in liberating the Cabindan territory. They also requested economic support for the Cabindan people, along with military support.

But the request that upset Barbara the most was the one regarding the handling of Brent's release upon the receipt of the demands.

It stated, "As soon as the agreement is signed and satisfaction is obtained on the social demands for the immediate term, Mr. Swan will be delivered in the hands of Jesse Jackson or the former president Jimmy Carter." It was signed by Jose Tiburcio Zinga Luemba, president of the central committee of FLEC/PM (military police).

"I remember reading the agenda and seeing release into the hands of Jesse Jackson or Jimmy Carter," Barbara said. "And that was scary because we knew that wouldn't happen.

"We're also thinking, Brent's not going to have a chance because how's Chevron going to do all this?" Barbara said. "That's what our feelings at home were."

The family back in Maine and Florida had lots of questions even before the arrival of Brent's first communication and confirmation of FLEC as the kidnappers. The day Brent wrote the "most difficult letter of my life," Melanie addressed many of the unanswered questions in her notes.

Melanie's Notes—Day Five—October 23, 1990
The Louisiana division of the FBI has contacted Gary Weber and been to see him. He told them everything he knew. They didn't

seem to know anything or offer any information. At first they contacted Chevron Oil in California, then PHI. [Melanie wrote as an addendum to these notes in 1996 that "This seemed to be the theme with the FBI—they never gave us any information, but always wanted to know what we knew."]

Mom decided not to give any information to Mike Daniels (Bethel Citizen) this week.

The Kinshasa division of FLEC has denied responsibility.

Questions we have at this point:

Will paychecks continue to Barb?

Are searches being conducted in the area?

Was the man Brent replaced politically active?

Are all divisions of the government working together? (FBI, Secret Service, State Department, Embassy)

If FLEC doesn't have him, who does?

Reactions: We are wondering who has Brent? Did he witness something and has been taken to prevent him reporting it? Has he gotten into trouble somehow? Will anyone ever come forward?

According to Melanie's notes, FBI agents came to question Barbara on October 25. However, Barbara has no recollection of this happening, but Melanie's notes state that Barbara called Maine at 6:50 p.m. and told them the FBI had questioned her about Brent's political activities and his relationship with the locals in Cabinda.

Melanie's notes also indicate Gary Weber told Barbara that PHI would most likely hire a negotiating committee to go to the meeting between FLEC and Chevron.

"Gary feels that none of the people from PHI will be allowed back into the country," Melanie wrote on October 25. "Gary seems to have information prior to everyone else telling us. Wonder why?"

Despite one reporter's dogged attempts to get the Swans in Maine to talk to the press, largely, Brent's situation was ignored after the initial reports. Although Barbara and Brent lived within fifty miles of Gainesville, Florida, the daily *Gainesville Sun* did not pick up on the fact that Brent lived within their readership area. Another very real form of terrorism was taking place in Gainesville during the fall of 1990. During the last week of August, someone brutally murdered five college students. In October, the murderer remained at large, and the one and only suspect had been ruled out when his DNA did not match samples at the crime scene. Terror and fear became very close and quite personal to the lives of anyone living within the vicinity of this college town.

Regardless, the Swans in both Florida and Maine decided they would not speak to the press no matter who called because they did not want the people responsible for Brent's disappearance to have any information about them.

"It felt like the reporters were turkey buzzards, circling around, never leaving us alone, getting in the way," Melanie explained.

The family also needed to keep the phone lines free to wait for the next call. They did not have a cell phone or call waiting or not even an answering machine right at first.

"There was nothing worse than rushing to the phone, heart pounding, to hear 'This is the *Advisor*,'" Melanie said. "We also didn't want to be rude, so we wouldn't think of hanging up on someone. We tried gracefully to get out of answering questions."

The Swan family knew very little about FLEC, except to be told that they usually did not harm those they kidnapped. Melanie remembers the family feeling great relief at receiving Brent's letter despite the morbid mention of New Hampshire's slogan.

Melanie's Notes—Day Eight—October 26
"Red Letter Day"
Barb received a letter from Brent via a fax machine at the bank! Stuart Hatcher [U.S. State Department] *read the letter to Mom over the phone. Barb verified that it was Brent's handwriting. A representative from FLEC came to the Zaire Embassy with a letter from Brent, which seemed to hold lots of clues.*

The State Department was going to try to do some deciphering to see if they might find their location. They feel he has gone into Zaire. He seems to be under no immediate threat. There was supposed to be another meeting the next day (Saturday) at 11:00 a.m. They were going to try to get pictures and a tape of the people when they come back to the Embassy. Mr. Hatcher will copy the letter and mail it to Mom. Mom called Gary to ask about what to do about the news article that came out in the Lewiston Sun *today.* [Melanie does not recall what this comment means.] *Finally, some contact from Brent! It's very encouraging. Things are moving forward!*

Melanie said receiving this letter marked a turning point for the family. Even though they had been worrying about the little things such as his glasses and his job, they really did not even know until the letter arrived if he was alive, but no one in the family would consider the possibility of his death out loud.

Melanie noted the family in Maine was also concerned about the "Live free or die" comment. They speculated about Brent's state of mind and the possibility that he might try to escape and get himself killed in the process. The letter may have brought relief, but it also brought its own set of new anxieties for the family.

Negotiating with Terrorists

The day the Zaire embassy and Barbara received the letter from Brent and the list of demands—day eight in captivity and the one-week anniversary of his capture—Brent and the soldiers marched to the new base camp.

Also on this day, Brent received a letter from the president of FLEC, Jose Tiburcio Z. Luemba. The president commended him for his cooperative behavior, stating the length of his stay with FLEC would depend on how well negotiations proceeded with the U.S. government and their associates. He promised to visit Brent within a week.

Perhaps Tiburcio counted on the U.S. policy, which denounced the Cuban military presence in Angola. Since 1976, according the State Department's "Background Notes" brochure from 1987, the United States made it clear that relations would not resume with the Angolan government until United Nations policies regarding Namibia were followed and until Cuban forces were withdrawn. The State Department recognized UNITA as "a legitimate nationalist movement that cannot be excluded from a role in the political life of Angola," according to the brochure.

Further it states, "The United States supports UNITA's struggle against Soviet/Cuban imperialism, and, in this regard, in providing it with appropriate and effective assistance."

All diplomatic negotiations between Angola and the United States ended in 1985 with the repeal of an amendment in the United States that forbid aid to UNITA. The Reagan administration supported this group who wanted to put the MPLA out of office.

However, the State Department did not forbid U.S. companies from operating in Angola. In 1987, they set forth a request for these companies to "consider U.S. national interests as well as their own in making business decisions."

The last lines of the "Background Notes" brochure give the strongest warning, yet points to the quest for profit making as the overruling motive.

"These companies are also alerted to the risks involved in doing business in the midst of a civil war. Direct bilateral assistance to Angola is prohibited by U.S. law."

Chevron's presence in Angola must not have been viewed as "direct bilateral assistance" despite the fact that the U.S.-based company pulled that oil up out of the ground off the shore of Cabinda, creating profits for Chevron and the Angolan government as well. In fact, the production of those offshore oil rigs provided the majority of Angola's income and had since 1966 with the discovery of the petroleum fields.

Gerald Bender, Angolan scholar, suggests that the relationship with Angola came as a result of U.S. politics, but those politics never interfered with the disruption of oil flowing out of the ground.

Karl Maier, a journalist in Angola since 1986, writes in *Angola: Promises and Lies* that it is the discovery of oil that will keep Cabinda tied to Angola forever, despite the best efforts of FLEC.

Sympathies for the total independence of Cabinda ran high in 1986, according to Maier as he spoke to Cabindans and the soldiers of FLEC. FLEC's modis operandi at this time consisted of stopping buses, mostly to and from Malongo, and emptying them of its passengers and forcing them to walk to their destinations. Then they would burn the vehicles. Maier writes that these calling cards of FLEC can be seen on the sides of the roads all around Cabinda.

CHAPTER 5

Life at Base Camp

Lewiston Sun-Journal (Lewiston, Maine)— *"Locke Mills man feared kidnapped in Angola"*

BETHEL (Oct. 26, 1990)—A Locke Mills native who has been working in Angola, Africa, has reportedly been kidnapped, although details concerning his abduction remain sketchy.

Brent Swan, a former resident of this small Oxford County village in Greenwood, is the son of Denise Swan, the town's deputy clerk, and Hugh Swan, the town's fire chief.

"It has been hell for us," said Mrs. Swan. "We don't know anything."

The only information the Swans have received is through their son's employer, Petroleum Helicopters Incorporated (PHI) in Lafayette, La.

Mrs. Swan would not comment on her son's situation for fear of jeopardizing his safety. "We don't want to say anything that might harm him," she said. "Our hands are tied."

Swan was kidnapped a week ago, according to Nyda Nodvorsky of the United States Bureau of Consulate Affairs in Washington, D.C. "We are still actively working on the alleged kidnapping and at this moment no one has claimed responsibility," Nodvorsky said Thursday.

Nodvorsky said that because the United States does not have an embassy in Angola, U.S. officials must work through neighboring countries that do have diplomatic relations with the country.

—

PHI, based in New Orleans, provides helicopter transportation for companies that operate oil-drilling rigs. The company owns 29 bases in the United States and two in Africa.

Swan was working in the Angolan base, flying workers to offshore rigs on the African coast.

A former Portuguese colony, Angola is in the midst of a long-running civil war.

Nodvorsky said officials are awaiting word about Swan's whereabouts from UNITA (National Union for Total Independence of Angola), one of the main factions in Angola.

Nodvorsky said that initially the Swan family had requested that Brent Swan's abduction be kept low key. However, Nodvorsky said that she has read news accounts of the incident in Washington newspapers.

Swan worked on helicopters and lived in Angola, according to Nodvorsky, who referred further questions to the African consulate in Washington.

The African consulate could not be reached for comment Thursday afternoon.

Gary Weber, a representative for Brent Swan's employer, verified that Swan works for PHI, but would not say whether an abduction occurred.

"It's a touchy situation," he said, adding, "We're not releasing any information at this time."

Depression Becomes a Companion

While Brent became accustomed to the second base camp, he began receiving regular packages from the embassy in Zaire. Brent remembers that Antonio Bento Bembe, secretary general, seemed to be one of the runners because when he returned to camp, he often came with a black pouch filled with letters. But instead of making him feel safer or more confident regarding his release, the letters he received began making him angry almost immediately. The embassy sent him a care package on October 29 with a note from his family, but not written by them—he could tell immediately. It was typed, and Brent saw it as a feeble attempt to raise his morale.

Mr. Swan,

   The following is a note from your family:
   Everybody in the family is pulling for you. It was great to get your letter. We hope you come home soon, but please write again in the meantime. We all love you very much. Barbara, Mom and Dad, and everyone sends their love.

"It made me mad," Brent said. "I knew they couldn't tell me what was going on, but they didn't tell me anything. The anger was probably more directed to those who were supposed to be working for my release.

"All you're doing is sending a letter from my family. They weren't telling me, 'this is what we're doing.' Of course, now I realize that everything coming in to me was searched by FLEC and the same for what went out, but I still didn't know what was happening."

All Brent wanted were reassurances that someone was working on his release, but he was not hearing that in the letters, and he spent every day wondering if it would be his last. Even though Gerald Scott, with the U.S. embassy in Zaire, wrote in his letter that everyone was working on his release, Brent wished for specifics because he was fully aware of the U.S. policy of not negotiating with terrorists.

Every morning, Brent woke to the sound of his daytime guard Agostinho, putting his clip back into his AK-47 and loading the first round.

"I heard that sharp snap of that chamber of the first round first thing every morning before I could go to the bathroom," Brent said.

It did not help his condition to go to the bathroom under those circumstances, but a new latrine at least brought some level of comfort during his frequent trips as the diarrhea continued.

Brent's Diary—Day Twelve—October 30

   First thing next morning, my very own hole was dug about 150 feet away. I was sick of doing a duck squat. I got some poles and vines and lashed together a good old American latrine, something to sit on, the comforts of home.

Brent actually built the latrine with branches and vines they had cut down and stacked. He used boards they had lying around, which he used to create a semicircle around the hole. He used one pole to hold the toilet paper, but this confused the soldiers even when Brent asked for a roll of toilet paper to demonstrate.

"I finally told them it was a device to escape from FLEC, as a joke," he said. "This was just not a really good joke because they took it seriously."

Alfredo reached for his pistol resting in a holster draped around his shoulder, but Brent says he looked confused as if wondering when they should shoot the American.

"Here I was just looking for a little more relaxing way to go to the bathroom to help my diarrhea," Brent said. "But it didn't help. It just varied from very bad to worse to 'Well, I guess it's not quite so bad today because I only made a couple of trips.' The bad days came when I had to make six trips."

This new latrine that Brent built did help some, but the relaxing part vanished as soon as Agostinho loaded his gun each morning. And despite the fact the prisoner's bathroom had a palm frond roof that extended almost to the ground in the back, the front part was open and exposed to anyone who might care to look his way.

"I had no privacy," Brent said. "I was stripped of my dignity."

"I was trying to keep track of who was there, who left camp, how many of them were there," he said. "I tried to see who might let their guard down. Maybe I could find a hole or opening, if maybe only six happened to be around."

Brent received the letter from the FLEC president, the letter from the embassy, and a care package around the same time near the last few days of October. Whenever anything came into camp, he watched as a soldier wrote things down on a piece of paper. Then they asked Brent to sign for everything he got.

Despite the fact that he was supposed to begin taking the vitamins once a day, he was not allowed to take them as soon as they arrived. He watched as his guards took one vitamin out of the bottle and gave it to one of the young soldiers who swallowed the pill sent by the embassy.

"The soldier had to wake up the next morning before I was allowed to take the vitamins," Brent said. "They wanted to make sure what they were sending into me wouldn't make me act funny or do something to me."

Around this time, he wrote back home in response to the letters and care package and signed it "Will see you home soon?????????"

Those question marks represented the anger Brent felt building. Barbara wrote around this time that Gary Weber would be coming to Africa. Instead of making him feel comforted, Brent felt scared because if all they could send to negotiate his release was Gary Weber, just an employee of PHI, what hope did he stand of getting out alive?

"Send the marines, send the army, send the air force, but send Gary Weber?" Brent said. "What's he going to do? Stand by and wait for me to be released?"

By this time, Brent had figured out that FLEC wanted to deal with Chevron more than anyone else, and he knew the U.S. government would have little role in negotiating his release because he knew the policy.

Some of the soldiers contracted malaria during this time. Brent would watch as they took the vial of malaria medicine and dip one needle into it to inject a soldier. The camp "doctor" would then throw the needle in a pot of boiling water, take it back out, insert it into the vial again, and then inject the next soldier in line.

"I was in fear whenever I saw them do this that I would be next in line," he said.

But the care packages provided him with oral doses of quinine to prevent him from contracting malaria, so he at least remained safe from the contaminated needles.

Brent was asked to make a tape on November 1, which was sent back to the States along with pictures of Brent opening his care package from Zaire.

Birds chirp in abandon in the background of the tape recording, in direct contrast to Brent's voice, which is slow and deliberate. Occasionally, his voice breaks, and if tears had sound, his voice would be weeping.

Brent makes a tape for the folks at home on day 14 of captivity.

Brent's Tape—Day Fourteen—November 1

Good morning, Mr. Scott, Cabinda Gulf, family and friends. November 1, about seven o'clock in the morning. Sitting here in the building, and I guess the best place to start is in the beginning. FLEC did try to contact Cabinda Gulf with a letter, but they had a negative or no response to that letter and then they chose to capture an American and they got me, and as you probably are aware, it was approximately five miles south of camp where I was captured. I had no choice in the matter; it was a very smooth operation. I was not harmed in any way. We hiked a short distance, went through a marsh to a base camp, where I was allowed to take a bath, put on some long pants, long-sleeved shirt, and then we hiked for the next four days, taking short hikes of three and four hours at which point we ended up at the base camp on Tuesday early in the morning. I was treated quite well; the first hammock strung in the trees was mine. They treated me as best they could on the trail, and I'm treated quite well here at camp. They've expressed a reasoning for capturing me and that they wished to open communications between FLEC and between Cabinda Gulf.

They are very strong people; they are united, and they wish to make things better for everyone concerned in Cabinda. They wish to change the government, which is nothing more than we've seen in the Eastern Block countries of Europe. I really can't blame them. They've been out here in the jungle for fifteen years, and after being here nearly two weeks, I can see why they would want to get out. [Voice begins to break here as if fighting tears.] *They live in conditions that are not the best; they are doing what they can to make my stay as comfortable as possible. For their troops, they are well disciplined, well organized. The operation to capture me was well thought through and the operation, like I said, went very smoothly, at least from my standpoint. I think you will find that the general population of Cabinda and the city of Cabinda overall is that they are ready for a change.*

The information that I need to pass on to you in concern to the fact that FLEC has not been recognized as an operation in existence, but I can assure you that they are in existence, I'm here with them. As their operation goes, they are throughout Cabinda province; they know Cabinda province like the back of their hand. That was very evident in my travels to the base camp. They could cause a lot of problems. They would like to change the government of Cabinda peacefully, and they wish to do this as best they can with the help of the United States, the help of Chevron/Cabinda Gulf. That had they not chosen to attempt a peaceful change of government, then everyone in Malongo could be in my shoes. They would like very much to solve all of the problems in Cabinda, make a better place for all of its citizens. One point that they wish for me to add and stress the fact is that the general population of Cabinda is, stands behind Cabinda, and that FLEC wants very much to change the government as well as having all the people in Cabinda want to change the government. They, I recognize, known by the general population, that they are here, that they are fighting for them, and that they would choose very much to have a more democratic society and that with the general population supporting them, it would be very difficult to suppress them.

Mr. Scott, I received your care package in full. Thank you. They are very concerned of my well-being, so concerned that the medications that were not in sealed containers have been taken by some of the troops to ensure that they would wake up this morning. They did, and I will be able to receive the medication. I received your letter. You seem hopeful that I will be home soon. That pleases me. As you say, you trust my personal relations with them are good as could be expected. I think we're getting along quite well. The gentleman that captured me and chose to point a gun at my head—a Mr. Senhor Loka—well, he and I are best of friends. I call him Miuto Bon Bandido, and it's kind of a local joke here at camp. Like I said, they treat me very well, feed me the best they can. We have had some local game that tasted pretty, well, it was even a little better than the porcupine.

The local potato, which is a root of an arrowhead family, very similar to a potato, but it's certainly not a Maine Russet. They have some greens, which is similar to the spinach family, and it's not bad either. I would take it that diarrhea is par for the course. That's what it's been. I realize that you're in contact with my family. I was very glad to get a note from them. I send my love. I also enclosed a letter that you may pass on, if you will. I think I've covered just about everything that I could pass on. If you get a chance to send some ointment or Caldecort or something along the line for an itchy ass (I hope your secretary isn't listening) it would be greatly appreciated. Like I said, I think I have covered everything that I can think of at this time. If I think of anything later in the day, I will add it. I have been, at one point, I wish to tell you that I have been moved from one base camp to another. It's about an hour and a half walk. It's a very similar camp. It has a small river, which is better as far as bathing goes. Other than that, I hope to be back in Malongo 'cause I'd certainly like to be turning a wrench on a King Air. With that I'll close and hope for an expedient agreement, and that my release may be very soon. I appreciate your help.

Mr. Scott, I've come up with some points I wish to add. It's a couple of hours later. I jotted a few things down here that I would like to pass on. Some of it important; some of it not. If you have any say in the matter at all, it's always a nagging thought in the back of my mind that the Angolan troops will try to get me back. If they can stay in their own territory or you can have any say in the fact that they stay in their own territory, I think things would go easier. A nagging thought is always that I'd get caught in the crossfire or something along those lines. I feel quite protected here. The FLEC troops have made me feel protected. However, remote the possibility is of Angolan troops finding me, it's always that thought in the back of your mind. The only other fear I have is what they call a scorpion, and it looks to me to be a well-fed, overgrown tarantula. Kind of a scary-looking fella. As I mentioned in my letter, I try to keep my mind at ease. This is nothing more than a camping trip with the Boy Scouts. I guess we all know what it really is. I've been working over here in Angola for six years, and I've got to say this is the first time I've seen any group of people either individually or as a group that walk and talk and take any action with a purpose in life. They have some very good intelligence. The camp in Malongo, the people here in Cabinda, and they are trying very hard here to do what they can with what they have.

I've had a chance to show them how to make an American latrine. My idea of taking a crap in a hole is hanging my balls between my ankles is, wasn't, my idea of a good, taking a good crap. So we made a latrine and lashed it together with some vines, and it seems to work pretty well. Little more comfort. Like I said, I do have diarrhea. I don't know how long a body can hold up to that. Feel pretty good except for that. The cut on my left ankle seems to be healing pretty good. It's still a little sore; it seems to be doing fine. I plan on using the ointment, which you sent, bandages, and been keeping it clean as I possibly can. I've been instructed as to how to make manioc bread from the manioc plant, and that was quite interesting. And Senhor Loka has taught me how to make a palm frond roof for the camps here. It's been quite an educational experience, I guess. And that's all I've got, so I'll hope to see you soon. And hope tomorrow brings a better day. This is sincerely yours, Brent Swan.

Along with the tape, Brent sent a letter to Barbara and his family. The tone in Brent's voice from the tape, added with the mixed signals in the letter, caused Barbara to be concerned for Brent's mental state. The following letter written on November 1 was faxed to Barbara on November 3.

Dear Barbara, Family and Friends,

Not to worry. I'm here with my brothers, and we together will change Cabinda. Personally, as I'm sure you know, I'd rather be turning a wrench on a King Air. Life does take its twists and turns. I know Mike Bouillion wants the King Air job pretty bad, but I never expected he'd go to such extremes. I'm sure a lot of people would pay good money to take a jungle safari like this. Bush Gardens will never be the same.

I'm sure Mr. Scott will pass on additional information and photos.

I try to ease my mind and that this is nothing but a camping trip with the Boy Scouts, and I guess in a way it is.

I Love You All,
Your Survivor,
Brent

A side note to PHI: Screw you, Mike. I will be a King Air mechanic again. Hopefully, in the near future. Yes, I still want the work over.

His bravado represented his determination to not let his captors win at any cost. It also meant that Brent had not yet lost hope—he still had a future if he imagined coming back to work upon his release. However, he knew it would be a battle to get Chevron to agree to his return to work if he ever made it out alive.

Brent was fully aware of the policy of this American company with ties in an African nation. He had seen the policy put into action in the past, and it meant that PHI and the other companies under contract to Chevron sent home several good workers.

In Malongo, if an American worker had a confrontation with one of the locals, for whatever reason, and the local became upset as a result of the situation, the American worker lost. No amount of excuses, reasoning, or innocence would change the minds of the managers. The American employee received a one-way ticket back to the States.

"We lost a lot of good people that way," Brent said. "People would come over to Africa, and they'd work for a little while and then get into some kind of trouble with the locals.

"It never had to do with not doing the job correctly," Brent continued. "It was just they got into cross fires with one of the locals, and Chevron's policy was if you're not going to get along, you're going to go home."

Brent called it their "quick and simple fix" no matter how talented or skillful a worker might be.

"So when I got into this situation," Brent said, "I figured this was the end of my career in Africa, and that I would never be able to go back."

His fight against his captors began with that simple statement in his letter home. He also worried whether he was still being paid by PHI and if Barbara was receiving the checks. He knew the policies of his company, and he knew he was not doing his job. It did not matter to him at the time knowing that doing his job had put him in this position; he still worried.

Life at Home

Melanie's Notes—Day Twelve—October 30

At 9:00 a.m., FLEC people came to the Embassy and took a package for Brent with boots, malaria pills, magazines, and cigarettes, high-potency vitamins, candy and a letter that Hatcher [Stuart Hatcher from State Department] composed as being from Brent's family.

Barb wrote a letter and faxed it to Gary. Not sure if it got into the package.

Barbara's letter did get into the package, but her intended purpose of offering Brent comfort and letting FLEC know Brent had loved ones awaiting his return did not hit the mark as Brent sank further into his depression. However, he managed to keep his sinking hopes from the members of FLEC as he watched their every movement without appearing to do so.

"I could tell he was very depressed," Barbara said about the tape. "Gary and Ed [PHI employees] kept asking me about secret messages. The FBI wasn't talking to me, so the only information I received came from Gary and Ed."

In fact, the PHI employees working toward Brent's release told Barbara they did not want anything to do with the FBI. After they heard about Barbara's first conversation with the FBI agents, Barbara said, "Ed went off his rocker and told me I didn't have to talk to those guys." She wondered at the time who was really helping to get her husband home.

The pictures of Brent opening his care package did not help lay her fears to rest. If anything, it made her more scared for Brent's safety.

Brent calls the photos taken by his captors proof of life. In this one, he gives the finger to the photographer.

"I kept searching his face for something that would tell me he was OK," Barbara said. "Then I noticed his clothes, and I wondered, 'What the hell is that yellow thing he's wearing?'

"It was frightening to see him—it's one thing to hear him—but to see him with the other people there . . ."

Several things become apparent in Brent's letter, although at the time they did not register with Barbara and the rest of the family. Parts of the November 1 letter and tape could be construed as Brent going over to the other side and sympathizing with his captors, not unlike what happened to Patty Hearst when she was kidnapped by the Symbionese Liberation Army in the 1970s, and she became an accomplice with her kidnappers.

Control Risks, an international consulting firm, worked with PHI. Control Risks' consultants are pulled from elite law enforcement agencies in the United States, England, Holland, and Australia. These consultants all have prior experience in countering crimes of kidnapping and extortion. Simon Adams-Dale, one of these consultants, sat in on most of the negotiations, and the other consultant, Christopher Gross, pulled together information on the effect of the kidnapping on Brent's mental state. Gross warned Barbara that Brent could become sympathetic with the causes of FLEC. The psychological term is the "Stockholm syndrome," which means the victim, in an effort to survive, goes to the side of the more powerful entity.

Rita Lawrence, a victim advocate counselor in Gainesville, Florida, explains that it is a fine line the hostage walks.

"Some people cross that line," she said. "They start out cooperating for survival's sake. That's what they are going to do to keep alive."

Brent's determination to go back to work as expressed in the letter might have caused alarm for Barbara if she wasn't so worried about other things.

Life became a little easier for Barbara around this time after PHI set up the fax machine in her home. Up until this time, she had to go to the bank in Chiefland to receive faxes, and she felt the whole world knew her business in such a public place. Privacy became very important to Barbara during this time as she found it difficult to know whom she could trust. She had learned to lean on Gary Weber and called him her "comfy pillow," but he had gone to Africa to help with the negotiations. That left her with Ed Gatza, who at least had a sense of humor as opposed to Gary's serious nature, but she did not know Ed as well and the change hit her hard.

The self-imposed ban on talking to the media continued. Gary and Ed both advised Barbara not to talk, and Stuart Hatcher with the State Department initially advised them to not talk before they knew exactly who had taken him.

"I didn't want to broadcast it either," Barbara said. "The *Gainesville Sun* never picked it up."

Since everyone around her was suggesting she not go to the press, and Brent's parents did not want publicity brought upon them, Barbara remained quiet. Both she and Melanie wonder if they did the right thing.

Melanie's Notes—Day Fourteen—October 31

FLEC reps came back to the Embassy and said they had dispatched the message. They are supposed to be back Friday or Saturday with an answer to Chevron's proposal.

An article came out in the Bethel Citizen *today. It was mainly rewritten from the* Lewiston Sun *article.*

———

Mom got a call today from the Voice of America, which broadcasts in Angola. They are wondering if we want to do an interview. They will broadcast in Portuguese so that the captors will understand. It's our decision.

Olympia Snow's [U.S. House of Representatives, representing Maine's Second Congressional District in 1990. Snow is currently a U.S. senator] *office also called to lend support. They restated some information we already knew and told us to contact Stuart Hatcher. They want us to let them know if they can do anything. Olympia apparently read a news item this morning and asked her office to call.*

Melanie believes their "helplessness and vulnerability" motivated the family to resist the press.

"We really wanted to just be left alone, to focus on the important communications with people working on getting Brent out," Melanie said.

CHAPTER 6

Deepest, Darkest Africa

Bethel Citizen

(Nov. 1, 1990)—*"Locke Mills man missing; believed hostage in Angola"*

While the attention of most Americans is focused on their fellow countrymen being held hostage in Iraq and Kuwait, political unrest on the other side of the African continent hit home locally last week, with the report that a Locke Mills native has apparently been abducted by rebels in Angola.

According to as-yet-unconfirmed reports, Brent Swan, 31, the son of Hugh and Denise Swan of Locke Mills, was abducted in Angola in the early morning of Oct. 19, as he was on his way to work.

Swan is a helicopter mechanic employed by Petroleum Helicopters, Inc., a New Orleans-based company that provides helicopter transportation for oil-drilling operations.

No one has yet claimed responsibility for the abduction—which has made the situation even more stressful for the parents.

"We just don't know very much yet. All we can do is wait," said his mother.

A former Portuguese colony, Angola won its independence in 1974. However, the United States regards its Marxist government as unfriendly and does not maintain diplomatic relations with the country.

The United States, in fact, openly supports the country's major rebel group, UNITA, the National Union for the Total Independence of Angola, which has been fighting for power for 15 years.

—

UNITA has denied any involvement in Swan's abduction and, according to published reports, has pointed the finger at another rebel group, FLEC, the Front for the Liberation of the Cabinda Enclave.

FLEC has been fighting for the independence of Cabinda, the region in which Swan was working at the time of his abduction.

According to Denise Swan, FLEC has a reputation for being nonviolent, and other hostages taken by the group reported that they had been well treated.

The Swan family, the State Department and Petroleum Helicopters, Inc. are all saying as little as possible about the situation, in order to avoid endangering the missing man.

But a State Department spokesman last week said, "We are continuing to pursue this at the highest levels."

Meanwhile, a thin yellow ribbon stays tied to a lamppost in Locke Mills.

Giving Up Hope

Gerald Scott at the embassy sent Brent a short note along with Barbara's letter on November 7, suggesting that progress had been made. He cited the example of Barbara's faxed letter as proof.

This three-sentence note sent Brent's mental state into a tailspin.

"What progress?" Brent said. "I just got a letter from my wife. Now how is that progress? We're not progressing here."

Things began to go downhill for him as he headed toward a full month in captivity.

"I had waited twelve days for any news at all since the last letters," he said. "Now I'm sitting here with 'We're making progress' because I've gotten a letter from my wife."

Even the care packages from the embassy did not help ease Brent's mind. When they sent a large bottle of bleach, it made him angry. The directions with the bleach told him to use a drop or two in a glass of water to make it safe to drink.

"I thought, how long did they think I would be there if they had to send that much?" he said.

Getting a bottle of one hundred daily vitamins and a three-month supply of malaria medication only added to his agitation and worry about his release.

Time played on his mind when he had been in captivity for thirty days. His thoughts fluctuated between "I'll never get out of here" to "I'll be so sick when I finally get out of here I'll never be well again" to "I'm going to be leaving here in a body bag."

Questions plagued him. How long would they keep him? Would they just keep him until he died? And as the diarrhea continued, he knew his body's ability to cope would be severely affected in a short time. As he continued obsessing with these thoughts, he managed to be aware of what he was doing, and he knew his mind was deteriorating as quickly as his body.

He kept telling himself he was just on a Boy Scout camping trip. Or he would imagine he was an explorer panning for gold in the little stream that ran alongside the camp—anything to keep his mind off of the situation and the endless questions with no answers. As he pretended to pan for gold in the stream, he would tell himself that if he found gold, he would never leave.

He would use these references in his letters home. He also liked to think that he was simply on safari in Africa as he camped in the jungle and panned for gold.

"I would tell myself that I just decided to take off a little time and enjoy a little safari here," Brent said.

All of these techniques served him well because he managed to keep his anger at bay, and his captors did not know his private thoughts; they did not know the depth of his hatred toward them. In fact, they viewed Brent as a friend more than an enemy.

On day twenty-five, November 12, Brent requested some paper, so they gave him a 5 x 6 notepad, and he began his diary. They noticed that he would write on the back of his letters using the pen that had been in his carry bag. He began conserving paper by sending back letters he had received with his responses written on the back. Then he began gathering information about his captors.

"I started talking with Agostinho about FLEC," he said. "He seemed fairly cooperative in providing information."

Then he began to write his story.

Brent's Diary—Day Twenty-five—November 12
Then I waited, no word till the twelfth. Hoping to hear good news like "OK, you go to Kinshasa now." What I got was a care package and "I think we're making progress."

—

> *Tail spin right into the ground. My reply was not good. I guess it's another twelve-day wait. I'm sure there will be more to this chapter as time goes on.*

Brent wrote a letter to Gary Weber. While parts of the letter seem upbeat, Brent was not revealing his true state of mind at the time. However, his fears about what was happening at home with his wife and his job are evident.

> *November 14, 1990*
> *Dear Gary,*
>
> *I heard you're headed this way. I hope you brought the Marines with you. I'm optimistic that I will get out of this mess. When?????*
>
> *I would hope that someone has thought to see that my wife is financially OK. I'm sure she has taken on extra expenses. I can only hope she's OK, but would ease my mind knowing.*
>
> *As you can probably guess, I could use some time with the wife at home immediately after release. I hope this doesn't surprise you, but I would like to return to King Base 575 and pick up where I left off. Kind of like falling off a bicycle, pick yourself up, dust yourself off, check out your equipment, and ride on. Will this be possible? If not, what are my options? I can only guess my wife's told you, "He'll never leave the States again." Give me a few days with her, she'll be OK.*
>
> *I hope you have a good trip over here, a prosperous one. Hope to see you soon. I am looking forward to joining the PHI family again.*
>
> *Regards,*
> *Brent A. Swan*

On this day, he still wrote with hope about his future and his release. The days to come would not be so bright.

Keeping the Faith

In Chiefland, Barbara tried to remain hopeful and sent a letter on November 4, attempting to do two things: bolster Brent's spirits and let the members of FLEC know that Brent had family back in the States concerned about his well-being. She had no idea the letters might have the opposite effect upon Brent's mental state.

November 4, 1990
Dear Brent,

This will probably be one of the most difficult letters I've ever had to write. There's so much I'd like to ask and tell you but am very limited on space and what I can say. I guess the important thing is that we keep hearing from you and know you are doing OK. Glad you are being treated well under the circumstances. You'll sure have some good tales to tell around the campfire about this trip!! I know you said you wanted to go on a diet, but this is not the way to do it. Try to keep your strength and general health up as best you can.

These past two and a half weeks sure have been long (can't imagine how they must feel for you). I'm trying my best to stay strong for you, but it's getting very difficult to remain so. You don't realize how many friends you have or even who they are, until a time like this. If it hadn't been for their support, I wouldn't have been able to cope as well. We have many people to thank when you are returned safely (I have NO doubts, it is when that bothers me). I'm surprised I have found time to unglue the phone from my ear long enough to write. Our line has been busy since this happened. Keep hoping to hear your voice.

My mom arrived on the twenty-fifth of October. She is here for the winter. I'm really glad she's here. Richard has been calling constantly, hoping to hear great news and feeling helpless like the rest of us. Sure wish we knew what we could do to speed this whole thing up, but we can only put our trust and faith in others more knowledgeable. This is not the kind of thing we deal with on a daily basis, and it is hard to just sit and wait. One thing for sure is that Gary Weber has been fantastic, keeping me up to speed on everything, and now he's going over there to see if he can help there. It's probably for the best, but I will miss the contact.

We have been having beautiful weather here, sure wish you were here to enjoy it with me. Great camping (our way!) and working on the house weather. I hope you are not getting too rained on, I know it's the season for it. Also watch out for the spiders you described, they sound nasty. I bet you never thought a Big Mac would sound so good!!

Your parents, grandparents, Mel, and Ross, all send their love, as well as all the in-laws. I truly hope to see you soon. I miss you and pray for your safe return home to me. Please take care of yourself, and remember, I LOVE YOU.

Barbara XXOOXX

Barbara's notes indicate that Gary left for Africa the day after she wrote this letter, which did nothing to reassure Brent that anything was being done to substantially help in his release efforts.

Melanie's Notes—Day Eighteen—November 5

Mr. Hatcher [Stewart Hatcher, State Department] contacted Mom to say he would send a transcript of the tape and a copy of the second letter. The Chevron people were going to leave on Saturday, but had not gone [to Africa]. They were going to go through Frankfort. They had established tomorrow, November 6, as the meeting date if Brent is released.

Barb got a letter from the president of FLEC today. He told her Mr. Swan was comfortable and in good health. She feels it is to win her support for FLEC.

Evening—Mom and Dad had been getting frequent calls with no message left on the machine. I was there and answered the phone for them, lying that they were not home. Mr. Ron Dox of the FBI asked for them and then asked if I was Melanie. All the time I was thinking, "How does he know my name?" My God, I'm lying to the FBI! I said I was a friend, just watching the house. He left his name and number. He just wanted to be in touch in case we got any information.

"I thought about this for a long time," she said. "Why had I lied about who I was? We lost trust in everyone. We didn't know if the people were working for us or against us. Were they working together or checking up on each other?"

Barbara became enraged when she read the letter from FLEC's president, Jose Tiburcio.

"The letter from the president made me very angry," Barbara said. "I thought the nerve, the gall, of these people. They don't think they're doing anything wrong.

"We're thinking at home they want to test how much Brent means to the government."

The letter, dated November 5, 1990, offers sympathy for the family's plight and concern for Brent. Tiburcio tried to assure her that Brent was well, despite the trying circumstances and living conditions. He told her he hoped Brent would be safely home within a few days.

Brent with FLEC's president Jose Tiburcio.

Melanie's Notes—Day Twenty-one—November 8
Gary and Simon Adams-Dale [Control Risks] were meeting with people from the French and Portuguese governments because they have dealt with FLEC. The French hostages had been released because they had given arms and money. We haven't heard how the meeting went.

At some point, they had brought pictures of Brent sitting on a stump. He is wearing his glasses and had Oreos. He is bearded. There were pictures of the troops and their flag also.

Friday is set as meeting date [the next day].

Melanie's Notes—Day Twenty-three—November 10

At 11:30 a.m., Barb called. Today's meeting went well as far as negotiations were concerned. They are down to two items that still need to be settled. They are addressing the refugee problem. Tribe members were displaced from their homes by Chevron. They refer to this as Genocide. They are getting Red Cross to provide medicine and food. They are saying they are not able to help them with the political issues (Cabinda's liberation). The Jesse Jackson and Jimmy Carter thing is out the window. October 23, 1990, is the date on the list of demands. Barb will send a copy of them to Mom. They will meet again on Monday, November 12, 1990, at 2:30 p.m.

Gary is impressed with Adams-Dale. He seems to know what they want before they say it. The meeting consists of Gary and his secretary, Chevron rep and his secretary, Adams-Dale and three FLEC reps (Mr. Zulu plus two others).

Today, the negotiating team is meeting among themselves with the Embassy people (Mr. Scott). They are sending another care package with candy, model planes, games, and cards.

We haven't seen the pictures yet and still haven't received the transcript of the tape and a copy of the second letter (from Mr. Hatcher.)

Wednesday, Barb is to be picked up at the Gainesville Airport by the corporate jet to go to Louisiana to meet Mrs. Suggs. An associate of Ed Gatza might come along to pick her up.

We've talked about keeping track of all these details thinking Brent might want to read them later. Maybe he'll even want to write a book and get rich!

The missing piece of all these notes is that with each call and new information, we play "what if" and "maybe that is why."

Our emotions go up and down with each new piece of information. Barb wrote a beautiful note to all of us, telling us she always felt welcome in our family and how much it has meant to her now. It touched all of us. Can't imagine how tough it is for Barb.

The day we first heard that a letter had come through was a great day. Until then we didn't even know where he was, who had him, or if he was OK.

Barbara managed to write another letter on November 13 that sounded hopeful and upbeat. Her impending trip to New Orleans to visit Carroll Suggs, the owner of PHI, and Ed Gatza, Barbara's PHI contact, lifted her spirits for a short time.

November 13, 1990
Dear Brent,

Well, here it is your break day tomorrow, and I guess you were right about it being a long hitch. I just hope it isn't much longer. Overtime takes a whole new meaning in this picture.

It has been awhile since I heard from you. Hoping to receive another letter from you soon. Hope to hear that you are still doing fine and are "enjoying" that camping trip still. Hardly a minute goes by that I'm not thinking of you. Even if you are not home by next Thursday [Thanksgiving], you can bet there will be a heck of a Thanksgiving dinner waiting for you when you do get home. We will sure have something to be thankful for.

I sure hope that the packages and letters are reaching you without much delay. Sounds like the care packages have some things in them to keep you busy and healthy.

Tomorrow we are going to meet Mrs. Suggs and Ed Gatza for lunch. They will pick us up in one of your "babies." Will enjoy the ride in one of the planes you work so hard on. I'll admit I'm nervous about the meeting but am looking forward to it. Mother is going with me. Just wish an occasion like this would have occurred under different circumstances.

Take care, you'll be home SOON. Everyone sends their love. Write when you can.

Love, Barbara
XXOOXOXO

While Brent tried to go back and remember everything that had happened in the previous twenty-five days, Barbara flew from Cross City, Florida, to New Orleans and met with the PHI people, including

Christopher Gross with Control Risks Ltd., hired by either PHI or Chevron to work to consult on Brent's situation. Gross had composed letters to U.S. senators that he had Barbara sign, "just in case." The letters were never sent, and Barbara does not remember what they said. However, she was asked to follow somewhat of a script in future letters to Brent. Gross gave her a "Draft Script for Mrs. Swan to include in her next letter to Brent Swan."

The Draft Letter

I don't know whether you see any newspapers there, but the position of the hostages in Iraq is terrible. I do try to understand our government's tough policy, but it's hard to bear and is now so real because of you.

[Leave a few sentences—discuss other matters.]

I hope that you get a chance to talk to the people you are with about our American ways and they to you about their lives and ideas. It must help relieve the boredom and at least you can say it's educational.

Melanie's Notes—Day Twenty-seven—November 14

Barb called after getting back from Louisiana. John Breaux [U.S. Senator from Louisiana] is on speaking terms with the President of Zaire. Mr. Scott [Gerald Scott, Embassy head] took notice when he was told Mr. Breaux was coming.

Barb was told not to expect Brent before Christmas.

Ed Gatza called Mom today, and Mrs. Suggs came on and spoke to Mom over the phone also. She is very impressed with Barb. They are willing to fly Mom and Dad down [to Chiefland] if they want to go.

I called Ed Gatza yesterday (Tuesday) about whether we could send letters. He said the more the better. We should fax them to all offices, and someone will get them through.

Barb sounded wound up after coming back from Louisiana today. Mom and Dad will probably not go to Florida on such short notice. They'll wait.

Melanie wondered why they ever waited so long to start writing Brent. "Seems ridiculous to wait so long to send letters," she said. "I think it was just part of the feeling helpless thing. Finally realized we had to speak up for what we thought was best."

Barbara remembers people telling her they were impressed with how well she was managing during this trying time. But she didn't feel as if she was managing at all.

"I was on autopilot," she said. "I just had to get through the day."

Cabinda's Problem

PHI told Barbara after the second meeting that Chevron was in control, which is something not felt after the first round of meetings where the negotiators acknowledged FLEC held the upper hand. During the second meeting, certain demands were discarded, such as the political expectations for Chevron to help free the Cabindan people. FLEC asked that Chevron negotiate with the U.S. government and major groups within the United States, such as the heads of the Republican and Democratic parties. Chevron told FLEC they had no such authority to serve as the liaison for FLEC. Chevron also told them they could not assist the Cabindans militarily as demanded.

The social demands for medicine, food, clothing, and money seemed more reasonable, and the negotiators for Brent's release promised to work with the American Red Cross in securing some of these items.

Melanie wrote in her notes that she remembered hearing the FBI was monitoring the negotiations carefully because of the legal issues involved in dealing with terrorists. She remembers at that point the family became very careful about not saying anything about what they knew regarding the lists of demands.

The members of FLEC maintained that the Cabindan people suffered a form of genocide at the hands of the Angolan government because of the miserable living conditions and level of poverty. Also, accusations of abuses by the Angolan military seemed a justification for FLEC's actions outside the law.

These fighters for the independence of Cabinda base their political philosophy upon something that occurred in 1885 when Portugal claimed sovereignty in Cabinda with the Treaty of Simulanbuco. This treaty recognized Cabinda as a Portuguese protectorate. Even in 2005, the Web site for the Republic of Cabinda calls itself a "Portuguese

Protectorate," with the words "FLEC" and "Portugal" gracing either side of the heading.

This treaty is often referred to in the arguments for independence. While Angola remained under the auspices of imperial Portugal in 1974, when it came time for the country's freedom, Cabinda representatives were not invited to Portugal to participate in the Alvor Accords. Only the three groups for independence of Angola went to the southern Portuguese town of Alvor in 1974 to negotiate the independence of Portugal's colonial holdings after its fascist government fell.

Jeremy Wells of Finders University states in his study on Cabinda and Somaliland in 2003, "FLEC, however, was not allowed to participate in these talks, the Portuguese believing that FLEC's interests were represented by the three independence movement groups from Angola in attendance (the MPLA, UNITA, and the FNLA)."

As a result, article 3 of the Accords annexed Cabinda into Angola, while remaining "an integral part of Angola" according to the *Washington Post* article "Cabinda: Politics—Let the People Decide" published in 2003. The *Post* maintains this took place without the representation of one single Cabindan citizen. Within several years of the Alvor Accords, FLEC had declared Cabinda's provisional government as the Republic of Cabinda.

Karl Maier notes in *Angola: Promises and Lies* that FLEC was mostly noted for its disruptive methods of gaining attention such as ambushing buses and trucks and forcing passengers to walk to their destinations and then burning the vehicles. Some of the factions within FLEC such as FLEC-Renovada were known for more brutal attacks with a reputation of torturing their captives.

In 1990, two other incidents occurred with connections to FLEC, although FLEC denied the first incident according to the MIPT Terrorism Knowledge Base, which cited the group as a "dissident faction" and noting, "The main body of FLEC publicly condemned the action," which involved the abduction of employees of the French-based ELF oil company. However, FLEC did claim responsibility for the abduction of the two Portuguese aid workers in Angola on September 20. They were released on November 15, 1990—Brent's twenty-eighth day of captivity—after intervention by the Portuguese and Zaire governments.

Melanie wrote in her notes about the release of these hostages: "Reports are that they had malaria. Gary and others were meeting with them to find out what they had done to get them released."

—

CHAPTER 7

The Good Hostage

Lewiston Sun-Journal

(Nov. 16, 1990)— *"Baker to meet African officials"*

WASHINGTON (AP)—In an effort to solidify support for U.S. moves in the Persian Gulf, Secretary of State James A. Baker III will meet this weekend with the foreign ministers of three African countries that are members of the UN Security Council.

He hopes to persuade them to support a resolution authorizing the use of force to expel Iraqi invaders from Kuwait. Baker last week lined up the Soviet Union, China, Britain, and France. They are permanent members of the Council and could have killed the resolution with their veto.

The three African countries are Ethiopia, Ivory Coast and Zaire. Enlisting them to support the Bush administration would give the toughened U.S. stance broader approval among neutral and Third World nations.

Baker's meetings with the African foreign ministers will be held Saturday in Geneva. He will fly to Paris to meet Sunday with the foreign ministers of Romania and Finland and hold another session with Soviet Foreign Minister Eduard A. Shevardnadze and British Foreign Secretary Douglas Hurd.

Later Sunday, Baker will meet President Bush in Paris for a 34-nation summit where a landmark treaty to reduce NATO and Warsaw Pact tanks and other non-nuclear weapons will be signed.

The following weekend Baker will go to Colombia to confer with President Cesar Gaviria. Colombia also is a member of the Security Council.

Baker, at a White House news conference Wednesday, said the administration had not decided to use force, but wanted that option to be credible in hopes of persuading Iraqi President Saddam Hussein to give up Kuwait.

Playing Charades

While the U.S. government dealt with the growing concerns in the Middle East, Brent sat in the jungles of Angola in the area sometimes called the "African Kuwait" because of its rich deposits of oil both on—and offshore. Cabinda's independence seemed as unlikely as Brent's release by mid-November. He wrote to Cedric Dumont, MD, at the embassy regarding his medical conditions. Six items dealt with his physical health with no major concerns. Item number 7 caused concern back home when it was finally faxed to Barbara on November 26.

"7. Mind—I'm losing it, I know it. I'm doing my damnedest to control it. Any suggestions?"

By day twenty-eight, November 15, Brent had caught up his daily diary entries. He did not want to stop writing.

"At lunch time, I didn't eat—'I'm busy, don't bother me, not hungry,' I told them. This really threw them," Brent said. "I guess they may have thought I was going on a fast, or was just going to starve myself to death. They got really concerned that I missed one of their lousy meals."

As much as the soldiers tried to make him comfortable, Brent always wondered when they might turn on him, which kept him in a perpetual state of anxiety and did not help his diarrhea.

Brent's Diary—Day Twenty-eight—November 15
I'm sitting here in their White House, Capital Hill. Camp is on the east slope of a hill. Behind me it rises sharply. This afternoon is a nice blue sky and sunshine on my back. In front of me is a kitchen fifty yards off. It's beside a small stream eight feet across. I bath in it, drink from it, (after boiling for one and a half hours), and dishes are washed in it. Between me and the kitchen is an eating

area. Though I'm fed under cover in the sleeping quarters. Troops get two meals a day at 9:00–10:00 a.m. and 6:00 p.m. I get three meals a day at 6:30 a.m., noon, and 5:00 p.m. More on what I'm fed later. Off to my right are two material buildings. I'll call them buildings, but they're marginal. Everything is made from what you would find in a jungle. The two material buildings and White House have clapboard sides split from trees here on site. All roofs are palm frond. I've been through some hellish rains, and I'll be damned why these babies don't leak. So far I've stayed dry through the storms. Sleeping quarters are approximately sixteen bed units, but there's always room for one more. There's one to my right and two to my left. They consist of an approximate eight to twelve pitch roof, eight to ten foot ridgepole, three to four foot eaves, twenty by thirty foot overall. Beds are elevated one foot off the ground by two poles running lengthwise, beds are bamboo slats tied with vines to the poles. There are two sets of beds per building. Mike Bouillon, your back would never make it as long as mine has. Even though I have a foam pad over the bamboo, it's been well used and is about wore out. So is my back. I guess anything's better than nothing. I must say all the members of FLEC are trying very hard to make my stay as comfortable as possible.

I guess you could say I'm their jewel of this muddy stream. They are very protective. Presently I'm sleeping in one of the quarters on the left, behind it is a hole for (she-she) piss. Way off to the right is a two-holer and that's all it is, two holes in the ground, the toilet. I was here about three days when I got diarrhea. This was real bad. Every hour all through the night. Like I said they are very protective. I get up, everybody gets up. The way to the toilet is secured then I can walk/run out and go. Had a couple of close calls. As you can tell, it was a long sleepless night. First thing next morning my very own one-holer was dug about 150 feet away. I too was sick of doing a duck squat. I got some poles and vine and lashed together a good old American latrine, something to sit on, the comforts of home.

My Daily Routine
Up at five thirty. Breakfast at six thirty. Nap (under mosquito net) until the sun comes out, and the bugs go away. Then every other

day, exercise, something I haven't done since high school. Fifteen minutes of calisthenics get that heart a pumping and them lungs a breathing. Then for the next fifteen to thirty minutes depends on how I feel, I pace my outer boundaries. Like a cat in a cage. A prisoner. A hostage, I am.

After I cool down and the troops eat, I take a bath. Lunch, then nap or read. Lately I've been writing. And I just made a big mistake. I cannot call myself a prisoner. There is a big difference because a prisoner counts the days to release. A hostage counts the days since capture and has no idea when release will be. Then it's suppertime at 5:00 p.m. Sit around the campfire a couple of hours.

During his daily routine, Brent also thought. Later he remarked that thinking was the only thing that remained his own, his only freedom. After he wrote about his exercise routine, he soon stopped it because he realized exercising made him thirsty, and he felt dehydrated. Drinking more water would not help, he knew, because it was not of good quality despite the drops of bleach he added to each glass.

He never stopped the pacing, like a caged animal at the zoo.

Not knowing when he would be released began weighing heavily on his mind. A radio had come in one of the care packages, so at night he would listen to BBC, South African channels, and Voice of America. There was never any mention again of Americano Brent Swan after that first time while still marching to the base camp.

Agostinho was assigned to Brent as his daytime guide the first day he came into base camp because of all the regulars at camp, Agostinho spoke the best English. However, it was the secretary for FLEC, Antonio Bento Bembe—Senhor Bento as Brent was instructed to call him—who spoke the best English of them all. Whenever Bento was in camp, Brent talked to him the most.

That first day in the base camp, Agostinho walked Brent around and showed him all the buildings, giving him some advice on how his time in captivity might go.

"He told me, 'We are not going to hold you two or three months,'" Brent said. "He also mentioned that how long I stayed would depend upon me."

Brent interpreted this message in two ways. First, he believed Agostinho was warning him to be patient, and he would be released as soon as negotiations had been completed. He knew the FLEC soldiers hoped the ransom demands would be met quickly.

However, Brent also heard an underlying message in Agostinho's words. If Brent did not want to continue to stay with them, he would have to commit suicide or escape. During this time, the words from the Eagles' song "Hotel California" began to play over and over again in his head.

"You can check out anytime you want, but you can never leave."

Brent wrote about his food on day twenty-nine, the day after a hard rain made the small stream a twelve-foot wide river. Oreo cookies came in his care package and even the soldiers of FLEC knew to eat the middle first, Brent noticed. He ate the meat of the gazelle and a small white-tailed deer and enjoyed them both. He also received a special item in the care package—a bottle of Jack Daniels. One morning, after a night spent drinking the whiskey, they fed Brent macaco, or monkey, for breakfast.

"They showed me half a skinned monkey, tail stuffed in its mouth with its eyes wide open," he said. "I violently vomited behind the closest tree. Dumped everything to dry heaves. I have never in my life gotten so sick, so fast as I did that day.

"They did not show me what we would eat after that."

He learned about manioc, a very versatile plant, brought to Angola by the Portuguese after discovering its benefits in Brazil during the peak of the plantations and slave trade. The leaves can be used as greens, and the roots can be eaten raw or fried or barbequed. The soldiers soaked the roots in the river for three or four days until they became soft. Then he watched as they "beat the living shit out of them," turning them into mush. The roots are toxic so the beating served the purpose of beating the poison out of them. The mush would then be rolled up in large green banana leaves and boiled for one hour to create a bread that could last a week before spoiling.

"Freshly made, it's kind of weird tasting," Brent wrote in his diary. "Gummy, chewy, and sits in your stomach like a rock."

One of Brent's kidnappers makes bread from the manioc plant.

They also cooked it with water to make a paste that became a glue to bind books or repair holes in the hammock.

"I've had some meals I couldn't even begin to identify, some not bad, and some right terrible," he continued. "You learn very quick when you get something good to stuff your face with all you can hold. You never know what the next meal will be.

"If and when I get out, may I never see another sardine."

Brent's Diary—Day Twenty-nine—November 16
New Chapter—The Political Side

The first letter of "help, get me out of here" was sent October 23, 1990. Reply on the thirty-first—Care Package. We'll see you home soon??????

On the first of November, I sent a letter to family and friends and a tape of all sorts of information. Note: Soon to me would be a couple weeks MAX.

Then I waited, no word till the twelfth.

Another Chapter—Thoughts

As time drags by, I have far too much time to think.

1. *The thing that keeps going over and over and over in my mind: I'm a pawn on a chessboard, and I only know enough about chess to know, not many pawns make the whole game. By trade, I'm an aircraft technician (or was). I took pride in inspecting and repairing aircraft. I am surrounded by, by trade, combat soldiers; they take pride in search and destroy.*

2. *I heard the song "Hotel California" this morning. Depressing. "You can check out anytime you like but you can never leave."*

3. *Will I ever get out of this place?????*

4. *I thought about this one a long, long time. What could or should I have done to prevent capture in the first place? Well, there's a lot of fore—and hindsight here. But what if I had just blasted around the bus and over the crest of the hill into the unknown. Probably a left field move. Might have worked though. They (FLEC) say and try to keep reassuring me that they don't want to hurt or kill any American. What if I had fought to the bitter end, unarmed, instead of surrendering? You wimp. Would I still be alive? Who knows. Maybe I could have saved a lot of people a lot of headaches. A couple of days ago, I finally came to terms with this and have shoved it out of my head. It came down to two hard cold facts that everyone including myself will just have to face. a. You were not there; I was. b. It's history.*

5. *Thoughts tend to go from good to bad. From the best blow job I ever had in my life, to MORBID. (I'll say no more.)*

6. *I'm just camping out.*

7. *Mark, may I never, ever, hear the words "weak moral fiber" or anything close to it.*

8. *I took my vacation at the wrong time (though I'd never wish this upon anyone else).*

9. *In addition to no. 8, was it the first day of rain or was I set up?*

10. *I don't like to reveal my thoughts, but if I hadn't, you might never have known.*

Brent wrote to Gary Weber on November 17.

Dear Gary,

I received your November 8 letter, believe me I had a lot more hair on top the 18th of October. Since then I have been pulling it out by the handfuls. Until today I could only guess that anything was being done. The reassurance is greatly appreciated. I'm glad you're reading between the lines with great interest. If some dark rainy night you think of something I could do to help, let me know. We're all getting kind of laid back and waiting for news from Kinshasa.

Regards,
Brent

He also wrote Dr. Dumont on this day, telling him, "My ass is sore enough it hurts to sit." And before he put down the pen on November 17, he wrote one more letter.

Dear Mr. Scott,

I can't thank you enough for the care packages. Sorry, but the two words "Home Soon" no longer have any meaning and haven't since a week ago. The boots you sent was a great idea, but much too large. I'm wearing 9 Sears walking shoe (leather upper), and I think they'll make the trip. That is if I'm not going to be here another six months. Please read the letters to Gary Weber. A rain suit would be welcome. If this is going to be awhile yet, then waist 33 inseam 31, T-shirt large, regular shirt medium, AA batteries, 35 mm. 400 ASA film, and insect repellent. I'm sure my locker in Malongo has been gotten into for undershorts and long-length socks.

I guess old Huck Finn got me going, but a writer I'm not. Might give my wife something to do and type this up, what a mess. I hope you can figure it all out. Happy reading.

See you sometime,
Brent

P.S. Please look into a possibility of direct radio contact, would need permission of use from President Jose and fresh battery packs for PT-500.

P.S. Just reread your November 13 letter. I'm hanging in here, buddy, till further news.

Even though he wrote these letters on November 17, they did not leave camp until November 22. He also gave FLEC his diary written up to that point, which Brent wanted to go out with the letters. He later discovered the diary never left camp.

During this period of time, Brent plotted in his mind how he might escape, but he never revealed to his captors his true feelings. He wanted to get involved with the young men and get as close as possible, getting them to trust him. Then he determined he would "blow their ass away and run for it." He began asking about their government and the different factions of FLEC. They provided all the information he requested, including their full names, not just the nicknames. Brent made a list of all the soldiers and the leaders with their titles next to the names. They seemed eager to share.

Brent helped them build and repair the buildings in the base camp. He would take the shovel from one of them and begin digging. The soldiers did not want his help, telling him the work was not for the officers or for him.

Brent and friend make palm fronds for the roof of one of the base camp's buildings.

Brent found the discussion of the Cabindan government tedious and too complicated for him to comprehend. He pretended to understand and acted interested, which allowed him to learn a bit about their culture. He even tried to learn their language.

The card game was the turning point in the trust beginning to form. They taught Brent the rules, and then he proceeded to beat them at their own game nine out of ten times.

"They never could figure out how I could do it," Brent said. "It started getting so bad I had to let them win, or they wouldn't play.

"But the point is they started to trust me because I gave them no reason not to."

The beds in the huts were terribly unstable until Brent devised a crude bubble level for them to use to balance the beds. He used a piece of bamboo split lengthwise with a little water in it, and they were able to level the poles to which the beds were lashed.

Brent tried to keep busy, but his helpfulness had another motive. He hoped that if the beds were level, the men would sleep sounder, allowing Brent a chance to put into place the escape plan that had begun to form in his mind. He thought if they were sleeping more comfortably, he could sneak out one night.

"I just knew someday in the future I was coming out," he said. "Either blasting my way out or sneaking out, I didn't care. Just out."

He managed to keep up this charade for the entire time of his captivity, even as his depression worsened. Brent listened to the explanation the symbols represented in Cabinda's flag: a red circle, not totally enclosed, green, yellow, and black strips with a white background. The white signified peace. The circle of red remembered the blood shed by the brothers lost in war. The circle would be completed once the peace returned to Cabinda. Yellow stood for the wealth of resources of the ground, and green for the wealth of resources above the ground such as the trees. And black represented the oil, gold, and ore—the wealth that would probably ensure Cabinda's ties to Angola as long as Angola had the support of such superpowers as the United States.

The soldiers wrote out their names for Brent and wrote out the names of the leaders and their positions. Brent then made his own list of "The 22 Most Wanted," the soldiers who had captured him and marched him to the base camp in his first few days of captivity.

Brent's Diary—Day Thirty-three—November 20

We spend the day reviewing FLEC's organization of government. It looks to me like they really got it together. But I'm of simple mind. In the afternoon, we heard their President will arrive sometime this week. FLEC address: Senhor Francisco Rodrigues, s/c Carlos Numes, Hotel Exelcior, BP No. 323, Boma, Republica Zaire.

Letters to Africa

Melanie wrote her first letter to Brent on November 19.

Dear Brent,

It's incredible that it takes something like this to get me to write to you! I wish I had thought of it sooner. We've just been concentrating on getting word from you to ease our minds, not thinking that you might be needing to hear from us, too.

I hope this letter finds you healthy and in good spirits. You can bet all of northern Oxford County is thinking of you and praying for your safe return. Your letters and tape sounded as though you were holding up OK. I trust they've gotten some medication to you for your discomfort (an understatement, huh?).

[Melanie writes several paragraphs about the news from home.]

I hope you're able to keep a journal. It might be worth asking for the materials if you don't have them. Not only will it occupy time, but might make you feel better, too. I'm sure it will make a great reading when you get home and will help us understand what you are going through. We are doing the same on this end, though some days are so hectic it's hard to keep things straight. I think you would find it worth the effort if it is possible for you to do it. We are hoping you will be allowed to write again soon as your letters make us feel a little better.

I'll close now. I want to get this faxed through every possible route. Hopefully someone will get it to you soon. You should know everyone is doing all they can to get you home as quickly as possible. Think positive thoughts and take care of yourself. We hope to get letters to you often now that we know that we can. We are all thinking of you and love you and are anxiously waiting for your return.

Love, Melanie

P.S. We will celebrate [Thanksgiving] when you get home. In the meantime, maybe you could explain this great holiday to your brothers in Cabinda.

Melanie's letter ends with a drawing from one of her first-grade students back in Maine and the words THANKSGIVING IS FUN as a title. Meanwhile, Barbara prepared for a Thanksgiving without her husband.

November 20, 1990

Dear Brent,

Still waiting on the word that you are doing fine and will be home soon. Hard to believe that Thanksgiving is this week. It will be a quiet one this year, and we will be thankful for any word we have from you.

Winter is here, I'm afraid to say. It is only about thirty-three degrees out there this morning. Glad I turned on the solar panel last night at the last minute. Never thought about the plants.

Wanted to let you know that I sent some pictures over, don't know when they will reach you. Just a few group family photos. Show them to the group over there, let them see how your home life is. I'm sure they will be able to relate to them, ours can't be that much different. Hope you get them soon.

Found out Mrs. Suggs's son goes to school in New Hampton, New Hampshire. That was a surprise, but he was headed down here for vacation last Friday, and Mrs. Suggs wanted to know if there was anyone I'd like to have come down. I asked your parents first, but your dad couldn't get the time off so quick. So Doreen, Adam, and Shannon [Barbara's sister, nephew, and niece] are here for a week! They had a great flight down in the King Air, and it was very exciting for them. They didn't have but twenty-four hours to make plans and pack. I'm glad they are here. It was so nice of Mrs. Suggs to offer to do this.

I got a copy of the pictures that were taken of you awhile ago. I was glad at least to see tables and benches, such as they are, better than nothing. It really hurt to see you over there like that, just praying that you are home soon.

Going crazy with the birds in at night already. But they are fun to listen to. The new saying is "Hi, Ducks." Marty's ducks are over here full time now; we have enough down in the yard to make a pillow or two!

Well, sweetheart, guess this is all for now. I'm thinking of you all the time. Take care of yourself, and you'll be home in my arms soon. Write when you can.

Miss you, Love you,
Barbara

Barbara also wrote a letter to Gary Weber and "Team" in Zaire on the same day telling them how much she appreciated the work they

—

were doing for "our cause." She felt particularly bad that they could not be home with their own families over the coming Thanksgiving holiday, and she hoped "they have turkey in Kinshasa."

On the same day, Bill Jennings, a helicopter pilot with PHI stationed at Malongo, received a reply from Amnesty International after he wrote them on October 30, requesting help in Brent's situation. The response from Amnesty International was less than he hoped for, and in his letter to Barbara, he expressed his frustration at the inability to do anything to help. He also expressed his anger at FLEC. Christianna Nichols, coordinator for Amnesty International's U.S. efforts in Angola, Mozambique, Guinea, and Equatorial Guinea, responded with sympathy to Bill's request, but said that her organization did not have authority over the kidnapping of a private U.S. citizen and an unofficial entity, such as Chevron.

El Presidente

On day thirty-three, Brent was told the president of FLEC would arrive within the next week. A flurry of activity began in the camp in anticipation of Jose Tiburcio's arrival, which actually occurred on day thirty-four.

The soldiers acted as if special company was arriving, and Brent found it puzzling and worrisome. Thoughts about why the president might be coming plagued him for the next twenty-four hours. And even after the president arrived, Brent was relegated to spend the day in his sleeping quarters while Tiburcio conducted meetings with the soldiers and leaders of FLEC, including Artur Tchibassa and Antonio Bento Bembe.

Brent's diary reflects his confusion and state of mind as they prepared for this head of state to enter base camp.

> Brent's Diary—Day Thirty-four—November 21
> *This morning their president will arrive. A multiple guess question?*
>
> A. *I will be released.*
> B. *A bullet through the head.*
> C. *Both.*
> D. *Neither*

Barbara, I love you.

The president is here, 7:55 a.m.

It's now 4:00 p.m. I have yet to talk to him. But I understand a couple of representatives from the U.S. returned today for talks in Washington. Or maybe Chevron personnel to San Ramon [Chevron's corporate headquarters in California].

May this story have a happy ending.

Brent wrote that he loved Barbara because he really had no idea if he would make it through the day. The soldiers told him he had to stay in his hut. He holds a picture in his mind of a man in a business suit walking across the bridge over the stream.

"The man is Artur Tchibassa," he said.

He met Tchibassa face to face when the president came to his hut later in the day, but then he had changed from the suit to a white T-shirt. The president was flanked with an entourage of approximately six men.

However, before this meeting, Brent's anxiety steadily grew, and he tried to discern what was happening outside of the palm fronds of his hut. Brent's daytime guard Agostinho was pulled to the meetings, and someone else guarded him for a short time.

"The president wanted to meet with all his higher ups, so I was assigned a guy that couldn't even speak English," Brent said. "He [the president] met with his troops there in the camp, and they had meetings all day long."

The White House at base camp could hold six to eight people, but there could be up to fifty people at any given time in camp. Brent always felt there was a perimeter outside the camp where soldiers stood guard. Almost daily, two or three soldiers would come into camp and fill packs with food and then leave again. Sometimes they might stay and others would leave. However, most of those on Brent's "22 Most Wanted List" stayed put in the camp at all times.

On this day, with the president in residence, Brent could tell soldiers were moving in and out, although he could not see the area where the meetings were being held.

After dark, the president came to Brent's lean-to hut dressed in an olive drab uniform with Tchibassa and others at his side.

"I was scared when he came into the hut," Brent said in 2005. "I didn't really know what he was going to do. He had met with his troops and now me."

———

Jose Tiburcio introduced himself and told Brent in fairly good English that he was working on his release. Brent learned that Tiburcio flew back and forth to London where his Jamaican-born wife lived.

They talked for at least thirty minutes. Tiburcio had learned from his troops during the day that Brent had been a patient and cooperative prisoner, and he thanked Brent for that.

"He talked about Cabinda wanting their freedom," Brent said. "And they wanted negotiations to go well. He said he wanted me to be released unharmed and in good health and back with my wife."

Brent asked when he might be released, and he was told that two representatives had just returned back to the United States. Tiburcio brought a care package with some items from the embassy. And that was it.

The next morning after more talks with his troops, the camp—including Brent—gathered for photo sessions. There was a ceremony with the raising of the flag and lots of saluting.

Brent is surrounded by some of FLEC's leaders. His captors not only gave him the photos when he was released, but also gave him their names. From left, unidentified, Alfredo Nhumba, Brent, Jose Tiburcio, Antonio Bembe, Francisco Rodrigues.

"The president left November 22, and I didn't get a bullet through my head," Brent said. "So I was thankful, and it was Thanksgiving Day back in the States."

CHAPTER 8

The Escape Plan

The New York Times

(Nov. 21, 1990)— *"Mideast Tensions; U.S. and Soviets Urge More Steps by U.N. in Gulf"*

BY ANDREW ROSENTHAL, SPECIAL TO *THE NEW YORK TIMES*—The United States and the Soviet Union said tonight that further United Nations action would be needed to get Iraq out of Kuwait, but they apparently failed again to reach an agreement on what concrete steps the Security Council should take to achieve that aim.

After three days of intensive discussions here, including a 90-minute meeting tonight between Secretary of State James A. Baker and Foreign Minister Eduard A. Shevardnadze of the Soviet Union, it seemed clear that the Bush Administration's stated goal of getting broad agreement now on a Council resolution authorizing the use of force against Iraq had proven harder to achieve than Mr. Baker had hoped.

The President leaves for the Middle East on Wednesday, where he will visit troops in Saudi Arabia, talk to King Fahd of Saudi Arabia and the Emir of Kuwait, and meet in Cairo with President Hosni Mubarak of Egypt. Clearly, he would have liked to take with him an agreement on a United Nations resolution on the use of force against Iraq.

Rambo Takes Charge

While the president of the United States attempted to get Iraq to withdraw from Kuwait and allow that country its independence, an American citizen sat in a hut in the rainforest of Cabinda imprisoned by soldiers carrying a Russian weapon, the AK-47. Brent would have liked some force used to secure his freedom, UN sanctioned or not.

Brent spent his Thanksgiving in the jungle writing a letter, and so did the president of FLEC. In fact, several letters left camp for the embassy on November 22, including those he had written on November 17. He also sent his diary in hopes it would make its way to the embassy.

> Brent's Diary—Day Thirty-five—November 22
> *Happy Thanksgiving.*
> *The President left today at noon, out with him I sent the first part of my "book" as well as several letters. I'm in hopes the more I send out, the more I'll get back. (Nothing since the fifteenth.)*

Brent began writing a letter to the embassy before his talk with Tiburcio and finished it the next day.

> *November 21*
> *Mr. Scott, Attn.: All*
> *Yes, I'm still here just kind of camping, out and the boredom is coming along just fine. I'm doing the best I can to keep my head on straight, and I guess at this point, that's the most important (as well as difficult) thing to do. I only hope my wife can do the same.*
> *I guess I'm finally coming to terms with the fact that they don't wish to harm me. But it's raising hell with my mental well-being just being here.*
> *I kept busy for a few days writing my "book" and the F-15 is assembled [plane model sent in a care package], engines ground run, flight controls checked—ready for take off. My next project is hacking out a runway. May I never finish that project—the trees are huge and the ax is dull. Hanging in here hoping for a breakthrough, any day. Now that would be fine.*
> *More later after my chat with the President.*

November 22

I had a nice chat with the President late last night. Seems to be a nice, down-to-earth kind of guy. He told me he wants to get things resolved so I can get out of here. I've almost got the feeling of not being wanted. Everybody says they want me out of here, yet here I am. He also brought me up to date on what's going on in Kinshasa, basically Round One went well. Everybody went back to their corner of the earth, and Round Two will start any day now. May everybody come out a winner.

I've given up on the runway project for bigger and better things; this muddy stream has a gravely sandy bottom, so I'm going to pass my time panning for gold. If I start hitting on some good nuggets, you'll have to come in here and drag me out. Right now I see myself coming into the Kinshasa outpost long since baldheaded, gray beard down to my waist, smelling no worse than I do now. My fortunes will be spent on a good pack mule and a bottle of good whiskey, and head back into the jungle. In case anybody's wondering, I'm just having a hell of a good time.

I do however appreciate all the hard work and headaches everybody is putting into this. Thank You. Good luck on Round Two.

Brent

P.S. Think survival: Gatorade, Campbell's soup, to hell with the sweets, bleach for drinking water, Bourbon, like Jack Daniel's (strictly for medicinal purposes): a shot a day keeps the worms away!

Brent realized the bourbon was the last thing he needed. It only added to his growing depression, which became more and more evident in his letters, which are filled with sarcasm and anger as the days wore on.

His plans for escape became more finely tuned as seen in this letter to Gerald Scott as he became bolder about his references to this plan. However, his captors did not understand the reference to "hacking out a runway," or they would have surely limited his letter writing or tightened their security.

Jose Tiburcio wrote a letter to "His Excellency, the ambassador of the United States of America to the Republic of Zaire, Kinshasa," on this same date. The letter thanks the ambassador for "the assistance that was extended to our delegation and that facilitated the mission."

The letter asks for the embassy's understanding of the Cabindan problem, stating that FLEC "remains convinced that the United States of America, defender of oppressed people and just causes, will not abandon the people of Cabinda, a victim of genocide."

He ends by stressing FLEC's reliance on the embassy "to bring both parties to an historical compromise that will seal a base for future relations between independent Cabinda and American businessmen."

Tiburcio also sent a letter to the president of Chevron, Mr. R. M. Matzke, stating that FLEC stood by the original demands and looked forward to further negotiations, with hope that the "Chevron Corporation will seize this opportunity that history has offered us."

Brent sent his own request to the embassy—at the request of Francisco Rodrigues—in a letter written on November 21, written on the same sheet of paper as the previous letter to Gerald Scott.

> *Mr. Scott / Chevron*
>
> *I have a request from Senhor Rodrigues for ten flags (dimensions and colors on a separate sheet). Also for reduced size flags 10 cm X 15 cm. Quantity, your choice.*
>
> *Portuguese training books on how to read, write, and understand the English language. Quantity, your choice.*
>
> *I have told them I/we would see what we could do.*

FLEC's white house represents their headquarters at the base camp during Brent's captivity. FLEC's flag is front and center.

Brent still had to write Barbara so that letter could make it into the pouch Tiburcio would take out to the embassy on November 22. On either side of the world, the letters back and forth did not generate as much good will as intended. The following letter made Barbara extremely angry.

November 22
Dear Barbara,

Sit down, relax, get your chin up, and quit using so damn many Kleenex. I certainly hope all had a good Thanksgiving. We do have a lot to be thankful for. Good, strong, close families, from what I hear, more good friends than we knew about.

I am in fair health. I hope all is the same at home. I hope you can believe me that the members of FLEC are also good friends. And as you know, good friends will never let you down.

I've had some tough hitches in the past, but none this tough, and on top of it, I will be putting in some overtime. I'm sure you know me well enough by now to know I'd never quit in the middle of a job and I'll do whatever it takes to get the job done. This hitch could be another week or a month, who knows. May future hitches go a lot smoother.

For you, try to do what you normally do when I'm gone, work what you can and try to keep from worrying about me. If you can't handle the customers, try a few stubborn nails on the back of the truck. Take a night out with the girls, relax, and enjoy yourself. We'll be looking back on this before you know it. I have no doubts.

As soon as you get a chance, call Levy County Health Department, explain the situation and ask for an extension on the septic permit. I'm sure they'll be cooperative. Tell him I'll finish it up as soon as I can when I get back.

Please tell Beth [Barbara's aunt who lived next to the Swans and was suffering from cancer at this time; she has since passed away] *I said Hi and I send my best. I hope she's getting better. There is a lot that can be done these days.*

I hope to hear from you again soon. I'll be home sometime.

Hey—get your chin up, smile, you are my rock, don't crumble on me now.

> *Forever and ever yours,*
> *I Love You,*
> *Brent*

P.S. Meat for the day is porcupine, river rat, or monkey. I have a choice, none of it is turkey or even close. It could be worse, at least it's fresh. You would be surprised at how good a quill pig really is. For this I am thankful. Read War and Remembrance.

For Brent, the letter represents the deterioration of his mental state. When he wrote the letter, he tried to imagine how it was for Barbara back home, worrying about him, but it was hard not to let his anger and sarcasm creep into the letter also. He was more concerned with developing his Rambo escape plan.

In his escape plan, he imagined his captors letting down their guard and leaving him alone in the hut for just a few minutes. On the table he sees two grenades, and he hides them in the roof of the palm fronds. When they return and discover the missing grenades, the soldiers search his area first before moving toward the main building. Brent then grabs the grenades from the roof and runs outside behind an embankment where he pulls the clips and throws the grenades toward the mess hall. He sees bodies flying and blood. Agostinho comes running toward him and trips on the embankment and falls to the ground. He has been hit with shrapnel.

Brent grabs the AK-47 and aims it at Agostinho's head and shoots, making sure he is dead before running away into the woods. He shoots guards at the perimeter of the camp and continues to run to safety.

In his thoughts, the plan worked itself out perfectly, but Brent still had enough of his facilities to recognize the flaws. The first problem came with execution. Here was a man who had never received military training, never pulled the pin on a grenade, never worked an automatic weapon, let alone an AK-47.

"I had fired a few rifles," Brent said. "But as for the AK-47? I knew there was a switch on it to go from firing a single shot to being fully automatic, and I only assumed there was a safety on it somewhere."

But that was a long way from actually finding the safety, getting it into a firing position, and being able to use it in a reasonable time frame before he was shot himself.

"The escape plan was more of a suicidal act," he said. "I figured I had maybe 1 percent chance of success, but I would go out in a blaze of glory, but at least I would be out.

"I hoped if I couldn't escape, I would be killed instantly."

After the president of FLEC left camp, Brent's thoughts of suicide grew until they occupied his every thought. The frustrations, depression, and anger stayed with him until the day of his release. He tired of the subterfuge required to maintain the relationship with the soldiers.

"I got sick and tired of playing goody two-shoes hostage and pretending I was into these people and what they do and pretending that I'm patient and on their side and that I'm interested in what they're doing, and I'm interested in their goals," he said in 2005. "I just wanted to get out of there, but I think I kept up a good front even though in my mind things were going downhill."

As tired as he was becoming, he still knew he had to try to keep up the appearance of being sympathetic with the goals of FLEC. He often wondered how long he would be able to do it.

"Maybe it could have been weeks or maybe I was within minutes or hours," he said. "I just didn't know."

Brent fully expected to be released after the president left, and when it did not happen, he began to lose hope that it would ever happen.

Perhaps compounding the depression was the boredom that began to set in. Brent had put together the model airplane; he tired of looking for gold in the stream; he had read the Bible and the other books that had come in the care packages.

"I made a note to read *War and Remembrance*, but to this day, I can't remember reading it or what was in it," said Brent about the reference in his last letter to Barbara. "I don't know what it was I was trying to get her to read."

Brent received no word for almost two weeks either. Gary Weber sat in Kinshasa waiting.

On day thirty-seven, orders came through to go back to the first camp. They walked slowly, and while Brent had no idea why they were moving, for him, the break in the routine was a relief. Again, he held out hope that going back to the first camp might mean his imminent release, but FLEC probably feared someone had tracked the president coming into the jungle.

He had to build a new latrine at the new camp, but he did a sloppy job on this one. His hands, accustomed to working on aircraft, had become soft, and working with the vines hurt. His captors noticed the sloppy job and made a comment to him, but he assured them it would still work just fine, and besides, he told them, maybe he wouldn't be there much longer.

"I was trying to be hopeful and letting down my guard to let them know I wanted to get out," he said. "But I never let down my guard as far as being cordial. I kept that façade up the whole time."

While the family felt some relief to receive word, Brent stopped doing everything, including writing in his diary by day forty. His mind had started to go.

"My body functioned because it had to," he said. "But my mind was wasted."

He wrote letters, but nothing happened, and he still remained imprisoned. He did not recognize any hidden meanings in the letters from the outside and took them at face value, which left him with no hope of ever seeing his wife again. Even when those hidden meanings were put into the letters, Brent was beyond comprehending what they meant.

"My mom wrote about my aunts and uncles, and she listed them all," he said. "One of the names was Sam, and I just thought, who's he? It never dawned on me to put Uncle in front of that name in the list."

—

Someone went to Malongo and emptied out his locker, and his clothes were brought into him. He searched the pockets hoping something would appear that would help him escape, like the prisoner searching for the file in the cake. He just found some notes and instead of comprehending that the notes were messages for him, he became more convinced that he would never get out.

Paranoia set in, and he imagined the shortwave radio had a secret transmitter in it. He stopped writing in the diary because he could not see any point in it.

"My time became consumed with an endless tape of what's my wife doing." he said. "I kept trying to finalize the escape plan."

And the tape of that escape played faster and faster in his brain. When he saw grenades on a shelf by a bunk fifteen feet away, the tapes played the same things over and over again: "How fast can I move? How fast do I need to move? Are those grenades alive? Have they been emptied? Will they work? How do you make them work? Do you just pull the pin and toss it like in the movies? Did they just set them there as decoys to see if I would try it?"

"I thought perhaps they might be testing me," he said. "At this point in my depression, I kept thinking so what if it's a suicidal move? And why put entries in a diary no one is going to read?"

Pumpkin Pie with No Sugar

Barbara managed to get through Thanksgiving Day surrounded by her family. Brent would have been home for this holiday if he had not been taking an extended leave with the members of FLEC. The mobile home on the Swan's property in Chiefland nearly burst at the seams with Barbara's mother, sister, nephew, and niece all staying under the one roof, along with Joyce, a friend from Tampa who had come for the holiday.

Barbara and her sister, Doreen, decided to make Brent's favorite Thanksgiving dish, pumpkin pie, in an attempt at normalcy. They worked side by side in the small kitchen, but when they pulled the pie out of the oven, both knew right away that something was not right with the holiday standard.

"I took a taste, and then I looked over and saw the sugar still sitting on the countertop," Barbara said. "So it was a different kind of holiday."

—

Chaos reigned, and Barbara remembers that her life resembled an unorganized heap of dirty laundry at this time. Thanksgiving did not prove to be any different. When her cousin visited, she took one look at the clothes strewn throughout the living room and said, "My God, I've never seen your house look like this! It looks like a tornado has gone through here."

Barbara had never had a husband being held hostage before either, so if socks hung from lampshades, she did not bother to notice or care. She searched that day for something for which she could be grateful.

"I knew Brent was still alive and holding up, but nothing was as it should have been," she said.

Just like the pumpkin pie sitting sadly on the cluttered countertop, Barbara's sugar, the essence of her existence in Florida, was not there.

By November 26, it had been two weeks since Barbara had received any word from Brent. She began to wonder if she would ever hear from him again when the letter came with the reference to her use of Kleenex to dry her tears. Because it had been so long since any word had come through, everyone analyzed the letter word by word. The folks at home, especially Barbara, knew that things had taken a turn for the worse for Brent.

"He's telling me to quit using so many Kleenex," Barbara said. "I thought, 'Where in my letters have I said I was crying my eyes out?'"

The entire letter made her uncomfortable as she wondered what was happening to her husband and what messages he might be trying to convey. After rereading it several times, she began to calm down and see it from Brent's point of view. She imagined that he was simply putting up a front for himself in order to survive.

The part of the letter about becoming good friends with his captors scared her because of what Christopher Gross had warned her about the Stockholm syndrome.

"But I convinced myself that Brent wouldn't do that," she said, "and he was writing it because he knew they were reading it."

Melanie's Notes—Day Thirty-nine—November 26
For the past two weeks, there had been no word at all. We were beginning to wonder if we would ever hear from FLEC again. Apparently they had not gone into the jungle until the seventeenth.

Finally (!) today, Barb received seventeen pages on the fax. FLEC has come back with several letters from Brent. One was written on the seventeenth and one on the twenty-second.

Brent writes that he has an airplane [model] and is now making an airstrip. He has lots of rashes and parasites. He also wrote another letter, addressed to the doctor, saying that he needs some different medication.

Is also panning for gold.

He told Barb to do what she usually does and not use so many tissues. He's counting the overtime hours.

PHI wants Barb to write some ads that can go into newspapers. It will be another way to get messages to him without FLEC knowing it. [According to Barbara, the ads were written, but never used.]

They are also passing word around to the locals and through the church that Brent is a good person. He's not a big political figure, just a regular person. They also are passing word that FLEC has been offered a good deal; they should take it.

Apparently, they took a box back to the jungle today with the letter and medicine from the doctor and (hopefully) our letters. We are so pleased to finally get some word again! It's been so long.

Melanie's Notes—Day Forty-one—November 28

The Embassy in Zaire has now come up with black-and-white pictures of Brent's capture. We are wondering where they have been all this time. Who took the pictures? We are suspicious if the Embassy is on our side. They knew that FLEC was meeting among themselves between the twelfth and the seventeenth. We don't know how they knew.

They are supposed to meet at 2:00 p.m. tomorrow.

The FBI called Barb on Tuesday, November 27. She had a three-way call between the doctor and an FBI agent. They talked for an hour about Brent's disposition. They wanted to know if he had been through anything stressful before. They asked about family tendencies.

Barb called afterward and was tired, so she didn't talk too long. Dad was home to receive the call.

The doctor was a psychologist at Quantico in Virginia, and along with the agent, they questioned Barbara for over an hour. They asked about Brent's childhood. They asked whether he had a problem with drugs or drinking. Looking back on it, Barbara believes they were developing a profile. At the time, they told her they wanted the information so they could help Brent when he was released. Now she wonders about that because the FBI was not around when he was released, except to ask questions in the weeks following his return.

Barbara told the FBI what she could, but when she called Ed Gatza and told him, he came "unglued," Barbara said. This was the first time she had heard from the FBI since the very beginning of Brent's time in captivity. Previously, Ed had told her she did not have to talk to them if they called, but this call took her by surprise, and after all, they acted as if they wanted to help her husband. She would not have considered not answering the questions at the time.

Melanie's Notes—Day Forty-two—November 29
Gary called Ed who called Barb about 2:00 p.m. Barb called Mom at two thirty. They met today for two hours. The FLEC representatives asked, "How is Mrs. Barbara?"

In today's meeting, they still want military help but are being told they can't help them there. They haven't set a dollar amount or pushed for any money.

Gary has been sick with diarrhea. Ed is preparing to go over to replace Gary if necessary. Gary felt there was not as much tension in the air today. The meeting tone felt different.

Barbara's Notes—Day Forty-three—November 30
2:00 p.m., Monday, list of demands
Travel to United States for four representatives
Social assistance for 30,000/15,000 medical assistance /7,500 medical training

Five Mercedes trucks, three Land Cruisers, two Toyota pickups, four Porsche or Nissan cars, four Mitsubishi buses

Office supplies: two large Xerox copiers, four electronic typewriters, four manual typewriters, one thousand reams of paper, one hundred tubes of ink, one hundred typewriter ribbons.

Accommodations: two plots of land with houses, one in Congo and one in Kinshasa.

Commercial materials: two video cameras, one hundred blank cassettes, five 35 mm. cameras, twenty portable walkie-talkies, ten cassette recorders, one hundred tapes.

When Barbara first saw the list of demands, she thought, "Are these people crazy? Is that all Brent's life is worth? Xerox copiers and office supplies?"

Melanie's Notes—Day Forty-three—November 30

In today's meeting, they were demanding a whole new list of supplies: trucks, typewriters, copiers, and USA recognition, etc. They were not pushing for military or monetary help at all.

Ed, Gary, and Barb had a three-way call, and Gary was supposed to call back later today.

The total $$ amount of value for the things they want is 3.5 million.

Sid Anderson of Chevron is going back over because he has the authority to sign deals.

Dad has had some strange dreams since Brent has been gone. Weeks ago, he dreamed about this truck running itself around the yard bumping into things. He was watching from the porch and couldn't figure out what to do about it. The car was getting beat up all the time.

Recently, he dreamed that Central Maine Power had cut down all the bushes and trees across the road. They had piled the bushes and wood up neatly, but he didn't want it cleared.

The third one was that Mom made Dad drive up this huge pile of gravel to get out of the pit. They got caught right at the top and the truck was stuck and they had to squeeze out one door. They finally found a rope to secure it to one of the buildings on top of the hill.

I have dreamed twice that Brent called. The first time was about two weeks after his capture. He was calling from the jungle. At first an African talked to me; then Brent came on. He just wanted to let me know he was OK. He talked for a while and then had to go.

The second dream was about two weeks ago. Brent called to let me know he had been released. He was calling from Georgia, on his way home. We hadn't been told earlier because Brent wanted to tell us all himself.

Melanie's Notes—Day Forty-four—December 1

Barbara called at 7:30 p.m. after getting a call from Ed Gatza. He got information from Larry Paige of Chevron. Today's meeting lasted two and a half hours. They are still asking for the social assistance (medicine, food) for the refugees. FLEC representatives first said they had 30,000 refugees. They [Chevron] wouldn't accept this as true, so they finally settled on 15,000 as the actual number. They feel the real amount is 7,500. They brought a new list of demands on Friday, and they are still working on those. They continue to want medical training and food.

They are hoping to release Brent on a signature of this agreement. There is a possibility of Chevron agreeing to this list of demands. Christopher Gross and Simon Adams-Dale [Control Risks] are pleased with this agreement and how things are going.

Barb asked how long he felt it would be. After some time, he came back with two weeks.

Sid Anderson [Chevron] is going to arrive back over there at 5:00 p.m. on Sunday. They are hopeful that it will make a difference to have him there.

CHAPTER 9

The Roller-Coaster Ride

Norway Advertiser Democrat

NORWAY, MAINE—(November 29, 1990)—*"Donors announced for hospital tree lights"*

The following are Christmas tree lights purchased from the Stephens Memorial Hospital Auxiliary. The lights cost $5 each, and may be purchased in honor or in memory of a loved one or friend.

All proceeds go toward the Auxiliary's efforts to provide the hospital with needed equipment. The tree will be lit Wednesday, Dec. 5.

In Honor of Brent Swan by Ann Bickford [several more names are listed, but most in memory of].

The Last Letter

The day the Christmas tree was lit in Maine with a light twinkling in his honor was Brent's tenth anniversary with PHI.

Brent wrote what he considered to be his last letters—no matter what—on December 2.

> *To All Concerned,*
>
> *First I'd like to thank everyone for all that you're doing and have done. The care packages and letters have certainly helped to ease the pain. Thank you.*

Mr. Scott, I was in the Boy Scouts, and I already have earned all the camping and wood lore badges in the book. Had this trip been "my choice," it could have been enjoyable. Also somewhere along the line, I learned how to be "patient." But I never learned enough of it. Six weeks ago, you knew nothing about Brent Swan, and I'm sure you've learned a lot. Add this to your knowledge, when I stop being patient, I snap to the extreme opposite. It's not something I'm proud of, but it's the way I am.

Fact: My wife and I established a relationship in one evening, and it's grown to be everlasting. "Till death do us part."

Fact: I was brought here to establish a relationship and "the relationship is established." (Quote by President Jose, November 21.)

Yes, I have received letters from several—"We are doing everything possible to obtain your release." "We are working as fast as possible on this end." That's your problem, you're all "working" and you've worked it up as more complicated than it is. Get back down to the basics and look at the simple facts:

1. *The relationship is established.*
2. *The United States will do nothing for FLEC as long as they're holding a U.S. citizen. (I demand this, as would any loyal U.S. citizen.)*
3. *Chevron / Cabinda Gulf, if you break the relationship, you may as well "shut 'em in," pack and go home. I am on the inside, I have seen and I assure you FLEC could make you pack and go home.*
4. *For FLEC to maintain a good relationship, I must be released in good health. And they want the relationship worse than anyone.*

You have asked me if there is anything you can do for me. The answer is yes, QUIT WORK—Refuse to discuss—Refuse to hold any more meetings or conferences until I'm released. Someone has got to take the bull by the horns, and if no one out there is man enough to do it, I will. Presently, it's your option.

Live free or Die
Sincerely,
Brent Swan

When Barbara read this letter she knew her husband had gone to the "other side." However, Brent maintains that everything he stated that might indicate he was really fighting for the causes of FLEC, was merely a façade.

"I tried to make them [FLEC] think I could do some things for them on the outside if I was released," he said. "I knew FLEC was reading my letters, coming in and going out. The entire time, I never received a letter in a sealed envelope, not until the end."

Brent also admits that these letters were a little bit "Jack Daniels inspired."

"Don't ever send a hostage alcohol," Brent said.

The letter to Barbara was faxed to her on December 6.

Dear Barbara,

Sweetheart, December 18 has a special meaning to us, as well it should. I hope it continues to for the both of us. Forever and ever.

Most U.S. citizens will never be in my position, and most will never fully understand the New Hampshire slogan. I didn't, but I think I do now. I couldn't even begin to explain either on paper or face-to-face what it's like to be freedomless. But I'll try.

I love you.

It is said that a man can only show his love for one. If this is true, then my love for you is getting weak. My love for freedom grows stronger every day. I hope you can understand.

Life is not sitting under a palm frond roof twenty-four hours a day. The only thing around here exciting is when it rains and lightning strikes.

I do have a few options, and one is to just wait this thing out. So far so good. How long can I be Patient? Only God knows.

I love you,
Brent

P.S. I hope you can handle reading this better than I did writing it.

Scott Taylor, with Chevron's security office in London, and in Africa at the time of negotiations, told Brent after his release that when he read these letters, he was certain they had lost Brent,

"It's true the pen is mightier than the sword," Brent said. "And even though I was depressed, I knew somebody had to do something, and this letter got everybody's attention, and they did something."

Another Jack Daniels letter made its way to Gary Weber.

December 3, 1990
Dear Gary,

I hope you're feeling better. Please give my best to all those at Cardboard City and PHI. As I haven't worked since the first of September (except for one day) I'm sure my wife is close to the end of our savings. I need to get back to work to save what I have. When you don't work, you don't make any money, but I guess that's just the American way.

My life was dedicated to Base 575. Thanks for reassuring me, my life's gone down the tubes.

Presently I'm back at the first base camp. Have been here the last eight days.

Sincerely,
Brent

P.S. I'm in a world of doom, drunk or sober, it all looks the same.

Brent truly thought the regular PHI policy would apply to him because of what had been instilled in him during his orientation ten years earlier.

"Company policy was if you don't show up to work in three days, you're fired," he said. "I didn't show up for work for three days, and I couldn't make contact, and I had no idea if anyone was taking care of Barbara or not. I assumed my parents, family, or friends would help out, but I didn't know."

But he admits that parts of the letter regarding his job were written for FLEC, not Gary Weber.

Around this time, Brent remembers hearing the soldiers talk about Chevron and six million dollars, but he could not be certain if that was the ransom amount or the dollar figures made by Chevron on the petroleum coming out of the Cabinda oil fields. Francisco Rodrigues referred to Brent sometimes as the "six million dollar man," and so Brent had made the assumption FLEC hoped to get six million dollars upon his release.

Brent's letters of December 2 and 3 had not been received yet nor did he know that negotiations had advanced as far as they had despite minor setbacks.

Gary Weber wrote a letter to Brent on December 7, which came through Antonio Bento Bembe. Mr. Bembe had instructions from PHI to deliver the message verbally as well. The sweetest words possible came to Brent, "We have reached an agreement with FLEC/PM." The message also informed Brent that PHI was making the final steps in their commitment and hoped that Brent would be free shortly thereafter.

"My escape plan was out the window," Brent said about the news delivered by Bembe. "That letter was a milestone as far as depression goes."

As promising as it all sounded, Brent refused to get his hopes raised too far. After all, he was still in the jungle, and he still had to be delivered safely into the hands of the representatives who had negotiated this release. He knew that anything could still go wrong. Another five days passed before he received word via Bembe from Gary Weber that Brent was receiving his last batch of letters. Again the promise sounded hopeful, but he still remained under guard without the freedom to move about as he wished. However, Brent noted a change in the tone of the last letters telling him that a Zaire official would accompany him to the border to be met there by a U.S. representative.

FLEC rebels take a break from guarding their hostage.

Remaining Hopeful

Melanie's Notes—Day Forty-six—December 3
Meetings today didn't go that well. The FLEC representatives acted embarrassed during the meetings. They wouldn't lift their eyes. They didn't know why they acted this way.

"When I read the letters he wrote on December 2," Barbara said, "I thought, my God, something has got to be done."

December 3, 1990
Dear Brent,
Here we are, sweetheart—day four of round no. 2. I suppose the news is encouraging, but I'm advised not to get too excited. I'll get excited when I hear you're on your way home. The team does feel that they are making some good progress and hopefully things will break before much longer. Maybe you'll receive this letter out of the jungle!

I'm trying to carry on in a somewhat normal manner. Mom and I did the "shop till you drop" bit yesterday. Got my Xmas shopping done so I can get it ready to ship out. I even put up the window lights last night. My heart wasn't really in it, but I'm going through the motions anyway. If you're not home for Xmas, I'm at least hoping we can spend it together in a foreign country. It would be a first, and I wouldn't mind one bit.

I had a nice long talk with Mark Schumacher [PHI lead mechanic] on Saturday night. We must have talked for about an hour. He said the King Air misses you, hasn't worked right since this happened! Even was grounded for two weeks. He also mentioned that he hasn't been able to go anywhere on camp without being stopped by everyone he sees. Your family over there is so concerned and, like me, feels so frustrated and helpless by the whole situation. It really helped to talk to him. He even offered to come over and help me if I needed anything—even taking care of the birds, and he said he doesn't even like African Greys. Don't think it's necessary but nice to know he's there for moral support—along with everyone else. Had a nice surprise at work on Friday. Guess you know Scott Whitehead? His wife, Dora, sent me a card right after this happened, and Friday

I get a nice arrangement of flowers from them! It was such a nice gesture from people I don't even know.

Mom told me that the Brent influence on the puzzle table has been there. Heaven forbid if a piece gets in the wrong tray! Puzzles are helping our sanity. Wish you were here to help us.

About run out of room. Can't wait to see your bearded face and hold you close. Take care of yourself. It'll be over soon. Love you,

Barbara
XXOOXOXO

Melanie also readied a letter on December 3 to send in what hoped to be the last letters they would have to write to Brent via his kidnappers. Melanie, a first-grade teacher, once again enclosed a picture of an elephant drawn by one of her students. The student wrote at the bottom, "Elephants have trunks so that they can pick food up from the ground and also from high in the trees. That's how they eat." Brent too had learned to be versatile during his days of captivity in order to survive.

Dear Brent,

We received your letters in the middle of last week. Barb is sending them to Mom for us to read. I've written this letter three times because things keep changing, and what I had written isn't important anymore. I finally decided this one will be sent to you.

It's great that you've been doing some writing. I would think it would help to pass the time. You know you don't have to write about difficult things, any topic will keep you occupied. How about the story of you jumping into the snow on the brook and having to be fished out? Or maybe, when you brought the male kitty, Paws, home! I've started writing some childhood stories, too. The first one was the fishing trip I went on with Rodney and Dad. The other one was when the house was re-sided. You could also write about future plans. Your letters are great reading, Brent, I think you have a knack for it. That, and putting airplanes together. Do you have just one model? We've been trying to think of things that could keep you occupied. Can you get any exercise? Would you like them to send any other games? A ball? Puzzles? I hope you are able to keep a daily journal. I think you might be glad you did later.

We don't know if you are aware of any current events. I'll give you a few highlights. Things are escalating in the Persian Gulf. The UN has voted approval for use of force to get Iraq out of Kuwait. January 15 is the deadline for withdrawal. U.S. troops are growing and many local people are being called as reserves. It's difficult to find anyone who is not affected in some way. Margaret Thatcher has resigned, and a new Prime Minister has been elected. It is now possible to walk from France to Britain for the first time since the Ice Age. The tunnel is large enough to go through now. A scientist has predicted a major earthquake for the Midwest tomorrow. Some people have left; some are celebrating. I'll keep you posted. It sounds quite peaceful in your corner of the world.

I spoke to Dave Tripp at Duffy's graduation (his son graduated, too). He is confident that you will make the best of the situation and will come away from it stronger than ever. We're counting on it. We are trying to continue on as usual, which of course is impossible. Some days are easier than others. The best days are when we hear that something is happening and we get your letters. I'm sure the same is true for you, except that you don't hear as often as we do. Life does keep going on here because it has to, but at the same time, everything seems to be at a standstill. We are hoping everything keeps moving forward at the negotiating table. I guess writing history takes time. I just don't understand why it has to be your time.

Be sure to speak up for yourself if you need anything. There are lots of folks working to be sure you're OK. Let us know what we can do to help you through this. Remember that we are all over here devoting thoughts and prayers to you. If comforts me to look at the moon and sun and know that this old earth isn't so big after all. It's the same moon and sun shining on you. You'll be back home soon. I'm sure. Remain hopeful and keep busy.

All my love,
Melanie

Melanie's Notes—Day Forty-seven—December 4
They met today for hours and hours. They have apparently settled on a dollar amount for aid and equipment, which is much less that the original 3.5 million estimate.

We are encouraged by the news. They may even sign an
agreement under the condition that Brent is released tomorrow! It
may take as much as a week to get him out of the jungle.
They are meeting again at 8:00 a.m. tomorrow.

Melanie said at this point the moods had changed in the family, as it seemed that each day brought better and better news. However, Brent heard nothing as he continued to wait. Barbara received a letter from Elizabeth Ann Swift, the deputy assistant secretary with Overseas Citizens Services with the U.S. Department of State on December 4. The letter attempted to assure Barbara that the "State Department, together with the U.S. embassy in Kinshasa and the Federal Bureau of Investigation" were doing everything "within the bounds of U.S. Government policy to secure your husband's release."

She included in the packet specific information on Angola, FLEC, and Zaire and the U.S. government policy on hostage taking. As Brent entered into his sixth week of captivity, the State Department finally sent something tangible along with information from the National Organization for Victim Assistance or NOVA. This booklet had been written specifically for families who had been affected by hostage situations in the Persian Gulf.

Melanie's Notes—Day Forty-eight—December 5
Estimates now are that Brent could be on free soil by the
fourteenth !! Halleluiah!! Barb is hopeful they'll be together by the
eighteenth after all (it's some kind of anniversary for them). They
estimate four days to get Brent out now.

They feel that if they can show purchase orders for the items
demanded, that they will release him. They are still talking on a
few points, mainly that they want to come to the USA. They are
trying to tell them that if they do, the FBI will arrest them for
taking Brent hostage.

The FBI doesn't seem to be helping much right now. They
want to know how much money they have settled on. They think
it might be breaking international laws.

They met last night 2:00 p.m. our time (8:00 p.m. there).

Barbara has taken a leave of absence. She has thirty days for now.
If she wants a longer leave, then she can make out another request.

The other letters in the package to Brent came from his parents and his grandparents. These letters could have been written to any relative who was living away. They contain newsy items—not all of it positive—and no mention of Brent's situation. The snow had started in Maine, and life continued. Perhaps that is just what Brent needed to hear at that time.

Melanie's Notes—Day Forty-nine—December 6

Barb received two more letters today. Brent sounds really down. Pretty depressing to hear this. Apparently he has been moved back to the first base camp again.

Gary caught a couple of FLEC guys on the street and talked to them about what Chevron had listed and had started doing (outside Embassy).

We sent out letters today from Melanie, Grammy Noyes, Mom.

There are some points they are still trying to settle. Coming to the USA is one of them.

Barb will call us again tonight.

Thursday night, Mom went up to Eric's [a relative] to receive faxed letters. Two came through. Nothing more. They are having problems getting some of the equipment. They can't order it. This may produce some delays.

Mom tried to get a hold of Ed Gatza. He is apparently moving into a new house. Stuart has been in touch every day.

There is a helicopter at the ready if they need to get him out faster.

Barbara was riding the roller coaster at this point, not knowing when he might be released or where or how. Brent still knew nothing, which may have been for the best, so his fragile state of mind, bereft of hope, would not be tested unnecessarily. As it was, when Brent finally received official word of his impending release, he would not allow himself to believe it until he was safe with Gary Weber and in Zaire.

Melanie's Notes—Day Fifty—December 7

We got the other two letters from Barb today. She faxed them up to Eric's. He brought them down on Friday a.m.

Barb wanted to know what we thought of them. Brent sounds pretty angry.

They had taken the Embassy car and gone back into the jungle. They took a letter from Gary to Brent telling him that it will be soon. Hopefully he will be comforted by it. This might make it quicker to get it, and get back again.

We still haven't received the pictures of the capture. Stuart has sent Barb information on Cabinda, Zaire, what his job consists of. With this was a letter from a woman that seemed to be Stuart's superior. She said to call anytime.

Barb is ready to ship out if they say they are ready to have her come over. She would like to be there as soon as he comes out of the jungle. Ed hasn't acted on it at all. We are looking at the fourteenth now as being the day he's released and the eighteenth as the fourth day to get him out. Gary plans to stay right there, even though Ed is ready to go.

We've figured out why he had his travel bag with him. He was probably taking it back to the hangar with him to store until he came back.

We're wondering what Bunda has to do with this. He won't talk to any of the investigators. He's also reassuring PHI that they [FLEC] wouldn't hurt him [Brent].

They might want to take Brent to a hospital in Germany before coming home. He won't have to go through any interviews afterward.

The Governor [President of Zaire] claims he had never heard of FLEC. It's hard to believe considering they had a phone number and a post office box. He would probably like to have Cabinda be a country because then Zaire might annex it.

Despite the encouraging news coming to Barbara, she was becoming increasingly angry and frustrated with PHI who did not respond to her requests to fly and meet Brent.

Barbara said by day fifty-two, her anxiety had increased because it did not seem as if anything was happening toward the promised release.

"I was arguing with Ed at this point," Barbara said. "I was determined to meet him even if it was only halfway to London. I had a passport. Ed told me he didn't want me to do that."

Melanie wrote to Barbara on December 9, this time with talk of what would happen when Brent finally arrived home.

Barbara,

I just finished reading Brent's last letters. His mood has definitely changed, though I think his anger and depression are normal. It sounds like he's getting damn sick of being there and wants everything to come to a conclusion now. I can't say that I blame him. I guess I'd be surprised if he didn't react this way. It's harder for us because we'd like to think he's happy and content. Of course, he won't be until he gets home.

I've been encouraged by all the talk in the past week of Brent's release. We seem to be preparing for it much more now than we were earlier. I try not to count on the dates they are throwing around, just in case there is another delay. But, it is getting closer and closer to being over with. Hang in there a little while longer.

Ross and I have talked about coming down to see you both after Brent comes home. Of course, we are anxious to see him soon, but we want to give you time alone. We'll wait and see how things go. I want you to be sure to tell us if you need more time alone together when the time comes. We will understand. There will be many more days for us. I'm sure you will both be exhausted too and will just need time to rest. Our minds will be eased just to know he is at home with you.

Mom and Ross have both said you are worried about how to approach Brent and what to say when you finally see him. I'm sure the anticipation is making it seem harder than it will be. Everything will fall into place and will feel natural. Brent won't care what you say or do as long as you're there. I'm just so glad he's got you, because I think your relationship is getting him through it.

Hopefully, the coming week will bring some good news. My thoughts are with you.

Love, Melanie

Melanie's Notes—Day Fifty-three—December 10

Barb called a little after six. Chevron has purchase orders for all but two large trucks. The FLEC people are supposed to be coming back out of the jungle tomorrow. She wasn't sure if they were going back with the car to pick them up or what. They haven't set a time.

They have plans to bring him out by helicopter to Moanda and then by Chevron jet to Kinshasa. There they will have a doctor *check him over quickly. He will then go by a commercial airline. He then might have to be put into a hospital later. (Maybe Paris, Germany or Atlanta.)*

Barb wants to go part way to meet him when he is released. Ed hasn't been very supportive of this idea. She was quite upset by his ignoring her request and planned to push it tomorrow when he calls back.

Barb sounded confident that FLEC would release Brent with the conditions as they stand.

When Ed called on December 11, Barbara told Ed she would just purchase her own airline ticket and go. Ed flew to Cross City a few days later and drove to Barbara's house for lunch in an attempt to calm her down.

"He finally agreed with me," she said. "He promised if he was hospitalized in Germany or London, they would send me there. I knew I couldn't go to Africa, and I guess that's what they were afraid I wanted."

However, plans were still not finalized, and the roller coaster ride continued. Brent still waited, not knowing for sure when he would be marched into Zaire.

Melanie wrote her last letter to her brother as a hostage on December 10. After reading his letters, she decided she would take a different approach. And as Brent said he wrote his letters to get a reaction, she realized later that she hoped for a reaction from his captors. She hoped FLEC would understand that Brent had a family back in the States who cared about him and missed him greatly.

Dear Brent,

I read your last letters this weekend. You sound very angry, and I don't blame you. I think anyone would feel like you do in your situation. There has been lots and lots of talk and little action, at least as far as you're concerned. We are told that things are being settled little by little. It's not fast enough, but you will handle it because you have to, for your own sake. You're going to have to draw on strength you never knew you had. It's there, Brent, dig deep and find it. I won't pretend to know how hard it is for you. I know the times I have felt pushed beyond my limits did not feel good, but I got through them and the other side makes you realize how very much you can withstand. Trust yourself, your feelings are normal. You've done well to stay patient this long. There is a light at the end of the tunnel. We've seen it. Every day brings you one day closer to your release. Take it one day at a time and feel good as each day passes that it is one less you are still going to have to get through.

There will be many, many happy days when you get home. Concentrate on those. You still have your home, wife, family, friends, and pets. Life will be good again with or without Base 575.

There are many happy people returning home from Iraq and Kuwait today. All hostages have been released there. Hopefully the wind is blowing toward Cabinda. Our Midwest is safe; there were no quakes. The storm has passed here and the flooding did not do much damage. Winter has set in here, the ponds are frozen and it's getting colder by the day.

We are anxiously awaiting your return. It is coming. Hang in there. Cry, scream, rant, and rave if it helps, but please don't do anything to put yourself in greater danger.

We love you and want you home.

Love,
Melanie

On December 11, Barbara was faxed an "Outline Release Sequence," which set the steps to occur over the next week resulting in Brent's return to the United States. The date for the actual release was set for December 15 to 17, with Brent's departure home a day or two later. But before that could happen, FLEC would receive the negotiated items, including equipment and vehicles.

December 13
Dear Brent,
What can I say?? It looks like our day is finally here again, and it will be special still, even with new meaning. You should be in the grasp of the "team" as you read this, and hopefully before long in mine. I have enough hugs and kisses to give you from everyone, I won't be able to let you go for a week . . . then I can start on mine!!

I told Gary to have you call me at the first available phone possible. The doctor can look as you hold the phone to your ear. Can't wait to hear your voice, even with all the people I've talked to in the past two months, it just isn't the same. Wherever I am at the time of your release, believe me, I won't be far from a phone.

I was glad to hear that the last part of your trip is planned to be done in a vehicle. It'll save some wear and tear on your feet and your energy. Hope it works out.

I'm going to keep this short and sweet. Before long I'll be with you, and this will all be behind us.

See you soon. I love you!

Love,
Barbara

CHAPTER 10

Day Sixty-one

Lewiston Sun-Journal

WASHINGTON (Dec. 14, 1990)—(AP)— *"Progress reported in Angola talks"*

Representatives of the two warring factions in Angola met Thursday with three outside mediators and a joint statement issued afterward reported "significant progress" toward reaching a cease-fire in the country's civil war.

Joining the Angolans at the talks were officials from the United States, the Soviet Union and Portugal, the former colonial power in Angola and site of the five rounds of peace talks held thus far this year.

"We believe that significant progress has been made, and that the prospects for a successful sixth round of negotiations in Lisbon early next year have been enhanced," the joint statement said.

The statement said the delegates were favorably impressed by the friendliness of the atmosphere created by the two Angolan parties as well as by the seriousness of their approach to the negotiations.

Out of the Jungle

Meanwhile, negotiations between the representatives of FLEC, Chevron, and PHI continued through December 13, with plans finalized for Brent's release. Gary Weber faxed Ed Gatza a "situation report"

—

141

after final meetings. Barbara received her faxed copy on the evening of December 13. Gary reported that the plans seemed to be fairly certain.

The arrangements called for Brent to be released to Gary Weber and Scott Taylor of Chevron in Moanda, Zaire, on the evening of December 18. Mention was made of a collection team consisting of Gary Weber, Scott Taylor, a U.S. embassy official, and embassy doctor for a meeting in Moanda after Brent's safe return.

The report does specify the items to be delivered to FLEC, but the first items came to them on December 13, with future deliveries scheduled for December 28 and February of 1991. The last delivery consisted of a truck, buses, and humanitarian aid. After the meeting, FLEC and the negotiating team met with the director of UNHCR to perfect the arrangement of Chevron's procurement and distribution of humanitarian aid. UNHCR, the United Nations High Commission for Refugees, oversees any action to protect refugees worldwide. The report further states that the negotiators had every confidence that FLEC would cooperate because they feared for their own security, as well as that of Brent's, during the release process.

The agenda for the final stage of Brent's journey out of the jungle included meeting Barbara in Atlanta and then flying together to New Orleans where he was to be admitted to Tulane Medical Center for a full checkup.

At FLEC's base camp in Angola, Brent woke early on the morning of December 17. He had received word that he would be released that day, so he rose early from his prisoner's bed. For Brent, knowing a release date changed his status to one of hostage to prisoner. His sentence had been announced. He packed his carry bag and was ready for the journey out of the jungle by 6:30 a.m. Then they fed him breakfast; then they fed him lunch and still no movement toward his release. In the afternoon, Brent attended a ceremony with the rest of the troops.

"They poured a capful of whiskey in the ground for the brothers who had died," Brent said. "It was my Jack Daniel's, but I had given it to them. I knew the whiskey wasn't doing me any good."

Brent wondered how much longer he would have to wait for his release.

He watched as Lourenco put on a clown act at the ceremony. Brent could not understand what he was saying or doing, but he laughed along with the rest at his antics. However, Brent had another image of

—

Lourenco etched in his mind. That image resembled nothing of the clown performing for the troops.

"I still have his profile in my mind," Brent said, "as he sat in the lamplight one night and told me how he killed Angola soldiers. He told me all these things I did not want to hear.

"He was a warrior, he was a killer, he was a terrorist, and he was feared by the Angolans."

Sometime in the morning, they brought Brent the radio from the truck. He tried to use it, but the battery was dead. The soldiers showed him a map with thirteen red dots on it, which Brent surmised were the camps of FLEC throughout Cabinda. He recognized two of the dots as the base camps where he had been held.

"I asked them about the red dots," he said. "But they claimed they were encampments of FAPLA, but they wouldn't tell me where I was.

"They knew negotiations had gone well, and they knew I was in better spirits, so they were willing to show me the map of their camps even though they wouldn't admit it.

"But two of those red dots are where I put the two camps when I did it for the FBI," Brent concluded.

The day continued to drag on for Brent on December 17. During the ceremony, one of the soldiers returned Brent's diary to him—the diary Brent thought went out in the mail on November 22. After the ceremony, he expected to be fed, but dinner did not come. Finally at 6:00 p.m., Brent began the walk to the Zaire border with his captors. He learned along the way a truck would meet with them at the border at 8:00 p.m. to carry him to Moanda and where representatives from the U.S. government, PHI, and Chevron would meet them. When Brent arrived with the soldiers to meet the truck, no one was there to greet them.

"That was pretty scary," Brent said. "I had been with FLEC, and I'm still with FLEC, and you really don't know what's going to happen.

"You really just don't know what's going to happen," he repeated.

Despite the fact he had a letter from Gary Weber saying an agreement had been reached, Brent would not feel safe as long as the men walking with him carried AK-47s.

"They still had the guns," Brent said. "I just didn't know how it was going to play out."

Finally, several hours later, the trucks arrived after getting lost and driving down Africa's potholes, which they call roads. But he was still not free yet; they still had to drive to Moanda. Brent rode in the backseat of one of the trucks next to Antonio Bento Bembe.

The dirt roads leading to Moanda were rough and mountainous. They stopped by some abandoned buildings, which at one time had been a Red Cross shelter during the Angolan revolution of 1975 when refugees fled into Zaire from the war-torn country. The buildings resembled bunkhouses, and Brent noted they seemed much better constructed than the stone and brick houses of the locals surrounding the area. When they began traveling again, Brent noted that many of the FLEC soldiers remained behind, and he went ahead with just a few men. They crossed railroad tracks and entered Lukula, Zaire, on a paved road.

"That was enough right there to help anyone locate where they were on a map," Brent said. "We came out north of this area and traveled south. I could pinpoint this on a map later. Then we turned and drove west. We went all the way to the docks, and I could see the boats on the Zaire River."

He noticed the rapids and falls on the river and realized they had risen in elevation further than he had thought.

As they drove into Moanda, the men in the truck with Brent became confused about exactly where they were to meet Gary Weber. They drove around the downtown area and then back out on the streets on which they had originally entered the city.

Brent remembers that at this point, Artur Tchibassa got on the radio. Brent later identified him as the "negotiator" and the driver of the truck. Tchibassa spoke in French over the radio. After receiving the correct directions, the truck arrived at the designated spot where Brent saw Gary Weber of PHI with another man introduced by Gary as Scott Taylor of Chevron. Brent did not notice anyone else waiting with them.

"I got out of the truck and met Gary," Brent remembered about his first moments of freedom. "I shook his hand, and he said, 'You're not getting away with just a handshake.' And he gave me a big bear hug."

"I remember Scott Taylor saying to Gary, 'Why don't you take Brent and go back to the safe house, and I'll take care of these guys.'"

"So I went with Gary and got into a pickup truck and drove through a gate and drove off," Brent said. "I never looked back."

Gary drove him to a Chevron staff house where Brent spent his first few hours out of the jungle.

Brent's Diary—Day Sixty-one—December 18

A very short day with FLEC

I was released at 4:00 a.m., African time, today.

FOOD, REAL FOOD, GOOD FOOD. I remember Gary asking what I would like for breakfast. I think I said anything but sardines. After a glass of COLD orange juice I had breakfast, then hit the shower—a nice long hot shower—and it felt real good. Then I called Barbara. Had my first checkup with the doctor. Then called Mom and Dad. Flew to Kinshasa. Spent the day. Talked to FBI. Had second checkup with doctor and nurse, tetanus shot, cream for my behind. Called Barbara again. Tried to sleep, no way wound right up. Nice lunch. P.M. flew to London sliver of the moon setting. Sleep. Woke up while stuck in desert of North Africa. Sleep.

He drank and drank anything that was cold, which caused a bit of a problem while flying from Moanda to Kinshasa on a "twin otter" without a bathroom on board. By this time, Brent was joined by an entourage of people, including a woman from the embassy. He ended up having to fill two of the vomit bags with his urine in order to survive the flight. He was most impressed when Gary Weber took those bags from him for disposal.

In Kinshasa, Brent saw another doctor and made another call to Barbara. He talked with the FBI agents and someone from a local church group paid him a visit.

Waiting on the Home Front

Melanie's Notes—Day Fifty-seven—December 14

Plans are being fine-tuned for transportation out. Brent will be flying from London to Atlanta on Delta and then on to Tulane University Medical Center, in New Orleans. There is an expert there on tropical diseases.

Ed met with Barb today to explain why they felt it was best for her to not go overseas to meet him. (In case of changes that need to happen in flights, plans they might have to miss each other). They want to rush Brent through to a doctor that will be able to treat him for a longer period of time. They also feel he will want to get to the USA as soon as possible. They have reserved a suite for Brent and Barb near the hospital on an outpatient basis. They may also be able to get counseling, if necessary, there.

Gary will also go to this medical center, as he has been sick with dysentery for twenty days.

Ed is supposed to be going with Mrs. Suggs to deliver cookies to workers on bases tomorrow. He hoped to be back in touch with Barb on Monday.

The point of release is Moanda. The contact time is 6:00 to 8:00 p.m. He will be able to be cleaned up, checked over there, and make a call to the USA. He'll be flown to Kinshasa. He'll fly into Gatwick in London. Will leave London at 11:00 a.m. on the nineteenth to Atlanta.

Though we are encouraged by all these plans, it is difficult to place too much hope, knowing things could still change. We won't be completely relieved until Brent is home and healthy again.

His job future is still unsure.

Day fifty-eight and fifty-nine passed with no word. Melanie's notes on both days state, "No news this weekend—guess that's good."

Melanie's Notes—Day Sixty—December 17, 1990
Tonight is supposed to be the night Brent is released and picked up by car. Mom expects a call at about midnight to notify them that he has reached Moanda.

As Barbara prepared to fly to Atlanta to greet her husband, she received a paper from Ed Gatza called, "Post Incident Behavior." Christopher Gross of Control Risks Ltd., out of Bethesda, Maryland, had prepared the paper for PHI with the goal of giving some advice on the possible reactions both the Swans might have as a result of Brent's release.

Gross predicted that Brent would feel temporarily euphoric upon his release, but Gross warned that this feeling could quickly dissipate into one of depression and mood swings. He recommended that Brent receive medical treatment despite any protests to the contrary. Gross also warned that Brent would most likely have questions about what had been done for him during his captivity and indicated that Barbara, not PHI, should be the one to dispel any of his concerns or anger regarding the lack of movement on the part of PHI to secure his release.

He also cautioned that Barbara would feel some anxiety upon Brent's release and warned that she had also been a victim in this situation. Gross's references to the now recognized symptoms of post-traumatic stress disorder (PTSD) are quite advanced for its time since much of the research into this disorder did not take place until the 1980s when large numbers of Vietnam veterans began displaying disturbing and violent behaviors when triggers of their time in a war zone surfaced. Putting the research into practice takes time.

Barbara's concerns for her husband sometimes outweighed her relief at his pending release. A letter from the "Cabindan brothers" not only made her angry, but resentful that they believed their world would be perfect once Brent gained his freedom. The paper from Christopher Gross made her apprehensive about what might be in store for the future.

By the time Brent called his wife in Chiefland, Florida, she was pacing the floor and answered the phone before it even finished its first ring.

"It was very overwhelming to hear his voice and know it was him," Barbara said. "We probably didn't talk too long, probably couldn't, too emotional. Very overwhelming. I told him to call his mother, but he told me he had to eat first."

Melanie's Notes—Day Sixty-one—December 18
We got the call last night right on schedule!

Brent called Mom and Dad at about twelve thirty. He had just had a checkup by a medical doctor. He said he was "in damn good shape." Mom and Dad had waited up for the call, though they tried to nap, but couldn't. He called Barb about 10:30 p.m., Monday night. Then he had his checkup, then called Mom and Dad. He had been up for twenty-two hours when he called. He still has a rash on his "butt," and his ankle hasn't healed. Gary planned to be at the meeting point by three so they wouldn't have to wait for the car. Brent said the car didn't get there until after he did at about 4:00 a.m. Brent sounded good. Mom and Dad were sharing the phone, both talking and listening at the same time. Brent wondered if they had two phones.

Barb called later in the morning. Brent has been made an honorary citizen of FLEC. Barb received a letter of apology from

FLEC today via the Embassy and fax. She's not impressed. Brent's horoscope made reference to his being on solid ground and having been on a long journey. Today, Brent is going by charter to London from Kinshasa. He had called Barb again from Kinshasa.

They have a VIP room requested in Atlanta for Brent and Barbara to meet. They had also requested a wheelchair. We were worried by that at first but guess it is just a precaution in case he is tired. He might also have to walk a ways to connect flights to New Orleans.

Mike Daniels [local reporter] called Mom today. He had gotten wind of Brent's release. She told him to call PHI or the State Department. We expect an article in tomorrow's paper.

The Righteousness of FLEC

During the final ceremony at base camp, the soldiers presented Brent with a Certificate of Nationality issued by the Front of Liberation of Enclave of Cabinda (FLEC) Military Position (PM). It is signed by Jose Tiburcio, Antonio Bento Bembe, Artur Tchibassa, and Mauricio Nzulu, and five others, including Francisco Rodrigues.

Certificate of Nationality

We, members of central Committee of F.L.E.C./P.M., legal representatives of Cabindan people in war, we're freely decided by the present Certificate, to confer on Mr. Brent Swan, American citizen, the Nationality of Cabindan citizen assuming that he has lived and experienced the misery of Cabindan fighters during his two month of stay in bush.

For the future generations that will have upper hand in Cabinda when it will enjoy its freedom, will may them to consider Mr. Brent Swan a genuine Cabindan citizen with no differences with those Cabindans of origin in rights and privileges.

We freely deliver to him the present certificate which testifies it is worth while to him to have the merits above mentioned.

A makeshift passport had been put together for Brent for his entry into Zaire, which states that Brent Swan is a member of FLEC. Brent was given letters. One was faxed to Barbara on December 18 with the title "Today is December 17, 1990, In the Bush of Cabinda–King Base. It's the departure of Mr. Brent Swan."

No signatures are affixed to this letter, which praises Brent's ability to carry the word of the Cabindan people to the United States. Brent is described as a savior. It begins with "We're deeply convinced that Mr. Brent Swan carry a lively sense of our goodness."

As the note progresses, it is clear they hoped Brent would help them once he was released.

"After six years of work in Cabinda, Mr. Brent Swan knows to what extent Cabindan people has been undergoing a life in harshness. And Mr. Brent knows many more now because you have the chance of living with representatives of Cabinda people who claim the right for self-determination of Cabinda. In addition, Mr. Brent Swan had long time to hear from the legal representatives of Cabinda."

Toward the end of the note, it becomes clear the authors are writing to Brent. "We'd not like Mr. Brent Swan to consider the months you stayed in our bush as a period of captivity. Please, think it over deeply; consider other people's impressions, and you will discover what does it mean. In our opinion, all this time has a deep sense, and it's just meaningful."

While they thank "Mr. Brent Swan" at the end of the note, these fighters for the Cabindan cause do not see that they have done anything wrong by holding Brent at gunpoint for sixty-one days. While their intent may have been only to bring attention to their cause, they forgot to inform Brent that his life never really was in danger there in the bush.

FLEC's reputation for being a group that did not harm its hostages probably hurt them more in their negotiations than anything else. The United States was not immune to acts of terrorism. However, FLEC hoped that the taking of a Chevron employee would bring them wanted attention, but it did not. The news of the capture of Brent Swan barely made a ripple in the newspapers back in the States, and while the family may have been grateful for this while Brent was held captive, it may have been the one thing that allowed FLEC to not make their cause an international concern for debate. No one had ever heard of Cabinda, and now in 2009, only those European countries that have taken up the cause for Cabinda's fight for independence are aware that there is dissent in Angola. While FLEC may have received some form of humanitarian aide from Chevron, as well as a few trucks and office equipment, it was not enough to bring the Cabindan people out of the severe poverty in which they lived. And it did not bring international organizations into the region to save the people as they hoped.

Jeffrey D. Simon discusses the role of the terrorist in his 1994 book *The Terrorist Trap: America's Experience with Terrorism.* While the political leaders would like to place alienating terms upon the terrorists in order to force the public to view them as crazed individuals with no goals, the reality is quite the opposite.

"Terrorists are the not the faceless enemies that we have become accustomed to reading or hearing about," Simon writes, "but rather are individuals who become so committed to a particular cause that they can justify in their own minds, and sometimes in those of their supporters, the terrorizing and killing of innocent people."

Simon cites the cliché "One person's terrorist is another person's freedom fighter" as more than just a tired, worn-out phrase, but as the essence of the concept that continues to haunt governments when dealing with these terrorists acts.

Thus, the members of FLEC did not see the act of taking Brent Swan at gunpoint a terrorist act, but rather they viewed it as a noble act, which would serve the purpose of saving their people. This sense of the "ends justifying the means" infuriated Barbara Swan when she received a short note from Jose Tiburcio, president of FLEC, faxed to her on December 18.

"Mr. Brent Swan will find security in Cabinda whenever he like to live there," the letter states. "Besides, we'd never like to lose him because he is now a Cabindan citizen. We had Mr. Brent Swan like an angel who came down in hell to take us up to the heaven."

Brent looked out the window as the plane lifted off the runway at Kinshasa. He saw the crescent of the new moon setting outside the left side of the jet, marking the end of his stay in the African jungles—two complete phases of the moon later.

Brent is finally released and is flying home via London. He looks out the window of the plane and sees the crescent of a new moon, the second one since his capture.

CHAPTER 11

Coming Home

Bethel Citizen

LOCKE MILLS (Dec. 19, 1990)— *"Brent Swan freed in Angola, is flying home"*

A Locke Mills family was granted its Christmas wish a week early. Hugh and Denise Swan learned early yesterday morning, Dec. 18, that their son Brent, 31, had been released after having been taken hostage for 60 days by antigovernment rebels in Angola.

Brent, who was unharmed by his ordeal, called his parents from Zaire at 1:30 a.m. (our time) to tell them he was free, safe, and on his way home.

Swan had been abducted on Oct. 19, as he was on his way to work. He was employed as a helicopter mechanic for Petroleum Helicopters, Inc. (PHI) a New Orleans based company that provides helicopter transportation services for oil-drilling operations.

Swan had been working in the Cabinda region of Angola. He told his mother yesterday that he had been abducted by anti-government rebels affiliated with FLEC, the Front for the Liberation of the Cabinda Enclave.

When it was first learned that Brent had been abducted, his mother said the family hoped FLEC was responsible, since the group has a commitment to non-violence.

Denise Swan said she did not have a great deal of time to talk with her son yesterday, but that he did assure her he had been well treated and was in good health.

A spokesman for PHI said Brent is being flown to Atlanta, where he will undergo a thorough examination at Tulane University Medical Center.

Brent is then expected to join his wife, Barbara, at their home in Chiefland, Fla.

Brent has a sister, Melanie Ellsworth, who teaches at the Woodstock Elementary School, and a brother, Ross, in Scarborough.

His mother said that she and Brent's father hope to be able to visit him soon.

She also gave her heartfelt thanks to all the people who have supported the family while Brent was in captivity.

"People have really been so good to us," she said. "We want to let them all know just how much we appreciate everything they've done."

The Celebration

A picture of a Christmas Star with Brent's name on it appeared in the *Bethel Citizen* on December 19. The caption reads, "LUCKY CHRISTMAS STAR—The Christmas tree in the lobby of the Bethel Savings Bank is dedicated to Americans serving in Operation Desert Shield, but it also has a star for Brent Swan, who had been held hostage by rebels in Angola. His family learned only yesterday that he has been released."

Brent traveled by chartered jet to Gatwick Airport in London where he called Barbara. He asked Gary Weber to order a red rose for Barbara. He boarded a plane on Delta airlines headed for Atlanta, sitting in first class. Looking back at that time years later, Brent realized he must have certainly challenged the sensibilities of the airline by allowing someone looking as he did to sit in the first-class accommodations.

Brent's Diary—Memories of December 19, 1990
I certainly must have looked out of place. I was wearing blue jeans, T-shirt, fully bearded, wearing my hat from FLEC with a big feather stuck in it. My carry bag smelled very bad. It had sat in the hut full of smoke for two months. I didn't realize how bad it was until I picked it up one day after being home for two months. It still smelled bad.

So here I am, a tramp straight out of the woods settling into a first-class seat. Everyone else is getting their suit jackets hung and probably wondering how the heck this guy can afford a first-class seat. I received a lot of strange looks. It probably didn't help any that the nurse accompanying me sat beside me. She was everything a guy would want in a nurse, good looks with a comforting smile. She had told me no alcohol and the best thing I could drink is lots of water. I knew she was right, but I wanted to enjoy first class a little bit. No luck, she insisted no alcohol; it doesn't mix with the drugs.

I had a window seat, and she had the aisle. Gary had a seat across the aisle. My selection from the menu was venison. I wanted to know what it was supposed to taste like. And it was very good. After dinner, my nurse insisted I get some more sleep. So much for enjoying first class. The Halcion took effect after twenty minutes, and I was in never, never land until our descent into Atlanta.

Now Gary had told me that Barbara and Ed Gatza would meet us in Atlanta and that Ed had everything all set up. I did not expect things to happen anything like they did. As we are taxiing up to the gate, everyone is getting their suit jackets on and straightening their ties. I was putting on my smoky hat and again looking like a tramp. The door of the airplane opened and a U.S. Customs agent came on looking for Brent Swan. He had his stamp in one hand and a single red rose in the other. He asked me for my passport, stamped it, handed me the rose, and said, "Welcome back to the United States."

I said, "Thank you, and these two are traveling with me." He stamped their passports as well. Everyone else in first class wanted their passports stamped as well, but he told them to exit the plane and proceed to the customs area.

Now I really got some strange looks, and I didn't care. I stepped off the plane into the loving arms of my wife, and got a big rib-cracking hug.

We then went straight from the gateway down onto the ramp, into a courtesy van to the awaiting PHI Saberliner. Next stop, New Orleans.

I can still imagine the thoughts running through the minds of the suits in first class. How come he can look the way he did and get such special treatment? Who was that guy?

Barbara had flown to Atlanta earlier in the day on the company jet with Ed. They spent several hours in the Delta Crown room waiting for the arrival of Brent's flight. Barbara's nerves kept her agitated despite her best efforts to calm down with several drinks.

"I didn't know what to expect," she said. "I was nervous and scared. Ed kept leaving me and coming back.

"Then he said it was time to leave, and we walked down through some gates and ended up at the doorway of the plane."

She grabbed Brent and then Gary and then back to Brent again.

"I couldn't let go of Brent once I got a hold of him," she said.

They were met by FBI agents in Atlanta, but neither Brent nor Barbara remembers much about what happened with them.

They managed to get on a PHI company jet and fly to New Orleans. Every time Barbara looked at Brent, she dissolved into tears. They both remembered staying in suites at the Clarion across from Tulane University where a doctor with a specialty in African diseases would see Brent the next day.

Melanie and the family back in Maine received reports on Brent's return from Ed Gatza.

Melanie's Notes—December 19, 1990

Brent went by chartered jet to London. Mr. Scott offered the couch for him to sleep and Brent took a pill to help him relax. It was supposed to take twenty-five minutes to take effect, but five minutes later he was ready to sleep. He slept about eight hours. He was going to sleep some more on the way to Atlanta. The flight to Atlanta was delayed a couple of hours. Ed called Barb early this morning to let her know. Ed and Barb were both going to be in Atlanta to meet Brent. He wouldn't get there until 5:30 p.m. or so.

Mom expects a call from them later tonight.

Marilyn Hackett from the Lewiston Sun *called Mom and Dad and left a message on the machine. She then called Ross. He told her we were not pleased with the way the story had been covered before. She called me, too. She was asking for a personal reaction from the family. I told her, "Obviously, we are very happy that he is coming home."*

She then waited a long time, waiting for me to say more. When she tried to get me to say we were relieved, I said I felt she was

trying to put words in my mouth. I told her I really didn't want
my personal thoughts and feelings published in the newspaper just
to make a more interesting story. It's not up to me to do that. She
also asked for a picture she could put in. She finally left a toll-free
number and hung up.

Melanie looked over her notes several years later and commented that she still feels sensitive to accounts "that sensationalize personal reactions to tragedies."

"Leave the poor people alone," she wrote in the margins of her notes from 1990. "Of course they feel sad, distraught, relieved, elated. All for dollars and higher circulation."

Brent had been undecided about whether to submit to the examination at Tulane, but he woke the next morning determined to get it over with. Perhaps they could help him with the rash on his buttocks, which did not seem to be going away as easily as the diarrhea.

Richard A. Oberhelman, MD, of the Tulane University Travel and Tropical Medicine Clinic, wrote a report on December 28, 1990, with a detailed report to Brent's personal physician. The report states the examining doctors found "Mr. Swan to be in good health, although we are continuing to follow him because of some clinical findings."

Those findings included a diagnosis for the rash as fungal. Stool samples appeared normal, although Brent had reported one incident of blood in his stool. Dr. Oberhelman noted that Brent should return to Tulane within the month for a follow-up examination while continuing to take the malaria treatment from the U.S. embassy.

When Brent and Barbara finally made it back to their property sometime before Christmas of 1990, they had little time alone to think about what had happened. A celebration ensued at their home in Chiefland the day they returned, and then family came for the holidays. Brent's parents visited in January along with members of Barbara's family. In those first three months, they went back to Louisiana several times, meeting with doctors and the FBI.

Brent and Barbara arrive back home in Chiefland to the delight of their friends and family.

By the time of Mardi Gras in February 1991, Brent had relaxed enough to attend some of the festivities when they returned for another checkup at Tulane. When they look back on this time, neither can remember talking about what happened.

"We were in a whirlwind," Barbara said. "For the first three months, we had no time to settle."

The Adjustments

Brent remembers his first night of freedom as one in which he slept very well. Barbara remembers something all together different.

"He paced and paced that small suite," Barbara said. "And it scared the hell out of me. I should have known he'd been sleeping out in the woods in an open hut, and all of a sudden we're in a city with all this traffic and in this confined little room."

Brent most likely was having the first symptoms of PTSD as he attempted to adjust to life free from the threat of death in every moment. Although studies had been completed and Christopher Gross had prepared a report on what to expect, no one had actually sat down with Barbara and explained what might happen and what she could do to help her husband adjust to life without a gun pointing at him.

David Hackney, with psychological services in St. Augustine, Florida, recognizes the symptoms of both a hostage and a soldier are very similar.

"What is normal to us is bizarre to them," he said. "Loved ones need to just recognize that the returnees feel very alien, suddenly living in a different emotional state.

"They are coming back from a place where they don't know who is a friend or enemy. Give them space and don't expect them to be the same."

Barbara remembers that Brent was very quiet during the first two days in New Orleans. They talked about the little things and just made an attempt to get through the Tulane examination so they could get back to their property in Florida. Without knowing what to do, Barbara did exactly the right thing. She let him go through his feelings of isolation and paranoia without judgment.

While Brent's diarrhea disappeared as soon as he began eating good food and drinking clean water, it still resurfaces as does the rash on his buttocks. Nearly twenty years later, any trigger that brings back memories or feelings of that time in captivity will also bring back the physical symptoms he had during this time.

Brent felt angry upon his release. He also felt betrayed by the U.S. government—his own country—because they did not arrest the members of FLEC as soon as he and Gary Weber walked around the corner in Moanda the evening of December 18, 1990.

"It is very common to take fears and turn it into something else," Hackney said. "The most common symptom is anger, and trauma reminders set off the survival mode behaviors, which are based solely on emotions."

Hackney also notes that what outsiders might deem as an overreaction is often just the normal symptom of someone suffering from PTSD because the brain is signaling for the body to protect itself.

Sometime in January of 1991, Brent did ask Gary about seeing a therapist. Brent said Gary put him in contact immediately with the doctor at Tulane who arranged for him to see someone in Gainesville. Brent began seeing a psychiatrist in March or April. Barbara went to the first visit, but PHI refused to pay for her visits after that. Just a few days before Brent's release, Christopher Gross had recommended in his report that "PHI is supportive of the idea of counseling for both Mr. and Mrs. Swan."

The report further states, "This [counseling] is an important feature of post-hostage treatment today. PHI may feel most comfortable in providing their own resource for this and Control Risks can assist in discovering if a suitable experienced person works near to the Swans, using our contacts in Washington DC."

Yet by the spring of 1991, PHI refused to pay for any counseling for Barbara, and Brent quit going soon afterward.

Barbara had been on leave from her job at Wal-Mart since November, but she returned to work in March of 1991. Brent worked around the house. PHI paid him for every day he was in the jungle, and then he went on sick leave. With the help of Gary, Brent decided that taking off the rest of 1991 would be a good idea although he knew he wanted to return to work "sometime" in the future.

Brent and Barbara had always enjoyed the outdoors, and during Brent's three-week stints at home during his PHI hitch, they often went camping in the middle of nowhere away from civilization. It is one of the reasons Brent probably fared better than the average person while in the jungle. He often thought about his time in captivity as just another camping trip. The first time Barbara and Brent managed to get away after his release was in the spring of 1991 when they went on an overnight camping trip to the Ocala National Forest. They found a spot near a lake but not totally isolated.

After they fell asleep, a deer walked by outside the tent. Barbara remembers that Brent jumped up. It scared Barbara because she realized that her rugged husband who always enjoyed being outside was scared by the noise outside the tent.

"It was pretty scary until he remembered where he was," she said.

Brent remembers the intensity of his emotions until he became awake enough to realize it had just been a deer that disturbed his sleep.

"I didn't know who was coming after me," he said. "But we got through it, and it didn't traumatize me or take away my love of the outdoors and camping and hiking."

For the next several months, Brent worked at a dairy farm next door occasionally, to give himself a sense of trying to stay active and working.

"If I didn't try to keep myself occupied with something, the days were just filled with thoughts of FLEC, and I was desperately trying to push all those thoughts aside and just not think about it," Brent said. "It was a form of therapy. I wanted it all to go away."

Waiting for Justice

Brent received a letter from Bunda, his assistant at the airport in Cabinda City. The letter had been written on January 17, 1991. Bunda told Brent that he was listening to his [Brent's] Stevie Nicks' tape.

"I felt guilty the day you were kidnapped," the letter says, "because you had asked me if the road was good still, and I said, 'Yes.' I am deeply sorry for that, my boss and friend."

Bunda said there had been a "joke" in Cabinda that said Bunda had information about the kidnapping.

"That broke my heart," Bunda wrote.

Brent remembers meeting with the FBI on January 7, 1991, in Gainesville. The agents asked him to recount the story of his kidnapping.

"I told them, 'Well, I was kidnapped by FLEC, taken into the jungle and held sixty-one days and released,'" he said. "They told me they needed a little bit more than that."

So Brent gave them details. He had developed the film in his camera, and he had the photographs the FLEC members had given him. He identified the members of FLEC by name.

"We went through the entire thing of where I thought they had taken me, and I drew a map," he said. "The FBI did not take anything from me at this time."

In the latter part of January, Brent returned to New Orleans where he met with the FBI once again. At every meeting with them—including the one in Gainesville—Gary Weber was present. At the New Orleans meeting, federal prosecutors flew in from Washington DC including Jennifer Levy. Levy asked Brent what it would take to get him to Washington to testify against his kidnappers. He told her she could start with a steak dinner.

"She still owes me that dinner," Brent said.

Brent remembers a reluctance to cooperate with the FBI in 1991 because he just wanted his life to get back to normal. He asked at one point if he had a choice on whether the charges could be dropped or if he could press charges himself against FLEC. He was told he did not have the ability to make that decision.

"I wanted to go back to work," he said. "I wanted to go back to Malongo and do the same job I had been doing. I wanted my life back as it was, and I felt if the United States intervened in Cabinda with the oil, we'd end up in the same situation we were ending up with in Iraq with the oil wells there and the fighting, and I wouldn't have a job."

Today, he also sees in his reluctance a certain empathy with the goals of FLEC. He viewed them as freedom fighters with similarities to the revolutionaries of the United States who pulled away from the British.

"I may have felt some sympathy," he said. "But I was angry and confused too. I wanted very much for justice to be served."

On the one hand, he wanted the members of FLEC to be responsible for what they had done to him, but he wanted to go back to work and not have any trouble. He did cooperate with the FBI by giving them information, but he never confirmed to prosecutors whether he would testify or not.

"I did express to the FBI that I did not want to stir up a hornet's nest," he said.

The United States district court for the District of Columbia swore in a grand jury on January 16, 1991. An indictment was handed down on September 25, 1991, according to court documents. Four co-conspirators were named in the indictment. The indictment states these four men did "knowingly, willfully, and unlawfully combine, conspire, confederate and agree together to do acts which are an offense against the United States, that is: to unlawfully seize, detain, and threatened to continue to detain Brent Swan, a national of the United States, in order to compel Chevron Overseas Petroleum, Inc., to do certain acts as a condition for release of Brent Swan, in violation of 18 U.S.C. $1203."

The indictment charges that the co-conspirators met with representatives of Chevron on several occasions to leverage their demands for FLEC. The four men listed in the indictment are Artur Tchibassa, Jose Tiburcio, Mauricio Nzulu, and Antonio Bento Bembe. Brent was rather surprised that those actually holding him hostage were not listed. Laura Ingersol, the prosecutor, told him the U.S. government felt that if they took out the top leaders of FLEC, the bottom would fall out. Brent surmised in this case, if the top was taken out, the bottom would just move up.

"I was angry with the FBI," Brent said. "I had been told by Gary Weber that the FBI had nothing to do with my release."

After conversations with Gary Weber when he was released, Brent decided the FBI wanted to deal solely with Barbara during the time of Brent's captivity.

"I believe, based on what Gary told me, that the FBI wanted Chevron to say, 'Brent doesn't work for us, he works for PHI,'" Brent said. "And the FBI wanted PHI to say, 'Brent's just a mechanic. We've got lots of mechanics, and we've already replaced him, but maybe you can get his wife to come up with some money, maybe she can help you that way.'"

Brent drew from his conversations with Gary that the FBI wanted Chevron and PHI both to pull out of the negotiations.

"And Gary said there was no way they could do that, they had to stay in contact with them [FLEC]," Brent said. "If they didn't stay in contact with them, they would lose me completely."

Gary Weber has not responded to any requests for interviews for this book.

Brent's anger began almost immediately upon his release when his captors were not arrested in Zaire. Whether or not the FBI knew about the transfer of Brent into the hands of Gary Weber and Scott Taylor is unknown, but for Brent, the fact remains that no one received any punishment for keeping him in fear for his life for two months.

So despite some reluctance on his part, he did cooperate and give them information upon his release. He thought with all the evidence that he provided, the arrests would come quickly, but again he was disappointed.

Jennifer Levy called him in January of 1991, to tell him about the grand jury and that made him angry also because he had specifically asked that all contact be made with Gary Weber and not him. However, the U.S. attorney's office had an obligation to tell Brent directly. Again, his anger rose, yet no one pushed for him to see someone about the anger and anxiety.

As the years passed, Brent and Barbara simply assumed nothing would ever happen to these men, and they only spoke about it in passing, wondering what had happened to all the evidence against them.

Brent decided by the fall of 1991 that he wanted to go back to work. For the next decade, they became busy with their lives and did not dwell on the what-ifs of the case.

It was over, and only occasionally would Brent bring out the box containing the memorabilia of his two moons as a hostage in Angola.

—

Chapter 12

Back to Malongo

PHI News, Second Quarter 1991

"A Unique Experience"

Unique and sometimes bizarre experiences are not uncommon in the history of PHI. One of the most unusual happened in Angola, Africa, when Brent Swan was taken hostage near the company's base of operations there. The incident ended happily with Brent's release. We recently received this letter addressed to "PHI friends and fellow employees," from Brent's wife Barbara.

"Not too long ago we had a very difficult time when Brent was taken hostage in Angola. I was so amazed how fast people rallied to give support. It's hard to express how much we appreciated the cards, letters, calls and moral support. It really helped carry me through. The genuine caring was overwhelming and makes one realize what a great bunch of people we have here.

At the time, Brent could not even begin to imagine what was going on, on the outside, but now he is so amazed and grateful for the PHI family support. Needless to say it was a very Merry Christmas for us, [and it brought] back the true meaning of the season.

Again, thanks so much for all of your prayers, caring, and support. It meant so much."

Not Allowing the Enemy to Win

As life in Chiefland settled back into a normal routine, Brent began to think about returning to his job—a job he loved and now missed. When he voiced his intentions out loud, Barbara did whatever she could to discourage him. But even as much as she dreaded what could happen if he returned to Angola, she knew she could not keep nagging him about not going back. She knew her husband too well.

Even FLEC understood that Barbara might be reluctant to let Brent return, but in the letter that so angered Barbara from the past December, Jose Tiburcio urged her to reconsider because "[Brent] is kind enough to everybody there just as Cabindan people in Malongo witness."

Even though security changes had been made at Malongo as a result of Brent's capture, it came as little comfort to Barbara, but she understood her husband's desire.

"Brent kept saying it was like riding the bike," Barbara said. "He kept saying he had to prove something, and it would mean his life was back like it was.

"It was still difficult for us to accept."

Rita Lawrence, an advocate counselor with Victims Services and Rape Crisis Center in Alachua County, Florida, says the struggle for Brent came from his love of the job and his unwillingness to give it up.

Lawrence, who works primarily with victims who have been traumatized for a day or an hour, says she encourages victims to "not let the bad guys take more from them than they already have."

"I encourage people to do what they love and to challenge the fear slowly," Lawrence said. "Even if it's just walking down a hallway that scares them."

Brent drives his truck to the Cabinda Airport before the kidnapping. Going back to Angola after his release means he is challenging and facing his fear.

For Brent, the first step down that long hallway came when he went to Louisiana and began working on helicopters in October 1991. But that did not satisfy him as working on the King Air had, so he convinced Gary Weber to send him back to Malongo by November.

"I told Gary that if PHI could not send me back," Brent said, "then how could they send anyone there?"

When Brent stepped off the helicopter in Malongo in November 1991, the reality hit him. He never thought they would really let him go back, but there he was standing on the pad and looking at Malongo for the first time in a year. Of course, his arrival differed upon his return. This time he had not been allowed to drive from the airport. However, everything else remained nearly the same. His coworkers were all there, and his job did not change.

"They had a cake welcoming me back," Brent remembered. "I had a piece of cake, but I was pretty much in shock, disbelief, and denial that I was even there.

"I must have played something right because I wanted to prove to others and myself that I could do it."

Brent said before he could return to Malongo, Gary Weber made him promise one thing. Brent was never to talk to anyone about the kidnapping and his release. Brent agreed, although in later years, Brent has wondered why he agreed.

"If anybody asked me a question, I'd flat out tell them I couldn't answer," he said. "I never signed anything though. There was never really that threat that I'd lose my job, but if I wanted to go back, I couldn't talk."

Brent felt that he had shown that he would be closed-mouth about the ordeal because he had shut out the press upon his return and did not pose a liability to PHI. Both Barbara and Brent felt that Chevron made the request that he not talk publicly. The company had gone against U.S. policy in giving the members of FLEC a ransom, and the FBI had seemed more interested in what the negotiators were doing than the kidnappers, both Brent and Barbara thought. They understood the reluctance on the part of Chevron to discuss their role in his release. And Brent knew that without their interference, he might either still be in the jungle or worse.

"I didn't want to stir things up," Brent said. "Anyway, how do you play a game you've never played before?"

One reporter from Lewiston, Maine, had dogged both Brent and his parents. Brent and Barbara unplugged their phone, and the elder Swans threatened to call the police if she continued to call. After that, the story died away, and Brent went back to his routine—except this time, when he left for Africa, he called Barbara from Paris and then again when he reached Malongo. Every Saturday morning after his return, Barbara would call him by calling the Chevron headquarters in San Ramon, California. The call would be transferred to Malongo by satellite.

"I'd wake up sometime between 4:00 a.m. and 6:00 a.m.," Barbara remembered, "and he'd be waiting for my call."

Then when he began the journey home, he called once he reached Paris and then again in Atlanta. Things may have returned to normal, but life would never be the same.

And so Brent got back on his bike in order to show the members of FLEC that they had not won. However, the members of FLEC had no idea that Brent felt terrorized by them. They believed they were doing their duty to Cabinda. One of the kidnappers even wrote Brent at Malongo for several years, as if they were pen pals or Brent was an older brother who might be interested in his life.

The first letter was written in July of 1991, from Agostinho, although Brent did not receive it until early 1992. Agostinho wrote that he had heard that Brent had returned to Malongo, although it would be another four months after the letter was written before Brent went back to Angola.

In the letter, Agostinho requests that Brent help his younger brother, Francisco Manuel Bambi, find employment at Malongo. The second letter was written on January 12, 1992, and Brent received it from a Cabindan named Ival in early February.

"I am convinced that neither the oceans or the rivers can't be obstacle for cutting our relationship," he wrote.

He told Brent he had heard that Brent had done well for Cabinda and that "Brent Swan was a name that would not be removed from the story of Cabinda."

Brent did not respond to either letter, but he did copy them and turn them over to Chevron.

"It was a little scary," he said, "but it wasn't like I actually saw him, and I didn't know where he was located. I knew that most of the Cabindans who worked at Malongo were supporters of FLEC."

Barbara worried more about this close proximity than did Brent. She feared that those workers living in the compound with Brent were friends or family with his kidnappers.

But with the security tighter, Brent did not think about his safety very much. Scott Taylor, with Chevron security out of London, assured Brent that he had told FLEC to not have any of their members contact him.

"I knew he was still in contact with them [FLEC members]," Brent said. "He told me they had never given them the requested plane tickets [to the United States]. One time, Scott came to Malongo and said he was going to meet my 'buddies.'

"He didn't say about what, and I didn't pursue it any further."

Barbara assumed it meant that the payoffs to FLEC continued, but neither of them knew any of the details. Brent received one more letter from Agostinho in 1995. By this time, Brent assumed Chevron was not doing anything about the letters, so he did not bother to turn it over. Neither did he respond.

While Brent was in Malongo in September of 1992, Joe Sala, from African affairs, arrived from Lisbon, Portugal. He told Brent that he had been in contact with all the factions of FLEC and wanted some further information about FLEC-Renovada from Brent. Joe asked Brent about the clothes his captors wore and the type of weapons they carried. He asked about their food and if all the food was made in camp for troops there. Brent cooperated, although he did not know really with whom this man might be associated.

Brent's initial feelings of anger regarding his kidnapping had dissipated somewhat as he became involved in his work back at Malongo. However, with Joe Sala's inquiries, Brent felt the first feelings of distrust of the government—and any of its officials—begin to form, although he never let on how he felt, just as he had done during his days as a hostage.

Barbara also fought feelings of anger during this time. Her anger remained focused on the members of FLEC for most of the 1990s.

"The nerve, the gall, the arrogance," Barbara said about the letter sent to her from Tiburcio after rereading it several years later. Her anger rose to the surface swiftly as she swept her hand in front of her like a knife cutting through air.

Brent also becomes angry when talking about this letter from Tiburcio. At one point, the letter states, "Guess what do we mean."

Brent's made a note on this letter sometime after his release, revealing the depth of his true feelings. The members of FLEC never knew how much he hated them during the time of his captivity.

"May you hope I not bring down the wrath of God and throw you back to hell! Guess what do I mean," he wrote in the margin of the letter.

The anger is a normal reaction, according to professionals who work with the victims of life-threatening situations. Psychologist David Hackney has treated hundreds of veterans returning from war zones. He describes the brain as functioning on two levels: emotional and rational. When a person goes into survival mode, it is that emotional side that works the hardest. One of the most common symptoms for someone who has lived continuously in survival mode is anger, which can surface at inopportune times once back living under normal conditions. Mistrust becomes a common part of the victim's life. Barbara and Brent did not realize they were suffering from the symptoms of PTSD as they attempted to put back the pieces of their life.

"Some people take years to reveal symptoms," Hackney said. "In one case, I treated a Vietnam vet who, twenty-five years after returning, saw something on television that reminded him of an atrocity his unit committed. That's when his nightmares began."

FLEC and Angola at War

The Center for Strategic and International Studies released CSIS Africa Notes in the early 1990s. "Angola in Transition: The Cabinda

Factor" by Shawn McCormick outlined the history of FLEC, providing information on their strategies and movements before and after Brent's kidnapping.

McCormick writes that in June 1989, after an abortive peace effort between Angola and FLEC, a faction of FLEC broadcast its intent for a "national liberation struggle until Cabinda becomes independent."

FLEC, with a base in Portugal, asked for a referendum on self-determination of Cabinda, with voting to be monitored by the United Nations and the Organization of African Unity. No such referendum has ever been held, but shortly after making the demand, FLEC began kidnapping foreign workers in the enclave of Cabinda.

They began on April 27, 1990, by kidnapping thirteen French citizens and ten Congolese employees of Elf Aquitainem, a French oil company. Within hours, most of the hostages were released. After discussions between French military officials and FLEC, the rest of the hostages were set free by May 10. In any of the accounts of this kidnapping—including from the MIPT Terrorism Knowledge Base—FLEC received nothing as a ransom except notoriety. This kidnapping and subsequent release of the hostages without harm led many to assume that FLEC would not harm Brent.

Then there was the kidnapping of the Portuguese employees of a Portuguese firm, which occurred on September 10, 1990.

A representative of the responsible FLEC faction told reporters in Kinshasa that "We want the issue of the independence of Cabinda to be negotiated in Lisbon by the Portuguese government—the former colonial powers—and members of our movement," as reported in the CSIS notes.

These notes also claim that it was a different faction who kidnapped Brent. This represented the first time that an American citizen had been taken hostage by FLEC, and according to published reports, it may have been the first time that FLEC had received any type of monetary support.

After Brent's release, military attacks on the Angolan government by FLEC continued throughout 1991 and into 1992. Prior to Brent's return to Angola, one thousand Cabindan employees of Chevron went out on strike. They asked for better wages and improved working conditions, but FLEC seemed to be supporting the negotiations, according the CSIS notes.

—

The month that Brent returned to Malongo, the Angolan government moved fifteen thousand more troops into Cabinda and imposed a dusk-to-dawn curfew. However, that did not affect the American and other foreign workers at the compound. After Brent's kidnapping, no one from Malongo was allowed to travel the roads in Angola. Brent and his fellow mechanics were flown by helicopter to the airport in Cabinda City.

Even the pope attempted to intervene in what some predicted as the next battlefield in Angola even as peace negotiations were under way between MPLA and UNITA. Pope John Paul II visited the Cabinda airport to conduct a mass in June of 1992, according to Shawn McCormick in the CSIS Africa Notes, *Angola in Transition: The Cabinda Factor*. Before an estimated crowd of ten thousand, the pope asked for cooperation between all the factions in Angola with a plea to "resolve the problems of Cabinda without violence, but with peace and dialogue, respecting the people and their concerns, but also keeping in sight the needs of the entire country."

Soon after Brent's return to Malongo in 1991, Chevron hired air surveillance teams to fly over the area at night. The oil company found they could keep insurance costs down by employing this service. The Cessna Sky Master aircraft used infrared cameras installed on the wing so they could get thermal images of the ground at night. These cameras were on loan from the State Department, Brent said, and flew irregular hours over the tropical setting, lush with banana trees and palms.

Despite the efforts to keep Malongo and its workers safe, FLEC continued its guerrilla tactics throughout much of the next decade.

Unlike other rebel factions in third world countries, FLEC maintained a strong profile in Cabinda because most Cabindans support the efforts of self-determination. This support has come at a high cost to the civilian population in the form of kidnappings, rapes, and deaths. A report from the Institute for Security Studies (ISS) in August 2003 suggests that the toll on Cabindans came at the hands of both the separatists and the Angolan government.

Cabinda City is home to the majority of the Cabinda's population. Census figures from 1995 put that population at six hundred thousand with estimates suggesting over half of that amount are in exile in neighboring countries. However, ISS suggests population figures are "highly unreliable."

Outside the fence of the airport, Brent remembered Cabinda City as the true "cardboard city" of Angola, rather than the hastily built structures within the gates of Malongo. Brent had been told that the peak of Cabinda City's popularity came in 1975, seven years after the discovery of oil. In those beginning years, as the discovery of the rich fields became known, most of the oil employees lived in Cabinda. As the civil wars began with Angola's independence from Portugal in 1975, those employees began moving to the capital of Luanda for security measures. Cabinda City simply became an air station for them as they flew from Luanda to Malongo and the offshore rigs.

Despite the fact that the United States did not enjoy diplomatic relations with Angola in the 1980s, the Reagan administration actively encouraged investment in Angola. The *New Republic* editorial states, "In the last five years, the U.S. Export-Import Bank has approved three loans for Angolan oil and gas projects totaling $227 million. Since the United States does not have diplomatic relations with Angola, the loans required approval by the National Security Council. In each case, the loans were judged to be consistent with U.S. national interests. Angola may be Marxist, but today the United States is its largest trading partner—thanks in no small part to the Reagan administration."

The editorial further states that Chevron's investment in Angola by 1986 totaled $600 million. Most of that investment was put directly into the oil operations in Cabinda. In 1985, Chevron paid the government of Angola $580 million in taxes and royalties. No wonder then that most of the money garnered from the oil fields never saw the light of an Angolan day. The *New Republic* reported that "at least 95 percent of Angola's oil ends up in the West; half of Gulf's production finds its way into U.S. refineries."

Cabinda, by all accounts, provided the majority of this oil, and Chevron declared in 1985 that Angola had the richest of oil depositories in all of west and central Africa. Today, it is second largest African supplier of oil to the United States, and new fields are being discovered each year. The quest for natural gas sources also will increase the value of Cabinda's natural resource base now that companies are being urged to process the natural gas rather than burn it off 24/7 as they had done in Malongo during Brent's tenure with PHI.

Cabinda Gulf Oil Company issued a memo on May 18, 1992, to all its employees, contractors, and visitors to Malongo, signed by R. K. Connon:

—

Threats against CABGOC employees and property have increased over the last four to six weeks. Employees have been notified of attacks on CABGOC buses, which occurred on March 26, April 1, April 7, April 20, and April 21. Five CABGOC buses and one contractor (NCCC) bus have been burned. No CABGOC or contractor personnel have been injured. Since these attacks, several new threats have been made. These threats are directed at CABGOC operations including facilities and vehicles (buses, trucks, helicopters and aircraft). Obviously, travel by any form of transportation to or from Malongo carries an increased risk to life.

On Wednesday evening, this week, there was a mortar attack on the Futila police force located one kilometer from Malongo Gate #1.

Safety of employees and contractors is and must be our greatest concern. CABGOC buses ceased operations for a brief period. Other modes of transportation in and out of Malongo have been restricted to essential personnel. Plans for the orderly departure of personnel are in place and will be activated if necessary. We will develop limited exceptions to policies on work absences to cover the current situation. Each employee and contractor should consider their individual circumstances and discuss their specific situation with their supervisor. We require all contractors to communicate this notice to their employees immediately.

We wish to make clear to all concerned that CABGOC'S position is and has always been one of total political neutrality. We believe that operations in Cabinda are of benefit to all Cabindians. We are committed to the people of Cabinda. We believe that the most effective way to resolve disputes among groups is by negotiation. We urge all concerned to dedicate themselves to a peaceful resolution of differences.

FLEC's Failure as a Terrorist Group

Unlike UNITA, who fought to wrest control from the communist regime, FLEC never gained the international recognition it sought for self-determination. The United States supported the efforts of UNITA to topple MPLA. Efforts to solidify the relationship became even more pronounced when communism ended in the early 1990s, although UNITA still did not have control of the government. MPLA simply switched its allegiances and attempted to hold elections in 1992. The struggle between the two factions continued for another decade until 2002 when peace was reached in Angola.

Acts of terrorism continued in Cabinda after Brent returned to Malongo. From July 6, 1992, to February 23, 1993, seven different individuals were kidnapped—all from European countries—and released. The Terrorist Knowledge Base notes that one of the hostages was released after FLEC was given food in a 1996 incident.

One incident occurred on January 2, 1994, when six mortar bombs were fired at the Malongo compound. One of the bombs hit the housing development, wounding a resident. Brent had not returned from his Christmas holiday in the United States when this occurred, but remembers hearing about it when he came back to Malongo. He did not share this and other incidents with his family. He remembers that quite often they would hear that a bus had been burned, but the rumor mill suggested the bus drivers had done the deeds in order to get new buses.

The mortar bombs were aimed near a section of Malongo reserved for Angolans from Luanda. Brent does not recall who was injured, but does remember that it was not a PHI employee.

"It was pretty disturbing, but we never got a whole lot of information on who claimed responsibility," Brent said. "But I wasn't alarmed and felt safe with the addition of more Angolan troops surrounding Malongo."

The Terrorist Knowledge Base states that FLEC took responsibility for the bombing.

From that point on, Brent remembers that security tightened within the compound, and an alarm system was installed on the control towers. They tested the sirens every Sunday afternoon. Brent remembers huddling with his fellow employees in the living quarters, which held Kevlar blankets and heavy gear to protect them from shrapnel. Mechanics were assigned to a helicopter for evacuation offshore. In the case of a real attack, the entire compound was prepared to move.

Kidnappings continued throughout the 1990s, with one resulting in a $500,000 ransom paid to FLEC by the Portuguese and French governments in 1999, according to the Terrorism Knowledge Base. The French in particular have often been noted for their sympathetic attitude toward terrorists who are attempting to bring political justice, according to an article by Mayer Nudell and Norman Antokol in *Security Management* magazine.

"The French have a long tradition of providing political asylum and respecting the right of the downtrodden to resort to political violence to redress wrongs," the article states. "Those deals have given terrorists considerable latitude to use French soil as a safe haven to plan operations or recuperate from them."

Several leaders of FLEC made their base on French soil and in later years even held meetings there without arrest even with outstanding indictments from the United States for the kidnapping of Brent Swan.

FLEC's tactics for gaining attention followed a pattern previously established by rebel groups. As long as there have been groups that have sought ways to gain power within a political structure, the act of terrorism has been one method for gaining that attention. Very few of these groups have ever achieved total success, just as pure forms of governments from communism to democracy have never truly been realized. Perhaps the Nazis, as a terrorist group, came closest to achieving their goal of ultimate power in Germany in the 1930s, according to the article in *Security Management* published in 1991.

This article outlines the stages of development of a terrorist group, regardless of its ideology. As these groups organize, it is the ideology that bands them together, and it is this philosophy which gives them the power that comes with believing their cause is the *right* one and all means justify the ends of achieving their ultimate goal, which is political power of some sort.

For FLEC, this ideology has never wavered since its inception in the 1960s, even before Portugal ended its formal relationship with Angola. FLEC, in its various incarnations and factions for forty years, has maintained that complete independence for Cabinda is its only purpose for existence. Its unwillingness to compromise with Angola is evident in its slogan "Cabinda is not Angola," which has been their tagline for decades. It was one of the first things Brent Swan remembers hearing after being taken hostage. "You are in Cabinda, not Angola," his kidnappers told him from the very beginning.

Once the group with its common goal has formed, financial support must be found; and since these groups are generally fledgling, loosely-organized young men, money is not available in abundance, particularly in a third world country such as Angola. So these groups begin by committing robberies to gain arms and money. Propaganda activities take place. Both of these steps would have been quite simple for FLEC to accomplish in those early years. Arms from Russia and the Cuban troops were either given to them or stolen. Angola's civil war meant that almost every man from an early age was armed and with some access to the materials to place land mines and to create havoc.

Convincing the Cabindan people of their message also would have been an easy task. Since the enclave itself never really was a part of Angola either culturally or historically, the Cabindan people have always viewed themselves as an independent entity. Since the members of FLEC were young men easily persuaded to join the ranks, many Cabindans probably had at least one member of their family living in the bush fighting for sovereignty.

Even though FLEC made it to the next step on the terrorist ladder, they have never really succeeded in moving from that level. Something in their tactics always failed, even to this day. At this next stage, the group must make a name for themselves and become visible, so their goals become public knowledge. Hopefully, these goals are valid enough for the public to take notice and perhaps even forgive some of the methods used to achieve success. Hostage taking and visible acts of aggression are most often employed at this stage with the hope that media attention will become so pronounced that the cause of the group becomes more paramount than the criminal activities associated with this stage.

FLEC managed the aggressive acts and the hostage taking, but never has their message achieved the type of international attention needed to push their cause for independence. In order for a group to succeed, they must not stay in this stage for very long or their methods are no longer effective. FLEC has been stuck in this stage for more than twenty years.

Three factors probably hurt their chances for making a successful bid for independence. Studies done on terrorists show that most of them are young and college educated. While the soldiers fighting for Cabinda's independence fit one side of the profile, they do not come close to fitting probably the most important part. The soldiers are young, but they are far from being educated. Of the twenty-five to thirty who guarded Brent during his captivity, only a few spoke English, making a global presence more difficult. Some of the incidents when his captors forgot their guns or knew little about the simplest of mechanical things, such as using a makeshift level for building a bed, show the lack of knowledge these young boys had.

This lack of education and naïveté probably hurt FLEC's chances of garnering much attention internationally. No efforts seemed to be made to bring in the media and publicize the kidnapping. They felt that just by taking a Chevron employee hostage, they would bring attention upon themselves.

From its inception, FLEC was a disjointed organization with many branches and no centralized center. Not until 2004 did the two remaining main factions come together to form one united FLEC. They met in the Netherlands to seal their partnership. The year before, several leaders of FLEC-FAC turned themselves into the Angolan government, allowing FLEC-Renovada a chance to form one strong voice in the fight for Cabindan independence.

A third factor also must be considered. Cabinda's chance for self-determination ended the moment Gulf Oil Company—later taken over by Chevron—who had been exploring the area for a decade, discovered oil offshore in 1968. It is highly unlikely that Angola, Chevron, and the United States would ever want to see a small country filled with angry rebels intent upon reaping the benefits of the massive reserves of oil on its soil come into power.

CHAPTER 13

Terrorism Has a Name

U.S. News & World Report

OFF THE CABINDA COAST, Angola (Aug. 9, 1999)—On the deepwater edge of Block 0, a 20-minute helicopter ride off the African coast, floats the most important moneymaker in Angola's intractable civil war. Nemba, the newest of 25 oil rigs operated by California-based Chevron, pumps $300 million of crude oil a year. "Out here, we know about the war," says Nigel Baker, the Texan platform boss. "But we're not part of the trouble."

Maybe not, but oil is certainly a big deal in the conflict. Angola's government and the rebels from the National Union for the Total Independence of Angola (UNITA) are bent on annihilating each other, and they are using money from oil and diamond sales to make sure they have the means to do it. A staggering 1,000 people a day died at the height of the two-decade-long conflict. Since fighting resumed six months ago, thousands more have been killed; as many as a million have been displaced. And things could soon get worse. The government is promising a new offensive that some predict could result in the total destruction of Angola.

A return to war means trouble for Washington. Angola's oil is worth an annual $3 billion and accounts for 7 percent of U.S. imports—a number expected to double in the next decade. The United States has always wielded strong influence in Angola, a former Portuguese colony twice the size of Texas. During the cold war, Washington backed

—

UNITA's Jonas Savimbi against a then Marxist regime supported by the Soviet Union and Cuba. Still, the United States wound up with the lion's share of oil concessions from the government it once tried to overthrow.

So Washington is throwing its lot in with the government, and American oil companies are following suit. Chevron will invest up to $5 billion over the next five years as slumping oil prices are offset by the size of potential finds. And the potential is great indeed, with Angola set to become Africa's biggest oil producer in the next decade. Experts say the oil fields offshore in the Atlantic are like spigots waiting to be tapped. "And the further out you go," says Warner Williams, Chevron's managing director, "the more oil you find." There is, of course, one other benefit to drilling at sea: Being far away from a war that the United Nations once called "the worst in the world."

Falling Off the Bike

Despite the warnings and continued threats from FLEC during the 1990s, Brent continued working his regular schedule with few changes until 1999. All of Brent's papers from his hostage days went into a box. Sometime in 1995, he noticed the faxed pages fading, and he decided to get everything into typewritten form in a computer with perhaps the intent to write a book at a later date.

"This bothered me," Barbara said. "At first I thought he just might need to download all the information in some form, but then I saw all the energy he was putting into it, and I was afraid that he was getting almost obsessed."

He originally called his diary—those entries he wrote while being held captive—*My Adventures in West Africa*. When he began looking over those pages in 1995, he changed the title to *Two Moons in Africa*, and he dedicated the book to his wife, Barbara.

"Without our love for each other, I would have gone the Rambo route in the jungle," Brent said. "Without her being here waiting when I was there, it would have been a whole different scenario."

He also continued to work on the house throughout much of the '90s, and on New Year's Eve 1999, they moved permanently into their

—

comfortable ranch-style home. The only reminder during the years of the kidnapping began on October 19 each year and lasted through December 18.

"He'd get very quiet," Barbara said about the anniversary time. "And there wasn't anything I could do to help. I didn't want to know. I didn't want to remember. I was in complete denial."

But still he continued working. Then in 1999, PHI sold the King Air, and Brent was reassigned to work on the helicopters at Malongo, just like any other mechanic.

Brent stands next to his King Air. When PHI sold the King Air in 1999, Brent lost the one thing that had made him happy in Africa.

"They stopped the contract with the King Air," Brent said. "And I wasn't working on my airplane anymore."

The job became more stressful because now he had to work with others, and no longer was he his own boss. He also saw that the Angolan mechanics had less training than he, and it made it difficult to do his job.

"I had been working by myself for fifteen years," Brent said, " and now I was working in Malongo, and things just weren't the same."

Brent left Angola in August of 2001 for an extended vacation that was supposed to bring him back to Malongo at the end of September.

By this time, the expense of the helicopters to transport the workers to the Cabinda airport had been cut to save money. Instead, the employees took a boat from the docks at Malongo to the airport. The day when he left for home in August 2001, he stood on the docks and turned around to look at the compound before boarding the boat. He asked himself if he would miss the place if for some reason he did not return. He suddenly realized he would not.

"I was reaching a point where I needed to find something different to do in my life," Brent said. "So that's why I looked back and asked myself that question. It ended up being my last trip there, but I didn't know it at the time."

Then sometime during the first week of September, Brent received a notice from Carol Suggs that she was selling PHI, and Brent knew changes were possible in a job that had already become a source of unhappiness for him.

Rita Lawrence, victim advocate, says it makes perfect sense that Brent began to have problems around this time, especially learning that the company would be changing hands and all that it might imply as far as a change in supervisors and job descriptions.

"Having new people in charge, new managers, if they don't understand, it means the victim has to tell the story again," Lawrence said. "And there is the chance the new people just won't understand.

"Trauma does not go away like grief can. Trauma is a whole different animal."

September 11, 2001

Brent watched the television news on Tuesday morning, September 11, 2001. He saw a video clip of what he thought might be a small piper or single-engine airplane.

"It didn't look like it had done much damage," Brent remembered. "I thought it was probably pilot error and didn't consider it much longer."

Barbara was at work, and Brent went about getting the upstairs bedrooms ready for carpet. Barbara's mother had the television on and mentioned a couple of times to Brent about what was happening as he went about his chores. However, nothing really registered — yet. Finally, he focused on what the television announcers were saying and realized that what he had seen earlier in the day had actually been a 767 hitting the side of a building. When he finally realized that terrorists had done this act, he tried not to listen.

"Things just started happening in my mind," he recalled. "I didn't actually realize what was going on, and I wanted to deny that it was even happening."

Barbara called Brent two or three times during the day, thankful that he had not been on one of those planes. The timing coincided with when he would have been scheduled to go back to Angola, and she knew he always flew on a 767.

Brent began stalling going back to Malongo and used vacation time to further his stay at home. He could not imagine getting on a 767 to fly back there because he feared losing control. When he ran out of vacation time, he began calling in sick.

He finally had the dreaded talk with Gary Weber sometime in early 2002, and Brent told Gary that he needed to retire "from aviation, from PHI, from Africa."

Brent made arrangements to have all of his things shipped from Malongo to the States, which took months to arrange. Finally in June, the crates arrived at Wal-Mart in Chiefland, carrying nearly one thousand pounds of Brent's belongings.

Brent went to Wal-Mart in early June to load his crates onto a trailer for transporting to his home five miles away. When he came home with his crates and set them in the yard, Barbara told him there was a message on the answering machine for him.

Joe Armstrong, with the FBI in Gainesville, had left a message asking Brent to call him back. The message said the FBI wanted to make sure Brent was still at this number. It had been eight years since Brent had heard anything from them.

"We hadn't heard from these people in how long?" Barbara asked. "And on the day Brent is picking up his last tie to Cabinda, he calls? Too coincidental."

"They knew," Brent said. "Somehow they knew, and I thought the phone was bugged."

Brent did not call Joe Armstrong back, but Joe called again later that day. This time, Brent took the call, only after verifying that Armstrong was really who he said he was.

Brent called the FBI number listed in the front of the phone book, which connected him with the Jacksonville office. They verified that Joe Armstrong was indeed an agent.

"He wanted very badly for me to tell him my address," Brent remembered. "I told him he had it on file. I never did give it to him."

Joe told Brent he was simply making the call to update his files. He had no information for Brent. Toward the end of the ten—to fifteen-minute conversation, Brent let his anger vent.

Armstrong's words infuriated Brent who felt the FBI never had any information; they just wanted his information. Brent remembers that his anger flared almost immediately upon hearing this man's voice. He flew into a rage and told Joe what he thought.

"You people need to get off your ass and do something with this case," Brent told the FBI agent. "Hell, I figured you had closed the case years ago and just never bothered to tell me about it."

Brent ended the conversation by asking Joe to do him a favor.

"Pass it on to Washington that I'm ready to play ball."

"I was outside the day he talked to Joe Armstrong," Barbara said. "But I could hear the anger in Brent's voice. I could feel it within a couple of minutes."

Barbara began crying and spent the rest of the summer near hysteria, not sure what had happened or why it happened so quickly.

"I began hyperventilating, which I'd never done before, and crying all the time," Barbara said. "I had no idea what had come over me and why the phone call was such a big deal."

"And Brent treated the call as if it was no big deal as he went off to Maine," she said. "And I was instantly a mess."

Brent continued his plans for going to Maine for the summer to help his brother.

The Blooming of PTSD

Days before Brent was scheduled to drive to his brother's house in Maine for the summer, Nada Alley with the FBI in Washington DC called. Brent classifies her as a profiler. She told Brent to stay tuned because the prosecutors in Washington might need to talk to Brent in the very near future. She offered no explanation. Brent went to Maine as planned.

"I didn't know what they wanted, but I figured it this way: this case has been open for over eleven years," Brent said about his decision to leave. "What is the near future to them? Tomorrow? Ten years?"

This time, the "near future" meant just that, as Artur Tchibassa was arrested in Kinshasa in the Democratic Republic of Congo on July 11, 2002; and on July 12, his indictment from 1991 was unsealed and redacted.

However, the Swans were not aware of this development until Saturday, July 13, when FBI agent Jennifer Snell called to inform Barbara that the FLEC negotiator, Tchibassa, had been nabbed. By July 16, Tchibassa was in Washington DC before a federal judge and entered a plea of Not Guilty.

During the summer of 2002, Brent and Barbara both went back into survival mode with full-blown symptoms of PTSD. But neither of them knew what had happened to them, and no one was there to help them cope.

With the opening of the whole nightmare once again, both Barbara and Brent began what victim advocates are beginning to recognize as "revictimization." It did not matter that they were safe on their property in Chiefland, nowhere near Angola and the members of FLEC. They were both back to 1990 and October 19 when Brent looked down the barrel of the AK-47 pointing in the window of his truck. Only this time he was looking down the barrel of a gun held by his own government, and Barbara could do nothing to protect him.

Rita Lawrence says that loved ones are affected most by the lack of control to protect the person they love. Barbara was just as helpless in 2002 when she heard the anger rise in Brent's voice while talking with Joe Armstrong, as she was when Gary Weber called her in 1990 with the news that Brent had disappeared on that road in Cabinda early one morning.

"The victim is feeling they are right back there," Lawrence said, "with increased hypervigilance, anxiety, paranoia, incredible mood swings, inability to sleep, inability to focus.

"The survival part of the brain has hijacked everything else. It's very good at what it does, and it's not going to pay attention to rational thought."

Psychologist David Hackney describes the brain as a computer with the brain usually working on two levels, the emotional and the logical.

"Normally, they work together smoothly, operating in harmony with many programs like a computer," Hackney explained. "Sometimes, other files are not available when working in one program as it is with Survival Mode. Other areas of the brain just aren't available.

"It's an altered state when faced with danger," he continued. "But resources from normal daily life are just not available to the victim of PTSD."

Barbara was home alone on that Saturday in July, already traumatized by Joe Armstrong's call a few weeks earlier, when Jennifer Snell, from the FBI in Washington, called on July 13. She wanted to talk to Brent, but Barbara was fairly certain that Brent had gone to a secluded cottage with his family for the weekend. He could not be reached by phone. Snell called back with Laura Ingersoll, the prosecutor, on the other line, and they proceeded to tell Barbara that Tchibassa had been arrested and would most likely be on U.S. soil within twenty-four hours. They could not answer her questions about what it all meant, but told her they just did not want either Brent or her to hear about it on the news.

"If I hadn't been a mess already, I was now really a mess," Barbara said.

She managed to go into work, but her manager sent her home soon afterward when he saw that she could not work.

When she managed to reach Brent, his response was, "That's great news." He did not understand why his wife could not stop crying.

"I felt pretty relieved, but surprised they had actually arrested one of them after all these years," Brent said about receiving the news. "I thought, finally, maybe some good will come out of this thing."

So he called Laura Ingersoll, and she gave him what information she could. Brent remembers Laura telling him that a judge in Puerto Rico—where Tchibassa had been flown after his arrest in the Congo—asked Tchibassa if he minded traveling to the United States to appear before a judge. Brent wondered at the time why Tchibassa would have any say in where he was flown since he was under arrest.

"She asked me a couple of questions like if I remembered Tchibassa, and at the time, I confused Tchibassa with Tiburcio who was the president," Brent said. "I figured if they were going to arrest someone, they would go to the top."

Ingersoll asked Brent to come to Washington so they could ask questions in an informal, comfortable setting to see how well Brent might perform if they went to trial. She told him that most of these cases never make it to trial because of plea bargaining.

"When I talked with Laura Ingersoll, she asked if there was anything I'd written down about this since I'd gotten out, or if there were any materials that we would have to turn over to the defense," Brent said. "There was no way they were going to get my stuff."

He called Barbara immediately afterward and had her put all of his materials from the kidnapping together and send it to him in Maine by the next day.

"When Brent called me, he sounded as if he was in a panic," Barbara remembered. "I was in very bad shape, and I got really pissed. I told him he better be working his ass off because it was going to cost $200 to overnight that stuff to Maine."

By the time the driver arrived to pick up the package the next day, she had worked herself into such a state that she sent the package to Maine, Maine, instead of Bethel, Maine. When the driver pointed it out to her, she still did not change it. She sent it off to Maine, Maine. Despite that, Brent still managed to receive the box the next day.

When he saw the pile of papers, he thought about burning them so no one could ever have access to what he felt rightfully belonged to him.

"It might be a pile of ashes on a mountainside in Maine, but it was mine," Brent thought. However, he did not burn it, but left it at his brother's place while he went to Washington on July 25.

He told Barbara to stay in Chiefland. He knew she was not coping well with the news, and the prosecutor had assured him the visit to Washington would be very casual.

The morning after he arrived, Nada Alley picked him up at the hotel in the pouring rain, taking him to the prosecutor's building where he met both Jennifer Levy with the FBI and Laura Ingersoll.

"They started questioning me by luring me in," Brent said. "They keep playing with your mind until you give up whatever information it is they think they need."

They started by asking him about Africa, and suddenly he felt himself returning to Cabinda. By that time, they had settled in the conference room; and from 9:30 a.m. until 1:30 p.m., Brent was interrogated about his kidnapping. They did not break for lunch.

Brent recalls those hours as ones in which question after question was fired at him. In an interview in 2005, he went back to that day as if he was going back into the jungle.

He recounted what happened that day on tape.

"*They dug out the big three-ring binder with all the photographs, all the things I had initialed and dated. They asked, 'Who's this guy?' It all starts to come back to me. Tiburcio is Tiburcio. They've arrested Tchibassa, and I don't remember meeting him that much. I didn't understand at this time when they were questioning what was actually happening in my mind. It was happening so fast. We covered a lot of ground. They asked me several things about FLEC. And I remember Jennifer Levy in this instance saying what a good memory I had. At 1:30 p.m. they were done with me and dropped me off at the airport for my 2:45 p.m. flight back to Maine.*

I walked through the doors at the airport with the sliding doors. And when the doors slid shut behind me, and I was disconnected from them, I crashed. From that point until about 4:30 p.m. or so, I don't remember anything. Absolutely nothing. About four thirty, I came to enough to know I was standing in the middle of the crowd, but I didn't have a boarding pass, and I hadn't checked in, and hadn't gone through security. I was just in the terminal building just floating around, I guess. Couldn't remember anything, and I had missed my flight. I called Laura Ingersoll and let her know I had missed my flight, and I still didn't realize what actually was happening. I didn't know what to do. She [Laura] said to go to the ticket counter and try for another one, and she would call the person in charge of flights. I got back to my brother's place around 1:00 a.m., just wiped out."

Brent ended up sleeping most of the next day, but when he did venture out to help his brother on his apartment house work, Brent was unable to do the simplest of tasks. His brother became upset with him, so Brent took off for a few days to commune with the mountains and nature. It did not help. During this time, he suddenly realized what Barbara had been feeling.

He never could get back to work on his brother's place so he ended up coming home. Once home, Barbara and Brent had difficulty functioning, and neither knew why. Barbara became even more frightened after Brent's return because of his demands. First, he told her they had to get a post office box and then an unlisted number. Barbara wondered if he would insist they go completely underground. She asked him, "What the hell did they say to you in Washington?" She wondered if the FLEC soldiers had plans to come after them.

"I never felt threatened before," Barbara said. "But we'd go in the car, and Brent would say, 'Don't say anything.'"

The only place Brent would allow Barbara to talk about it would be when they walked down their deserted rural road. Barbara's anxiety increased.

"I was totally paranoid," Brent said of this time. "I told my brother the FBI were in his house in the middle of the night. I didn't see anybody. I just knew they were there."

When Brent met with Laura Ingersoll, he told her that he was worried about his wife. Ingersoll eventually put him in contact with a victim advocate in Gainesville. However, as much as they liked this woman, she was not versed in federal cases and could not provide much information for the Swans on what might transpire during a trial, if one should be held.

Brent still remained in denial about his condition for the most part. He told everyone that he needed some counseling for his wife.

Prior to his interrogation in Washington, he met with Julie R. Breslow, the chief victim advocate at the time. She talked to Brent about financial help that he would be entitled to as a witness. For instance, if they needed someone to run a business while participating in the trial, financial assistance would be provided to the Swans. At no time did Breslow talk to Brent about any type of psychological help. He had to ask for that information from the prosecutor.

Rita Lawrence addressed the lack of help for the Swans in an interview in her Gainesville office in 2005.

"I think the federal government is really just learning how to deal with people," she said. "I don't think we're anywhere near where we need to be. A lot of study needs to be done to figure out how to help victims."

David Hackney says that studies dealing with victims of a traumatic event really did not start until the 1980s with Vietnam veterans who were having difficulty assimilating back into society. Laws addressing the rights and needs of victims were not enacted until 1982 with the Victim and Witness Protection Act of 1982 and the Victims of Crime Act of 1984.

When Brent was kidnapped, these laws were in effect, but the Swans did not know about them because those in charge did not inform them.

—

By 2002, when the worst of the PTSD symptoms began displaying themselves in the life of the Swans, no one knew quite what to do about it because the trauma had occurred so many years ago, and those closest to Barbara and Brent assumed the event had been forgotten and put away. They did not understand how it felt to be retraumatized. So Barbara and Brent stopped sharing with their family.

CHAPTER 14

Back into the Jungle

Press Release—U.S. Department of Justice

WASHINGTON, D.C. (July 16, 2002)—Attorney General John Ashcroft and Roscoe Howard, U.S. Attorney for the District of Columbia, announced today that Artur Tchibassa, who was indicted in 1991 for the Oct. 19, 1990 kidnapping of American citizen Brent Swan in Angola, has been arrested abroad and transported to the United States in the custody of Special Agents of the Federal Bureau of Investigation to stand trial in the U.S. District Court for the District of Columbia.

Swan, an aircraft technician for Petroleum Helicopter, Inc., (PHI), an American company under contract to Chevron Oil Company in Cabinda, Angola, was abducted on Oct. 19, 1990 by members of a group called FLEC-PM (Front for the Liberation of the Enclave of Cabinda – Military Position), a para-military organization whose objective was to promote the independence of the province of Cabinda from the country of Angola. On or about Oct. 25, 1990, a member of FLEC-PM had seized and detained Mr. Swan. On or about Nov. 3, 1990, a member of FLEC-PM delivered a letter addressed to Chevron Overseas Petroleum, Inc., demanding that Chevron meet with representatives of FLEC-PM. The indictment alleges that Tchibassa was one of the three FLEC-PM representatives who negotiated directly with representatives of Chevron and presented a list of demands to be met prior to the release of Brent Swan, including a demand for a financial ransom. From on or about Nov. 29, 1990, through Dec. 18 1990, Tchibassa and other FLEC-PM representatives met with Chevron representatives to negotiate conditions for Mr. Swan's release. Mr. Swan was ultimately released from captivity on Dec. 18, 1990.

Tchibassa, 47, was charged in the U.S. District Court for the District of Columbia on Sept. 25, 1991, by sealed indictment with the crimes of hostage-taking, in violation of 18 U.S.C. sections 1203 and 2, and conspiracy to commit hostage-taking, in violation of 18 U.S.C. sections 371 and 1203. Tchibassa had remained a fugitive since the kidnapping of Brent Swan. The charges against Tchibassa were unsealed on July 12, 2002, a day after he was arrested by the FBI in the Democratic Republic of Congo. Tchibassa will be prosecuted by the U.S. Attorney's Office for the District of Columbia and the Terrorism and Violent Crime Section, Criminal Division. U.S. Department of Justice.

"As President Bush stated in the aftermath of the September 11 attacks in New York, Virginia, and Pennsylvania, the war on terrorism must be fought on a number of fronts," said Attorney General John Ashcroft. "This arrest demonstrates the tenacity of the United States in tracking down persons charged with having committed terrorist acts against Americans, no matter how long it takes."

U.S. Attorney Roscoe Howard noted, "Our dedication to the cause of justice and our resourcefulness are our greatest strengths in fighting crime wherever in the world it occurs."

Tchibassa is scheduled to appear for arraignment before U.S. District Court Judge Thomas Hogan at the U.S. District Court in Washington today at 3 p.m. If convicted of all the charges, Tchibassa faces a maximum penalty of life in prison.

The Government's Star Witness

Brent wrote the "final chapters" of his book in October of 2002 in an effort to organize what he had accumulated. As he chronicled the happenings of the summer of 2002, he wrote, "Seek Counseling—Just like I got out of the woods yesterday!!!!"

His frustration is evident in the writings. He found out that the prosecution "stopped the clock" on due process for the accused's right to a speedy trial when they requested information from another country on August 22, 2002.

"As you can guess, they didn't tell me they were going to Great Britain to talk to Scott Taylor," Brent wrote.

He worked through the indictment, trying to include the things that had been redacted such as the names of the other co-conspirators listed. He worried that Gary Weber had been listed as a co-conspirator because he had negotiated with FLEC.

"I understand why I cannot be told certain things," he wrote. "But still, I am right in the middle of this whole mess. I didn't ask to be here. It bothers the shit out of me to have spent so much time putting all of this together and still all I get is bits and pieces."

His frustration grew with the lack of information coming from Washington about how things were progressing. From the beginning, the prosecutors had tried to assure him that this type of case rarely went to trial, but as the months lengthened, and the attempts to get Tchibassa to give out information about the others in the indictment failed, a trial began to look like a strong possibility.

In March 2003, Barbara and Brent headed for Washington as the prosecutors began to prepare for the trial—the trial that was not supposed to be—as Tchibassa continued to refuse any attempts at plea bargaining.

"To some extent, I wanted him to have to do as much time as possible," Brent said in 2005, "instead of getting out early with the plea bargaining."

During the trip, Brent ended up giving over more of his materials he had been hoarding. He gave them more photographs and corrected some of the information they had received from the FBI.

As they prepped Brent for the trial, he remembers his state of mind was "terrible," and the paranoia continued. During April or May 2003, the Swans met with a therapist in Gainesville, but they were not satisfied with her.

"We were actively seeking counseling by this time," he said.

Barbara's Trials

Barbara remembers the first time they met with a victims advocate in 2002. Brent had his leg across his knee, and he began unconsciously itching the spot on his ankle that had the infected cut.

"The immune system and the nervous system talk to one another," David Hackney said. "The brain mobilizes itself, and it's all interconnected."

Barbara said she calmed down after seeing the victim advocate in Gainesville. For the first time, someone recognized that Barbara might be having some difficulty with all of the events. The advocate stopped speaking to Brent for a moment and turned to Barbara.

"And how was that for you when they called you that day on October 19, 1990?"

The question hit Barbara so hard that it was as if the wind had been knocked out of her with a sucker punch to the stomach. She could not answer because the tears started.

"It was just as fresh as if it had just happened," Barbara said. "When the whole thing was happening [in 1990], my mind was a blank except for a few things."

After Brent returned from Maine in the summer of 2002, Barbara had a rough month, never wanting to let Brent out of her sight. If he left the house to go into Chiefland—five miles away—to run errands, she would panic, pacing the floor until he returned.

The first panic attack occurred before he even arrived back home from Maine. She had walked down the driveway to the mailbox when suddenly she found herself sitting in the middle of the driveway hyperventilating, near hysterics. Another time the panic attack hit while she was sitting quietly in a corner of her living room.

"I tried explaining this to Brent," she said, "but he didn't really understand the actual power it had over me until he got home."

Their first contact with Yvonne Bryant, a victim advocate appointed by the prosecution, came during the March trip to DC. The Swans look back and agree that Yvonne did one good thing for them and that was find a therapist in Gainesville who was knowledgeable and helped them deal with the crisis in which they now found themselves.

Both Barbara and Brent found they could no longer do simple things such as pick up the phone and call a therapist on their own. They needed help with the extra things required of them at this time.

Preparing the Witness

The prosecutors continued asking Brent questions—sometimes the same questions. Brent saw it as their way of making sure he would not change his story once on the stand. The Swans continued to see the victim advocate in Gainesville. On May 14, 2003, Brent met with Jennifer Snell of the FBI at the victim advocate's office to help put the photographs in order. The trial was scheduled to begin July 9, 2003. In June, the prosecutor's office called to tell them the trial had been postponed to September 3, 2003.

"We were hoping it would all be over in July," Brent said. "It was upsetting, and it put everything on hold for us for a while."

They had arranged for Barbara's sister to come and stay with Barbara's mother during the trial in July. They decided to go to Maine for a vacation instead.

By this time, Brent had figured out, with the help of his therapist, that when he talked of that time of captivity, he needed to be brought back out of the jungle afterward to avoid the type of situation that had occurred at the airport the year before. He asked the prosecution to do that for him to help lessen the effects of his testimony.

Barbara and Brent finally left for Washington on August 27—on yet another new moon—for the beginning of the trial.

When they arrived in Washington, annoyances began almost immediately for Barbara and Brent. The prosecutors told them to come prepared to stay through the entire trial, estimated at two to three weeks. They packed accordingly, bringing four suitcases. Two FBI agents met them as soon as they got off the plane, holding a sign with the word "Swan" printed on it.

"Looking back, we wish we had the nerve to just walk by," Barbara said. "Did they recognize us? It just felt so intimidating at the time."

As frightening as it all seemed, Barbara and Brent walked over to the two large armed men who took them to a four-door sedan. The trunk was not large enough for their luggage and so Barbara and Brent rode into the city with suitcases on their laps in the backseat of the car. They assumed they would be taken to the hotel to deposit their belongings, but instead, the agents drove them directly to the prosecutor's office.

The Department of Justice needed paperwork filled out so the Swans could receive cash, but Barbara and Brent just wanted to go to their room. Preparing for the trip and making arrangements for Barbara's mother in their absence was hard enough. And traveling to Washington had worn them out. Finally, they collapsed in their room.

The next day on August 28, Brent and Barbara arrived at the prosecutor's office; and as they sat down to begin the preparations, the fire alarm went off in the building, and they had to evacuate. This situation would be confusing and somewhat frightening for anyone realizing they sat on the eleventh floor of the building and would have to use the stairs to leave that building, but for someone suffering from the symptoms of PTSD, the effect once again put the Swans back in survival mode.

"Laura [Ingersoll] had just put her big wooden file box down on the table when bells started ringing and alarms going off," Barbara recounted. "Going down that staircase, we realized everyone but us has guns. Not a great way to start."

They went over to the FBI building for questioning. Brent was questioned by Laura and John Patarini of the FBI from 1:30 p.m. to 4:30 p.m. He had requested they bring him back out of the jungle after questioning, but they did not do that.

"That isn't what they want," Brent said in 2005. "They want to take you back to the scene of the crime and see if it'll jog your memory, and maybe you'll remember something new.

"I was already remembering way more than I wanted to, and I didn't want to be there," Brent continued about his first day of questioning. "When I'm there [in the jungle], I can't function."

The days of questioning continued until the day before the trial when Ingersoll did make an attempt to bring Brent out of the jungle at the end of the day. However, Brent remained trapped back in Angola for days while the prosecution prepared their case. On the day before the trial, Ingersoll's attempt to bring him out consisted of asking him who he saw at the Atlanta airport. Brent responded that he saw two FBI agents. Ingersoll countered with "Didn't you see your wife?" End of questioning.

"I was still in the jungle, and that question didn't do it," Brent said.

The Trial

Brent suffered from headaches that intensified during the days in Washington. He was taking eight to ten Tylenols a day to help relieve the pain. He remembers sleeping very little the week prior to the trip, and once in Washington, he says he did not sleep at all.

And so he began the trial in a very agitated state. He was on the stand from 11:30 a.m. to 4:30 p.m. on that first day.

Since Barbara had been subpoenaed to testify, she could not be in the courtroom while Brent was on the stand. She was directed to two little rooms down the hallway from the courtroom. One other person sat in the room waiting to be called. She attempted to complete a crossword puzzle, but remembers that she spent most of the day pacing the hallway.

Then Brent came out, and Barbara said, "He looked as if he'd been wrung through the wringer."

"I didn't want to push him," Barbara said. "But I told him if he wanted to talk, I was interested in Tchibassa's reactions. Brent barely remembered going in there and doing it."

That evening Jennifer Levy took Barbara aside and told her they would not be using her testimony in the trial because they could not have any emotion in the courtroom.

"Then why have the trial?" Barbara said. "Why put Brent on the stand?"

The Swans now believe that Barbara had only been subpoenaed to keep her out of the courtroom.

On the second day of Brent's testimony, the defense took over the questioning—the part Brent had been dreading the most. Brent described the defense attorney's questions as "short, sweet, simple." He told Brent he simply wanted to clarify a few things.

He was told he could step down. As he stepped out into the hallway to meet Barbara, he could not make eye contact or talk.

"He was like a zombie," Barbara said.

Yvonne Bryant, the victim advocate, met them in the hallway and asked them to come back to her office to process the paperwork. Before leaving the building, Barbara saw Gary Weber and went over and hugged him. They talked about the weather, but Brent did not participate in the conversation.

After completing the paperwork, Barbara said Yvonne looked at them and said she had them booked on a flight that very afternoon back to Gainesville.

"Look at him," Barbara told Yvonne. "I'll be lucky if I can get him back to the hotel room, and you want me to put him on a plane?"

Barbara could not believe that the one person who was supposed to be concerned about their well-being was so out of touch with Brent's state of mind that she would try to get rid of them without checking on Brent's mental state.

"She didn't care," Barbara said. "And on top of that, there was a tropical storm sitting off the coast of Florida. We probably wouldn't even be able to get into the Gainesville airport."

Brent believes that Yvonne's title had been misplaced. He refers to her as the "government's advocate."

"Victims should know this," Brent said. "They have a lot of power right up until the point they've given their testimony. As soon as you've given testimony, they don't care anymore. They dump you."

Barbara was horrified at the prospect of having to race back to the hotel and pack. They had been told they would be in Washington for the entire trial, but Yvonne now told them they would be leaving in a few hours.

"I had to actually say to the victim advocate, 'Look at him! No way can we travel right now.'"

Yvonne reluctantly told them they could stay in the hotel one more night. She booked a flight for one-thirty the next afternoon, Saturday, September 6. Barbara had to figure out how to get to the airport from the hotel on her own. There were no drivers waiting to take them. She could have used someone else making decisions for her at this time because Brent was not functioning well.

"Where was the escort for us back to the airport?" Barbara asked. "They were done with us, and they didn't care how we got home."

Yvonne Bryant never contacted them after that day in the hallway after Brent completed his testimony. The Swans had to call her after the September 12 verdict was handed down to find out what the jury had decided.

Donna Miller has been a victim advocate with the St. Johns County Sheriff's Office in Florida for ten years. She has been trained through Florida's State Attorney's Office.

"We're not counselors," Miller said about her role as a victim advocate. "We're a calming agent at the time of trauma, and we're listeners."

She maintains that each time something reminds the victim of the trauma, the senses become heightened, and rationale is exhausted.

"If I had been there after he took the stand, I would have let him process the stresses that came with the reliving of the event," Miller said. "What happened to him on the stand and afterwards is a revictimization."

Miller believes that victim advocates simply use the tools of basic human nature that include caring about fellow human beings and ensuring their well-being after being retraumatized.

—

"To not check on the victim," she said, "is a total disrespect for the office of victim advocacy."

When they called Yvonne on September 12, 2003, she told them Tchibassa had been found guilty on all counts.

"It felt good to hear," Brent said. "But it couldn't have been any other way. If they had come back with a not-guilty verdict after everything we had put ourselves through, I can't even imagine that scenario.

"Yes, he's guilty. We've known that for years," Brent said.

Sentencing would take place in January of 2004, which meant once again Brent would face Tchibassa in the courtroom. It would be Barbara's first chance to look at one of her husband's kidnappers.

CHAPTER 15

Facing Enemies

Press Release—U.S. Department of Justice

WASHINGTON, D.C. (September 13, 2003) —United States Attorney Roscoe C. Howard, Jr. and Michael A. Mason, Assistant Director in Charge of the FBI's Washington Field Office, announced that late yesterday a federal jury in the District of Columbia returned guilty verdicts, after a trial which began on September 3, 2003, against Artur Tchibassa, 47, formerly of Angola, on charges of hostage-taking and conspiracy to commit hostage-taking, in connection with a 1990 incident in which an American citizen was abducted and held hostage in the Angolan province of Cabinda for two months until ransom was paid for his release. Tchibassa faces a maximum penalty of life imprisonment. Sentencing will be before United States Chief Judge Thomas F. Hogan, on January 14, 2004.

In announcing the verdict, United States Attorney Howard noted that, "the jury's verdict demonstrates our continuing commitment to hold responsible those who seek to exploit Americans working or traveling overseas for political advantage. As the President said earlier this week in memory of September 11, we 'will not tire, will not falter, and will not fail in fighting for the safety and security of the American people and a world free from terrorism. We will continue to bring our enemies to justice or bring justice to them.'"

. . . The evidence at trial showed that, shortly after Mr. Swan's capture, letters from the then-president and commander in chief of

FLEC-PM, Jose Tiburcio Zinga Luemba, confirmed that FLEC-PM had seized Mr. Swan and was holding him, and demanded that Chevron meet with FLEC-PM representatives. There followed a month-long series of meetings between a Chevron-PHI team and three FLEC-PM representatives in Kinshasa, Democratic Republic of Congo (then Zaire), at which Tchibassa served as spokesman and lead negotiator for Mr. Swan's captors. FLEC-PM initially demanded a ransom package that included military equipment for 2,000 troops, but ultimately settled for a package limited to indirect humanitarian aid and miscellaneous vehicles and office equipment. When the negotiations temporarily stalled, Tchibassa and his two associates traveled back into the bush of Cabinda, where Mr. Swan was being held in a remote encampment. There, they and Tiburcio Luemba posed for photographs with their captive, which they later gave to the Chevron-PHI negotiators. After the negotiated agreement was finally reached, Mr. Swan was ultimately handed over by Tchibassa and his associates, on December 18, 1990.

. . . The indictment against his three codefendants was unsealed at the start of his trial. It charges former FLEC-PM president Tiburcio Luemba, as well as Tchibassa's two associates in the hostage negotiations: Antonio Bento Bembe, who succeeded Tiburcio Luemba as the president of FLEC-Renovada—the name assumed by FLEC-PM after the Swan incident—and Mauricio Amado Zulu.

United States Attorney Howard and Assistant Director Mason praised the outstanding work of the extraterritorial squad of the FBI's Washington Field Office, particularly Senior Special Agent Edward Montooth and Special Agents John Patarini and Jennifer Snell and former Special Agent Nada Nadim Prouty. They commended the excellent efforts of the many United States Office personnel who assisted in preparing the case for trial, particularly the staff of the United States Attorney's Office's Victim Witness Assistance Unit and Paralegal Specialist Barbara Necastro. Also commended was the work of Assistant United States Attorney Laura A. Ingersoll of the Transnational and Major Crimes Section and Trial Attorney Jennifer E. Levy of the Department of Justice Criminal Division's Counterterrorism Section who investigated and prosecuted the case at trial.

—

Preparing for Sentencing

Barbara Swan began taking a personal leave from her job in August 2003. She planned to go back to work sometime in October once the trial ended; however, when her doctor found a lump during a routine examination, her personal leave turned into medical leave.

The "lump" turned out to be ovarian cancer, requiring a hysterectomy. When she became upset at hearing the news, the doctor asked, "Why are you upset? We're going to get all of that out of there." That increased Barbara's feelings that no one understood.

Michael R. Johnson, MD, a psychiatrist, saw the Swans throughout much of 2003. Johnson wrote a letter to the courts in December 2003, outlining the impact of the trial upon the Swans' mental and physical health. His letter states, "During the period prior to the trial, her [Barbara's] symptoms [of depression] worsened to the point that she became unable to function at work and has had to take extended leave. She subsequently was found to have ovarian cancer that required surgery. It is not unusual for periods of severe stress to lead to the development of serious health problems including cancer and heart disease. I suspect that the stress of the events related to Mr. Swan's captivity contributed to her development of ovarian cancer."

The tumor contained all of the cancer cells and had not spread, and so what could have been a disastrous outcome turned out to be as good as could be expected with this type of cancer.

"They took twenty to thirty biopsies, and there was nothing else there," Brent said. "Everything came back negative."

She did not have to face chemotherapy, but she did have to face writing her impact statement for the sentencing. Both she and Brent spent the holidays of 2003 trying to assess what impact the kidnapping had on them. The prosecution put pressure on the Swans to have it completed by Christmas, along with completing a financial impact statement. They did the best they could, but both remember those holidays as one of the worst.

"It was a horrible year," Barbara said. "On top of trying to recover physically, I was trying to write this statement.

"I had an idea of what I wanted to say, but I was at the point where I'd be up at midnight or two o'clock in the morning on the computer only because it was in my brain, and I couldn't sleep," she continued. "The financial thing required digging up receipts and paperwork.

"It had become our life for so long," she said. "It got to the point where there wasn't a day when this did not come up in discussion somehow."

So many years after the event and so many years of not talking about it finally exploded into the Swans having to deal with it every moment of every day. They did everything the government asked them to do at a great cost to them emotionally, which in turn caused them great financial hardship. Neither of them could work.

Brent was still dealing with his treatment by the prosecutors in Washington and dreading the moment when he would have to return in January.

"Once they're [prosecution] done with you, they're done with you," he said in 2005. "You were a victim, but now you're not."

Brent managed to write an eight-page impact statement to the judge. He begins on page 1 by asking the question, "How would you feel if you were forced to wear a hat with a repaired bullet hole in it? FORCED TO WEAR A DEAD MAN'S HAT." He then wrote out the normal reactions to abnormal situations as outlined by the National Organization for Victim Assistance. He wrote next to the physical reaction of rapid heartbeat, "How could anyone watch a combat soldier fill a bus full of holes with a machine gun then point that gun at your head and not have a rapid heartbeat."

> Brent's Impact Statement
>
> *How has this crime affected me? Physically? Emotionally? Mentally?*
>
> *The least amount of impact would have to be physical. The initial capture consisted of a small cut on the left ankle. During my stay in the jungle, I encountered insect bites from ants, mosquitoes, and bugs unknown. The ankle cut became infected. I was able to treat this but a rash developed from the dressing. Another rash developed on the buttocks—this one stayed with me for months even after release and proper treatment. As with most skin irritations, they lead to an itch, the itch to scratching, and scratching to more irritation. The fungal rash of the buttocks continues to return to this day, and my ankle still itches from time to time.*
>
> *The physical impact appears to be minor as compared to say a missing arm or leg. But it's the physical impact that you don't see that*

is the greatest. A mind does not function without a body to support it. Nor does a body function without a mind to support it.

I set out to prepare this statement with three separate impacts: physical, emotional, and mental. But each has a direct effect on the other. All of which, I had been able to reach an acceptable level of control, but only with, at times, a lot of help. Prior to capture, I always felt I was in complete control. And most certainly in control of my own mind. No one should need help to control their own mind!

In the years since release, it is the emotions and the mind that have control. Most evident of this, with the arrest of Tchibassa and the continuing questioning by the FBI and prosecution. The return of the nightmares. Waking up in the middle of the night only to realize I had been scratching. Scratching hard enough on my legs to cause bleeding and scabs resembling ant bites. Scratching enough to cause the return of skin irritations to the ankle and buttocks. The physical impact returns, brought on, only by the state of mind. I had an acceptable level of control prior to the arrest. The arrest removed me and my wife from anything resembling a normal life.

I spent several months after being released trying to just cope with everyday life. I expected that arrests of this entire group would be made within hours of my release. When this didn't happen, I expected arrests to be made after turning over information to the FBI in January 1991. And again in New Orleans, after talking to prosecutors from Washington DC, as I remember, in February of 1991. I remembered every detail as close as possible for about four or five years. At this point, I gave up on the possibility of arrests ever being made. I had been told in New Orleans that I could not press charges, nor could I drop the charges against FLEC. I told myself that after five years, my case had been dropped into the bottom of a file cabinet to collect dust and cobwebs. I also took into consideration that FLEC had disbanded and regrouped by another name. What I could remember of an indictment being sealed, vanished. I took the assumption that FLEC had been dealt with by some covert military operation. I would never hear anything more about FLEC. I was perfectly content with those thoughts and very slowly continued to forget all the little details of the case.

Then the FBI calls, June 2002, just checking to see if I'm home. Instantly the anger returns.

Then another agent calls from Washington DC. This is starting to become harassment, just making sure you are home. Prosecutors might want to talk to you in the near future. I continue with my life. Plans have been made I don't want to change.

Finally the prosecutor calls from Washington, talks to my wife. An arrest has been made. This comes as a surprise to both of us. The last thing I expected was an arrest after eleven and an half years. I am not home. This hits my wife right away. She starts having trouble dealing with this. I think this is great—time for revenge, time to get even. Time for Justice to be served?

My first trip to Washington went quite well until I'm dropped off at the airport for my return home. I have just spent four to five hours without lunch, being questioned by the Department of Justice. I have been returned to 1990. Physically, I'm at Reagan airport in July 2002. I remember the glass doors closing behind me as I entered the terminal. Next thing I know, I'm in a crowd of people moving toward security. I'm standing still. No boarding pass. Over two hours have gone by. I've missed my flight. What happens next is everything I went through in 1990 and 1991. Physically, mentally, emotionally, I relive 1990. The flood of thoughts and emotions that instantly come back is overwhelming. I dealt with this the best I could and finally succumb to the fact I need help. I slowly start to realize that I can't think, can't concentrate, can't even keep up with day-to-day tasks. Everything you try to do just seems to be a gigantic chore. Why do my feet hurt when I put my shoes on? I can't even keep up with clipping my nails. More than you need to know. I find it too frustrating to get help, to pick up the phone and deal with others is more than I could cope with. Thank you for the Victim Witness Assistance Programs for finding help for my wife and I. The only problem is that Victim Assistance cannot bring back the last thirteen years of my life. I will never return to what I would have had today without the arrest. The thoughts and emotions continue coming even though the trial is over. Is there an end to this? Can't we just finish this? I no longer think this is great, a time for revenge, a time to get even. Time for Justice to be served?

In March of 2004, my Inspection Authorization (IA) renewal comes due. I have been out of work for over a year. The FAA will not allow renewal unless you have worked in aviation for the *previous three consecutive years. I have been working in aviation for twenty-five years, carried my IA for over ten. The loss of it is devastating. Since the arrest, I have slowly, and without realizing it, slid into a depression. A depression deeper than I have ever had to deal with. A depression I cannot deal with on my own. I take the doctor's advice and resort to medication. I hate the thought of having to take drugs. I also hate the thoughts that are overwhelming, incapacitating. I just cannot get FLEC out of my head, and **no one understands what I'm going through.***

JUSTICE

What is Justice?

When I was captured by FLEC, my RIGHTS were taken away from me.

When Tchibassa was arrested, he was given RIGHTS he thought he would never have.

When I was captured by FLEC, I was kept in a smoke-filled hut open to the elements.

Since Tchibassa's arrest, he has been kept in an environmentally controlled building.

When I was captured by FLEC, their doctor couldn't treat a small cut on my ankle.

Since Tchibassa's arrest, what kind of medical care has he received?

When I was captured by FLEC, I was given water with an awful taste, the color of tea, to drink.

Since Tchibassa's arrest, he has been given clean, drinkable water.

Since Tchibassa's arrest, he has been given clean hot water to bathe in.

When I was captured by FLEC, I was given a muddy stream.

When I was captured by FLEC, I was given food to eat that was far less than nutritional.
Since Tchibassa's arrest, he has been given three squares a day.

When I was captured by FLEC, I lost over thirty pounds.
Since Tchibassa's arrest, how much has he gained?

Since Tchibassa's arrest, he has been provided with a toilet to sit on.
When I was captured by FLEC, I had to make my own!

When I was captured by FLEC, I WAS NOT GIVEN A RELEASE DATE TO LOOK FORWARD TO!
Will Tchibassa be given the same?

When I was captured by FLEC, my torture lasted sixty-one days.
Since Tchibassa's arrest, my torture has lasted over ten times as long.

What is Justice?

ANGER

To say that Justice is keeping him from doing this again is simply not enough. He has taken our lives as we should know them, away from me, my wife, and family. I spent sixty-one days in the jungle. Had I been killed on day one, it would have been over. Finished for me, time for my wife, family, and friends to start healing. But no, I had to deal with the threat of death every day. How can I possibly put those feelings into words? How can I tell you what it is like to look death in the eye and think it's my only way out? RELEASE—DEATH—FREEDOM at last. (And then you make me relive this all over again.) I cannot begin to understand how my wife and family dealt with this. For the Justice Department to say that this crime is less violent than murder is injustice by itself. Those who make the laws, those who uphold the laws, those who set the punishment, and those who uphold the punishment DON'T HAVE A CLUE what it's like to be held against their will, in the jungle, on the west coast of Africa.

"No one understands what I'm going through." *I don't expect you to. To understand is to go through it. Just show me Justice. Prove to me that pledging allegiance to the flag of the United States of America for forty-four years can bring Justice for All.*

THE PUNISHMENT

To be forced against your will is worse than murder. Murder carries the Death Penalty. To be punished for something greater than murder is the death penalty sixty-one times, once for each and every day I was kept. For me, I knew I was a Dead Man. So if you can't give me justice than give me an eye for an eye. Place him upon the gallows just outside the courthouse. Let the Chess Men, and all the world, see a guilty terrorist with a hangman's noose around his neck. Let all the terrorists of the world see what the United States of America does to terrorists. We can only fight terrorism by terrorizing terrorists. A public televised good old-fashioned hanging. This is what we do to terrorists. And this is what we do for the victim(s). We give the victims the right to say when the rope comes tight. Would I let him lose thirty pounds over the next sixty-one days? How many days would I make him stand upon the gallows? How many times would I just toy with the rope, let it tug against his neck, let him think, will today be the day I die? How many days of torture does he deserve? Sixty-one days? Maybe I'll double it? Justice is not swift. **It is absolutely imperative for Tchibassa to not know when he will be released. To force him against his will, to not know what tomorrow will bring, this is the true punishment he deserves.**

I would continue to write hundreds of pages of how this has affected me, or how this has changed my life. Each and every reaction deserves three, four, or more pages. I think I've done well to get a few sentences a day. I'm tired of the headaches.

FINANCIAL IMPACT

Is Tchibassa responsible for all of my losses? I am in no way trying to stand up for him. He is a guilty terrorist. He owes me everything he ever had, including his life. But what about the United States—you? When I say you, I mean in broad terms, Department of Justice, FBI, Victim Compensation of Washington,

Victim Compensation of Florida, the system as a whole. You made the decision to arrest him. You had to know it could go to trial. You have to know it is not easy for the victims to have a mess like this thrown right back in our face. I spent eleven and a half years trying to close my mind and let the injuries heal. I have had a very difficult time dealing with all of this, not just the impact on me, but dealing with my wife and family. I have been removed from a profession I have enjoyed for twenty-five years: aviation. I will not go back to it until I am certain that YOU would feel comfortable riding in an aircraft I had been working on! You made the decision to arrest him. Shouldn't you bear the responsibility of returning me to aviation? I want more than anything to get back to where I was, prior to the arrest. No doctors, no drugs, no overwhelming thoughts of FLEC. An acceptable level of control. The financial impact of this began on October 19, 1990, and it will continue the rest of my life. Some relief has come for expenses incurred over the last eighteen months. Most of my specific losses are a direct result of his arrest—expenses just to be at trial, doctor's bills, prescriptions, and the traveling that goes with it, time lost out of work. Why should we have to wait for restitution from his prison wages? Haven't we waited long enough?

What is it about this that if he joins the prison work force he can get out on good behavior? If he had been good in the first place, he wouldn't be in there. Then I hear he only has to do 85 percent of his time. I'm sorry, but do you know how stupid that sounds to me?

What would you think, if I, in my profession, did only 85 percent of putting on that wing?

Barbara's Impact Statement

Barbara managed to get her Impact Statement written through long sleepless nights during the holidays of 2003.

This is by far the most difficult thing I have ever been asked to do. Since October 19, 1990, I have not been able to tell myself how I feel and how these past years and events have affected me. Now I am asked to put them on paper and not only try to explain to strangers but to one of the men who has done this horrible injustice to me and my family. In the past twelve years, we have tried to put this behind us. I will do my best to try to put it all on paper, to try to make others understand.

I will start in 1990 and just give you some ideas of what I was feeling back then.

I'm sure I was in a state of shock after I received the phone call that morning. When I had heard my husband had been "abducted," I did not understand the word. Wasn't that something aliens did? It seemed like it took me forever to collect myself, to make myself call my mother and mother-in-law. I was home by myself at that time, nobody to comfort me or talk to. I can still hear his mother crying over the phone. That was the hardest phone call I've ever had to make. I can remember details of that morning like it was today, not twelve years ago.

The fear for Brent was so intense, the fear of the unknown. Was he even alive???? My God, what has happened here? All these years I thought he was working in a secure place, how wrong I was. The only thing I was told was, "We don't know who did this or where Brent is. We'll call you when we hear more." I was to live with that for a week before we actually had word from Brent himself in letter form that he was at least alive. I was able to verify his handwriting, but what had happened to him since he had written it? Who were these crazy people and what did they want with my husband? Was he hurt? Were they beating him? What was he thinking? Nobody knew.

On a daily basis, I was wondering how I would make it through the day. I knew I had to be strong for Brent and myself. I was severely depressed, so anxious I couldn't think, couldn't sleep, and I drank Maalox by the bottle. I had to take a leave from work. How was I to be nice and smile at customers with this on my mind?

I had a terrible need to be in touch with anyone, felt like I had to be glued to the phone. As long as I was talking to someone, whether it was PHI, family or friends, at least I felt like maybe I was doing something. My mother left her house up north to come stay with me. She knew I couldn't handle this on my own. She ended up staying until June. It was a burden on her and the rest of my family for her to leave her home so quickly and stay so long, but what a great comfort to me.

After it was discovered that FLEC was the responsible party, my anger toward them was overwhelming, especially when they had the nerve to write to me!!! Disbelief that they would be so arrogant, to think they did not have a clue as to what they were doing to our lives.

When I saw the first set of photos that were sent—Brent being taken by gunpoint against his will through marsh and woods. Imagine how frightening it was for me and his family at home, but what about him? We couldn't even begin to guess at the horror and fear he must have been feeling. When I received the cassette tape, I could hear in his voice how depressed he was, sounded so despondent; I feared for his sanity and the fact he kept referring to the New Hampshire license plate slogan, "Live Free or Die." That really scared me. What was I to think? And I felt so helpless; there was nothing I could personally do to help him through this.

I couldn't help but think when he got home how different he might be. How was this going to change him, myself, our relationship, our marriage? Would things ever be the same again? What had we done to deserve this? Fear in all areas of thought was the norm.

1990 to July 2002:

Watching Brent around his "anniversary" date—He was always moody and depressed, very withdrawn, and quiet. Nothing had to be said. We both knew why he was feeling like this. What could be said anyway??? We couldn't change what had happened.

There was always added stress during the holidays as it was the time frame this event happened. Kind of put a damper on our holiday spirit all these years. The memories are always in the back of your mind. Except these past two years, they are right here, right now, consuming our thoughts and actions like never before. We have tried to go through the proper motions to set the holiday mood, but I know my heart was not in it. Things were done because I felt I had to, not because I wanted to.

Whenever the need to discuss this event in those twelve years came up, we referred to it as "the jungle camping trip" or something in a light term we could deal with. We thought we had pretty much put this behind us. We would wonder out loud to each other from time to time, "I wonder if they ever found any of those guys?" and that would be the end of the conversation, not worth dwelling over; it was in the past. Here we were, thinking we done such a great job of putting this behind us and being able to get on with our lives. We never knew how much one phone call could change all that.

We could never discuss this with his parents. They were and still are in complete denial. It's very difficult to deal with when you cannot talk about something so important in your life to your family and loved ones because they are afraid to hear about it again. They know the feelings that it brings back, and we do not have the luxury of denial. We have to face this.

July 2002 to present:

If twelve years ago someone had told me these events would come back to haunt me like they have, I never would have believed them. Now I know when I received the phone call from the FBI that Saturday night eighteen months ago that they had arrested one of those guys, I was right back in 1990. It was like a time warp, still is. I was instantly there again. Brent was out of the state at the time, and I could not get a hold of him, only made things worse. I was in a state of panic, major anxiety, fear for his well-being all over again. When I got hold of him the next day, I had not calmed down any. He had to cut his trip short and come home after a week. I could not handle it. It was like I was experiencing the event again. I knew I couldn't do it over again. One example I can give you is I was walking out my driveway to my mailbox. It's a tree-lined, quiet road, and I enjoy this walk. This one day, which was about a week after they had called, I found myself sitting in the middle of my road, hyperventilating, crying to the point of being hysterical. Happened that quick, no warning, and it took a long time to pull myself together. After that it was not an isolated incident; it happened many times. These feelings are very powerful and overwhelming after all these years.

After Brent got back home and we tried to get back to normal, I would panic and feel fear whenever he left the house, even it he was just going to the store or some quick errand. I would pace until he returned. I was so afraid something would happen to him.

I was having trouble concentrating on my job. I finally had to cut back my workweek to four days. I have worked for this company for fifteen years now. They needed and depended on me, but I could not give them my all as I always have. This has only added to my anxiety. I had to request a leave of absence in the middle of August to handle the stress of the trial. I knew I could not concentrate on work as well. I have yet to go back to work at my previous capacity. I know it will be at least until after the sentencing, and even then I do not know how long it will be. It weighs heavy on my mind.

I had trouble sleeping. I finally had to seek help in getting prescription sleep aid. I have had to seek counseling and am taking prescription drugs to control my anxiety and depression. I understand that it could take a very long time for me to be able to handle these emotions. I can see the need for counseling to continue for some time. How could life get so complicated in such a short period of time??

I find myself being short-tempered and the feeling of being mean to family and friends. This is not my normal personality. I do not like this but cannot help myself. Both my husband and I have to be careful of what we say to each other. My mother, who has lived with us for four years now, also feels the stress. At her age of eighty-two, I can't help but worry what effect this has on her well-being as well. It's impossible to live in the same house with someone and not share the stress of the times you are going through. It's so easy to hurt feelings when you're walking on eggshells, trying to be so careful of what you say—then instantly regret what you say—and trying to understand what each other is going through, thinking, or feeling at any given time. These feelings and stress to our relationship has just been since the last eighteen months. I imagine it will be awhile, if ever, for things to return to normal (whatever that is anymore).

My thoughts and feelings toward the Justice system:
First, from what I have seen and been through, I do not believe the "victim" has any rights. The seat to be in is the defendant's chair. He gets warm meals every day, fresh water to drink, air-conditioning, heat, hot showers, clean sheets to sleep on, medical care way beyond what he probably ever had before, new glasses, and a suit to wear to court. Compared to what I have heard, living conditions were like for him in his own country, he must feel

like royalty and assumes he should be treated as such. Let's put the "victim" life on hold for another six weeks while the defense tries to interview people on what a great guy he is!! Did Brent get any of these accommodations while he was at their mercy? I think not.

My husband and I had thought we had put this horrible portion of our life behind us, then this guy was arrested. Hell, all over again, only worse. Where are the last twelve years of our life we had?? We cannot get them back, and this time around, the feelings are much more intense because they had been put behind us for so many years. I have much anger at the defendant because he still does not have a clue what he has done to our lives, never will. I doubt we will ever be able to put this behind us. I have much anger toward the justice system, every time we get a call from Washington, doesn't matter who or what department, it is a trigger for us. The tears, anger, anxiety, fear, frustration, feelings of not making a difference.

I did not get my time in court during the trial. I was subpoenaed, I was prepped, I had all the facts and reminders thrown back in my face. I wanted to look the defendant in the eye, to have the chance to tell him what he did to me, my family, my life. Yes, I was frightened by the thought of doing so, but I was ready. I was under the impression that the impact statement would allow me that opportunity; now I understand it does not. Another reason to be angry with the justice system. Just where is this "Justice" and who does it benefit? For sure not the victim. Why not just take the word victim out of the dictionary? If I had gained a sense of accomplishment or relief because of the trial, I might feel differently. I have neither of those feelings for either myself or Brent.

Also during this whole process of pretrial and directly after my husband testified, I definitely had the feeling of being used. This feeling has not gone away. If anything, it has intensified. I have always thought of myself as being patriotic. I like flying flags on my property, using my right to vote, thinking I'm an honest, law-abiding citizen. I hate the thought of not feeling like that anymore.

One week in August, just before trial, I was so anxious and overwhelmed. I lost ten pounds in just one week. It is a frightening feeling to not be able to swallow because you are so tense and anxious. To be hungry and not be able to eat, to have to think about swallowing a pill for ten minutes before you can actually do it. I have since lost thirty more pounds. What I used to consider an enjoyable thing—eating a satisfying meal—I have not felt comfortable doing for months now. It is not natural to have eating become such an overwhelming task. I have never known the true meaning of stress before this past year and a half.

There are three more individuals out there the United States is looking to bring to trial. How are we supposed to get on with our lives if we have no idea when the next call will be??? If anything, this whole process has left me with bad feelings about our government and how "everyday" people who just want to get on with their lives are treated. There is certainly room for changes in these areas, and I sure didn't see anyone we were in contact with thinking along those lines.

Several years ago, I had no idea what "Post Traumatic Stress Disorder" was. The word "terrorist" was not a household word. Now I know personally what they both are and their true meaning.

One more point I would like to make here. People in Victim Services tell me I am a victim of this crime. I know I am. No, I was not in the hostage situation in Africa with Brent. However, I was a hostage as well in a different kind of jungle and circumstance. I was not released until I saw for myself he was safe and home with me again. Yet in the past eighteen months there have been many people and departments associated with the court or justice system I have been in contact with, and they seem to forget I exist. I have been going through the same type of emotional turmoil and reliving the horror the same as my husband is. When someone told Brent this is "just for the victim," it upsets both of us because what am I? We get papers in the mail addressed only to Mr. Swan; once again, I'm not included. Once again, I ask, "Where does the Justice for the Victim fit in?

Financial Impact:

I have had to cut my workweek from forty hours to thirty-two hours since the arrest was made in July 2002. In addition to the one-day-a-week pay cut, I have also lost vacation, sick, personal, holiday pay, and yearly bonus over this period of time. I have also had to take a leave of absence. It is very difficult to say when I will be able to handle full-time again, to handle the daily responsibilities I once had a lot of pride in doing for my company.

We paid out of pocket what we had to, to get to the trial. We had airline expenses to take care of my mother who is a dependent living with us who cannot be left alone. We had bills to take care of our animals while we were there, parking expenses, etc. To this date in December 2003, we have yet to see reimbursement for these expenses. Is this a fair burden on the witness or victim? This only makes the frustration level higher, adds more anger and distrust to the justice system.

Between my loss of wages and the fact that my husband has not felt confident to work has only added to the stress of the whole situation.

CHAPTER 16

No Satisfaction

Press Release—U.S. Department of Justice

WASHINGTON, D.C. (February 27, 2004)—Attorney General John Ashcroft, United States Attorney Roscoe Howard, Jr., and Michael A. Mason, Assistant Director in Charge of the FBI's Washington Field Office announced today that Artur Tchibassa, 47, formerly of Angola, was sentenced today before U.S. Chief Judge Thomas F. Hogan to 24 years and 5 months in prison on charges of hostage-taking and conspiracy to commit hostage-taking. Tchibassa was found guilty by a federal jury, on September 12, 2003, in connection with a 1990 incident in which the armed insurrectionist group he helped lead abducted an American citizen and held the American hostage in the Angolan province of Cabinda for two months until ransom was paid for his release.

In imposing the sentence, Judge Hogan noted that the long sentence was the most severe available under the United States Sentencing Guidelines, adding "I hope it serves as notice to others who would harm American citizens abroad."

"There is no greater priority of the Department of Justice than to protect the lives of Americans, here in the United States and abroad," said Attorney General John Ashcroft. "Today's sentence in the Tchibassa case sends a strong and clear message: Those who would target Americans living overseas will face justice in an American court of law and spend time behind bars in an American prison."

The hostage in this case was Brent A. Swan, an American aircraft technician for Petroleum Helicopters, Inc., (PHI), an American company under contract to Cabinda Gulf Oil Company, a unit of Chevron Petroleum Overseas Petroleum, Inc., to provide aircraft transportation services for offshore oil production.

. . . "This case shows our continuing resolve to hold responsible those who seek to exploit Americans working or traveling overseas for political advantage," stated U.S. Attorney Howard. "We will continue to bring our enemies to justice no matter how long it takes."

. . . Tchibassa, who did not testify at trial, spoke at length at the sentencing proceeding, not denying any of the facts presented against him but claiming that his role was only that of a purported "diplomat" and concerned "middleman" who sought nothing more than Mr. Swan's quick and safe release. Chief Judge Hogan rejected those claims, stating that they "ring hollow to the Court" in light of the "overwhelming and complete" evident of Tchibassa's complicity in the scheme to keep Mr. Swan captive while extorting the conditions for his release. In addition to imprisonment, the judge sentenced Tchibassa to five years of supervised release following the prison term, and ordered him to make restitution of $303,954 to the hostage as recompense for the cost of the consequences of his captivity.

. . . They [Ashcroft, Howard, and Mason] commended the excellent efforts of the many United States Attorney's Office personnel who assisted in preparing the case for trial, particularly Yvonne Bryant and Gregory Nelson of the Victim Witness Assistance Unit and Paralegal Specialist Barbara Necastro . . .

The Sentencing Trial

Despite the press release commending Yvonne Bryant's role as victim advocate, the Swans remember being told Yvonne could not attend the sentencing trial.

"She was nowhere around," Barbara said. "And no one else was assigned to us."

Brent remembers thinking that it was just as well because they both felt that Yvonne Bryant only added to their distress during the trial. Even the mention of her name had become one of those triggers for both of the Swans.

During the trial in September 2003, Tchibassa sat at the defense table as Brent testified, but Barbara had yet to face him since she had not been allowed in the courtroom at that time.

"I feel there's a problem in the judicial system," Brent said in 2005. "A victim should not have to face his terrorist or rapist again.

"You shouldn't have to go through that. You shouldn't have to be traumatized in front of a jury just to make a show, which is how I see it," Brent said. "They bring victims into the courtroom to make a show for the jury. There are other ways, and they shouldn't have to go through that additional trauma just to put a criminal behind bars."

But that is how the system works, both during the trial and sentencing phases. So with the impact statements written and the restitution documents filed with the court, Barbara and Brent prepared to go back to Washington for the sentencing trial—which had been postponed from January to February 27, 2004—where both would have the opportunity to give oral impact statements to the judge.

The Honorable Judge Thomas F. Hogan presided over the sentencing phase. Laura Ingersoll and Jennifer Levy represented the government and David Bos represented the defendant. Two interpreters were present. The judge announced that sentencing would be based upon the 1990 guidelines in existence at the time of the crime. Mr. Bos protested reference to Tchibassa in an "aggravating role" since the defense maintained he had been merely a spokesperson for FLEC during negotiations, not the planner or leader in the execution of the kidnap.

Laura Ingersoll addressed the problem with that view of Tchibassa, as shown in the transcript from the sentencing trial.

> *The fundamental mischaracterization that has pervaded the defendant's position on this issue is that he was somehow in the middle, he was somehow caught and trapped and that he wasn't part of, if you will, either team. In fact, he was availing himself of a technique that the Court heard testimony about at trial from some of the negotiators on the Chevron side, and that is that the spokesperson for a side at a—in a hostage situation doesn't want to be the decision maker. He wants to be the one who has to leave and go back and consult with others, so as to put himself in an apparent arm's-length from the final decision as to what the terms of a release will be. That's all this defendant was doing. He was*

playing the role, which he assumed on behalf of FLEC. He was not there as a diplomat, as the Court knows, he had no diplomatic status . . .

He was not there to help Mr. Swan in any regard, except the following: And that is that if their prize pawn was harmed, then they would lose the opportunity, not only to obtain the full ransom that they'd succeeded in extorting for his release, but also the opportunity to credibly engage in negotiations in the future, which they did, for other hostages that they took in the years to follow.

The judge asked Brent to "address the Court with your situation, as brought about by this hostage taking."

Brent managed to say a portion of his prepared statement. He does not remember what he said, but the court transcripts record the following brief statement.

"I don't have very much to say, sir, except I'd like you to know that working within the justice system has been very frustrating. It doesn't mean I wouldn't do it again. Terrorists will not win. I have but four words to say to the terrorists: Live free or die. Thank you."

"We had written down a bunch of stuff to say," he remembered. "But when I got up there—just being in the courtroom—my heart was pounding, I started sweating."

Even though he did not say everything he had written down, he managed to say, "Live free or die." And he was satisfied that he said the words of the New Hampshire license plate to the face of Tchibassa.

Then Brent sat down next his wife. Barbara wanted to speak. She had prepared herself to speak, but when the time came and the reality of sitting just feet away from one of the men who had kidnapped her husband hit her, she could not stand in that courtroom. She just shook her head in response to the judge's question, "Mrs. Swan, would you like to address the court?"

"She was crying so hard," Brent said. "She just couldn't get up. She never got there."

After each side gave statements, the judge addressed Tchibassa and allowed him to make his statement. While he spoke, Jennifer Snell from the FBI moved from the back of the courtroom to sit next to Barbara who continued to cry. She patted Barbara's hand as Tchibassa began talking.

Tchibassa's Statement at his Sentencing Trial

Your Honor, before I begin my allocution, I wish to, first of all, complete a duty I have, it is to ask for Mr. Brent Swan's forgiveness for everything that happened to him in 1990. I wish to do this in my own name, and I also wish to do this on behalf of the Cabindan people.

Your Honor, I know what freedom is, and I have known what freedom is since the age of five years because this is what the Cabindan people have been deprived of. I know what it means to be deprived—for somebody to be deprived of his freedom. I've been in prison now for nineteen months, and I really know what not having freedom is. I'm not in favor of this policy of depriving somebody of their freedom.

Your Honor, before I begin, I would like to tell you that I never participated in any way in the preparations nor in the execution of Mr. Brent Swan's kidnapping, because at that time I was not a part of that movement. And from the very first day when I went to the U.S. Embassy, I explained exactly that.

Your Honor, your honorable Judge, I'm not going to go into justifying here what the others did, but I would like to explain to you the reasons why I felt that I was forced, or that I had the obligation to participate in the negotiations.

From 1977, I came to the understanding that in order to achieve the freedom and independence of the Cabindan people, armed forces were not necessary, that in fact, it could only be achieved diplomatically and through political means, and since that time, I chose to only post my efforts in diplomatic—in the diplomatic and political sphere. I was somebody who was known and I was quite used to being in diplomatic circles, and people were very much aware of my way of operating and of my aspirations for the Cabindan people.

Before I begin to speak about the negotiations themselves, I wish to give you a little bit of background, in order that you can understand what the Cabindan people were facing in the year 1990.

Cabinda used to be under the Portuguese protectorate, and in 1974 it became occupied, politically and militarily, by the Angolans

—

219

in 1974. Cabinda does not have a common frontier—a common border with Portugal. Cabinda has two borders, one with the Democratic Congo Republic and the Congo of Brazzaville. The reason for the occupation by Angola of Cabinda is because of its oil reserves—it is called the Kuwait of Africa. And this oil is being drawn by the Chevron company. There was absolutely no social, school or medical infrastructure in Cabinda in 1990.

In 1990, young Cabindans had only two choices before them: They could either join the occupation forces and fight against their own people, or they could go into the jungle and fight together for the liberty of Cabinda. That war had already caused the death of over one hundred thousand people in Cabinda. Four-fifths of the Cabinda population was living either like that, in the jungle, or in exile as refugees in the neighboring countries. And the youth that you saw in those photographs, Your Honor, are people that either came into the jungle very early on in their lives or were actually born in that jungle.

And just to give you an idea of how important Cabinda is for Angola, Cabinda's resources represented 65 percent of Angola's national—domestic national product. There were 75,000 Cuban troops stationed in Angola and 70,500 in Cabinda. The population had no right even to food and they imposed food restrictions just to make sure that the people would comply with all of the restrictions that were placed upon them. After having explained this panorama to you, Your Honor, I'd like to just tell you what I believed was possible, even after all of this suffering.

In 1986, I did not flinch at being able to sit at a round table with the Angolan authorities in order to discuss the situation with Cabinda, and I did so up until 1989. And all of the ministries, the foreign ministries, the U.S., the European and the Africans, were aware of my role and my position in these situations with the Angolans. This is just to make you aware, Your Honor, that I am not a fanatic, I am a responsible man.

Your Honor, I'd like to now talk about Mr. Brent Swan's case and what I'm going to say is my truth. From the very beginning when I was first informed of Mr. Brent Swan's kidnapping, the first person who called me was my brother Tiburcio. After I spoke with him at length about this issue, I told him that it was a huge mistake because it was going to be a strong blow against the freedom of the Cabindan people. I convinced him, Your Honor, I told him Mr. Brent Swan needs to be freed immediately. And in order to illustrate my belief and actions in getting Mr. Brent Swan freed immediately, I asked my brother, Tiburcio, to avoid using any middlemen. It wasn't easy to convince my brother of this position. I told him, there's a need to go directly to the embassy, to reassure the embassy, to make it possible that there be direct communication between Mr. Brent Swan and his family, Chevron, and the embassy.

This, Your Honor, was my position from the very beginning of Mr. Brent Swan's kidnapping, and I don't believe that a bandit would have had that position. I love the Cabindan people and I love the Cabindan cause, but I didn't want other people to suffer because of the Cabindan problems. There had already been too many innocent victims.

We went to the embassy, Your Honor, we presented ourselves there, and I believe that this gesture was a very strong one. And from the very first day, the embassy did not want to receive the people from FLEC—FLEC-PM—and it was I, Your Honor, I was the one that reassured the American diplomats. I told them that they could verify my background, that I was well-known by the Department of State, that I had already had contacts with American diplomats in Brazzaville, and that I came from FLEC-FAC and that I was new in FLEC-PM. And they checked on this and they informed me forty-eight hours later that what I had said was correct.

Your Honor, we were all convinced that Mr. Brent Swan needed to be freed as soon as possible. My brother, Tiburcio, had given me assurances that this would, in fact, take place. And in order to confirm this conviction, the U.S. diplomat who came here to testify said that in the first eleven days they were certain that Mr. Brent Swan would be freed immediately. But after that, we saw that complications arose. I was able to determine that my brother, Tiburcio, did not really have control over the people on the ground.

We had a meeting with those people at the embassy who were in charge of this matter. We told them that they needed to suspend any negotiations and to allow us to go out into the field. Even though I'm a Cabindan nationalist, I had never been in that part of the country; it was the first time I ever went into the jungle and met with my brother's people.

The photographs that you saw, the photographs that were presented by the prosecution in this case, were the photographs that were taken on that occasion when I first went into the jungle, and this was something that was known by the embassy. It wasn't something that I did in hiding when I went into the jungle.

And when we got to this wild area in the jungle, my brother had a position completely or extremely opposite to mine. This can be explained because he did not have the political or diplomatic viewpoint or exposure that I had as to how to achieve Cabinda freedom. It wasn't easy to convince them to change their position. And this is the work that we did for three days. It took that long in order to demonstrate to them and convince them, that in order to achieve freedom for the Cabindan people, it wasn't going to be done by kidnapping people, and that we didn't need to have Chevron as an enemy, but rather, we needed to have them as our political ally. And we took steps to restructure the movement at that time.

The first day that I was there, I had to deal with all of the officers and all the divergent viewpoints and I knew that telling my brother we'd never be able to reach an agreement. And we set up a provisional structure in order to be able to have a credible partner, and this bore fruit.

When I went back to Kinshasa, the negotiations were not long. If it got more complicated within the first few hours of negotiation, Your Honor, it's because the first team wanted to act as a sort of police negotiator. But with Mr. Anderson's arrival, things went quite rapidly.

Your Honor, at the same time that we were negotiating with Chevron, we were in constant contact with the diplomats at the U.S. Embassy. And their message was quite clear to us: If you want the U.S. to assist the Cabinda people in achieving their freedom, you need to free Mr. Brent Swan immediately, and this advice was taken into account.

Your Honor, had I had the authority to free Mr. Brent Swan, this would have taken place within the very first hour of his captivity. Of course I was the spokesperson, of course I was an expert, but I did not have the power of decision. And all of the witnesses that came here said that Bento was the head of the delegation and that, always, agreement had to be reached with Tiburcio. Of course it was made—it was explained here that I would have to withdraw, but it was an irresponsible attitude because there was a moral responsibility. I needed to be a realist in making sure that the Cabindan cause would go forward, and part of this was achieving Mr. Brent Swan's freedom.

Your Honor, I know that you have heard a lot of testimony, that a lot of proof has been presented here, that you saw the negotiators' reports, but that does not really reflect the spirit of the negotiations as they took place. The atmosphere was quite relaxed. We spoke at length about political considerations that are not at all reflected in their reports. We talked with Mr. Anderson about the future of Cabinda. We spoke about what the U.S. could do to help Cabinda, but at no time did I hear any mention of that here, nor did I see any of that in the reports.

Your Honor, I know that I am not of such a superior intelligence; however, I believe that I am wise enough to know that when we conducted the negotiations, it wasn't a matter of putting down figures and negotiating for Mr. Brent Swan as if he was a piece of merchandise. Mr. Anderson acknowledged here that we acted responsibly and this was also acknowledged by the embassy.

Your Honor, had I not behaved in this fashion, you must realize that I never would have had any access to the embassies of the United States, of European countries, or of the African countries, had I behaved otherwise. I'm not going to cite here the names of all the high level people, that wouldn't serve any purpose. But I'd like for you to know that I was always received very well, either by American diplomats, either those that actually lived in Africa, or those that came from New York or Washington, as well as European diplomats. And I'm sure that if the prosecutors wished to do so, they would be able to verify that my reputation is quite good with all of these people in the different embassies of Europe and the U.S.

Your Honor, the photographs that were presented to you, the recording that was presented to you, these weren't elements that were used in order to convince the embassy that we, in fact, did have Mr. Brent Swan in captivity. It was at the embassy's request that we provided this proof to them.

Your Honor, if Mr. Swan spent so much time in the jungle, it wasn't because we didn't want to free him, but rather that the negotiations were suspended for a certain period of time because the Chevron delegation sometimes needed to go back to work.

Before I conclude, I'd like to say, Your Honor, I am not the person that has been described here. I love Cabinda greatly and I love people to have their freedom. I only had one concern in my mind, that this matter would be resolved and well. But in front of me, I had my brothers that did not have the same level of understanding that I did. I am a friend of the American people. I have always been received quite well in the U.S. diplomatic circles. I am one of the Cabindan diplomats that has always counted on the U.S. in order to obtain Cabindan freedom.

I am well placed to know and state all the things that the U.S. has done directly and indirectly in order to assist the Cabindan people in obtaining their freedom. In this matter here, I did not have absolute power. I was a spokesman, of course, but there were bosses, there were heads that needed to be consulted with and who made the decisions.

I personally wish to thank Mr. Scott from the U.S. Embassy, and Mr. Anderson for their participation in resolving this matter. And in Mr. Anderson's place, I wish to thank him quite respectfully, because during the course of the negotiations, as well as during the time that he testified here, he always remained the same person.

Your Honor, I dare to believe that in a few statements I have been able to give you an outline and made you understand that I am a friend of people's liberties. And I ask Your Honor, as a man respectful of law, that you would take into consideration the circumstances, the ten-year circumstances.

I wish to address the man that you are, who has a heart beating like I do. On June 16, I will be forty-nine years old. I have been married to the same woman for twenty-six years. I have seven children who want to see me with them. In a few moments, Your Honor, you are going to make the decision over my life. You will be alone among men and God. And, Your Honor, I request—I ask you to make the wisest decision possible in my regard, and I hope that you will allow me to continue, one day, with obtaining and working toward the obtainment of freedom for the Cabindan people and to share time with my loved ones.

Finally, I wish to say to you, Your Honor, I wish to give you my sincere thanks for your concerns for my health during the course of my incarceration here. I'd also like to thank and provide my greetings to all of your assistants. Once again, Your Honor, quite simply, thank you."

Artur Tchibassa (in white T-shirt) sits at the table with other FLEC members at one of the base camps where Brent was held hostage.

The Judge's Verdict

Brent said a year later that Tchibassa's words were "comical, sad, and hollow ... and he was going to jail."

The judge concurred. "His position that he was a middleman trying to resolve a difficult situation, seems to be, to be nothing more than this—a shell game as old as the hills, where people have deniability—where they wish to have deniability, who are the front spokesmen and negotiators for terrorists groups. They always take the position, 'I didn't know what our military arm was doing. I wasn't aware of it, and I just tried to help release the fella. And that's why I spent several weeks trying to negotiate a lot of money and products for my people.'"

Judge Hogan did not buy the "innocent negotiator" claim. He referred back to Brent's impact statement and the terror he felt in the jungle and the terror he still feels today.

"He [Brent] has lost his employment, he has become debilitated, unable to work. His wife has gone through the same process of reliving this terror again with this trial, and now with the sentencing, and has also become ill as a result. And they find themselves, Mr. Swan finds himself, unemployed . . . twelve years after his kidnapping . . . where he has life, life as a young man, has essentially been taken away from him."

The judge said he had no choice but to impose the penalty that would give the strongest message possible to terrorists abroad who took U.S. citizens captive. As a result, he decided it appropriate to set sentencing at even the higher range than recommended by Laura Ingersoll. Tchibassa was sentenced to twenty-four years and five months with restitution of $303,000 paid to the Swans out of wages earned by Tchibassa in prison. Any unpaid portion would be attached to his release conditions.

Just before setting the sentence, Judge Hogan said, "It seems to the Court that the sentence is entirely appropriate for the type of actions that occurred here in depriving Mr. Swan not only of his freedom for two months, but basically of his life. He and his wife have never led a normal life again, and it looks like they never will."

CHAPTER 17

Waiting for the Next Call

Motion of protest of the Cabindese Government in exile

From www.cabinda.org—(March 20, 2004) We, the Liberation Front of the State of Cabinda (FLEC) all of the citizens of Cabinda as well as the president of Cabinda in exile; condemn the subjective and unilateral decision of the government of the United States of America for sentencing Mr. Arthur [sic] TCHIBASSA, a combatant for the freedom of Cabinda, to twenty four years and six months of isolation and a fine of $300,000.

We recognize the actions of MR. TCHIBASSA as a legitimate plea for the liberation of the people of Cabinda from Angola. Angola has commenced unsavory alliances with American oil companies such as Gulf, Chevron and Texaco. These companies have managed to systematically plunder our oil reserves while the people of Cabinda, who are the rightful beneficiaries of any profits of oil, live in abject poverty and misery.

If acts of terrorism occur at the oil site of Malongo, which is located twenty kilometers away from the capital Tchiowa or if oil sites are sabotaged off the coast of Cabinda, we cannot be held responsible. If such instances occur, it is the sole responsibility of the government of the United States of America and its biased, unwarranted decision to hold Mr. TCHIBASSA captive.

As a result of the urgent need to continue our objectives, the government of Cabinda will meet during the month of April, most

—

likely the 25th, with all members and sympathizing friends in Paris, France. It is our hope that we establish appropriate and equitable solutions for the unconditional liberation of Mr. Arthur [sic] TCHIBASSA.

Cabinda is not Angola!

Long Live Cabinda!

The Next Call

With one of the four indicted men of FLEC put away in the United States for nearly twenty-five years, Brent and Barbara attempted to go back to their lives. However, they now knew the possibility existed that the next call would bring news of another arrest and another trip to Washington to try to convict. Life did not become any easier.

While Barbara was at work on Friday, June 24, 2005, her mother had gone out to lunch with Barbara's uncle Arthur. Barbara's mother is ambulatory but must carry oxygen with her at all times, and getting her in and out of the house requires the help of at least one person. When the two returned from lunch, Brent was assisting. As they brought her through the door, the phone began to ring, which Brent ignored. He said, "That's what machines are for." Then he heard Yvonne Bryant's voice in his living room. Just the sound of her voice sent him reeling. He turned down the volume and let her message go to tape.

> *"Hi, Mr. and Mrs. Swan, this is Yvonne Bryant from the U.S. Attorney's Office here in Washington DC. Um, I have . . . I'm calling you because I need to give you some information. Uh . . . there's been another arrest made, and I need to, I just wanted to let you know . . . uh, please feel free to give me a call at your earliest convenience."*

She left her number, but Brent had no intention of calling her back. Instead, he left the house and lost track of the next three hours. Brent taped his recollections of that day.

> *"Events that I can remember the afternoon of June 24. In the afternoon about one fifteen [answering machine recorded 12:45*

p.m. as the time], I got a call from Yvonne Bryant, saying they had made another arrest. Then I don't remember until later in the afternoon coming to my senses—my vision was blurry, and I was shivering and trembling. I was curled up on the floor of the barn. I remember making it over to a five-gallon bucket sitting there, crying, wishing I had a phone so I could call 911. [His voice cracks on the tape; later, I asked Barbara why he wanted to call 911, and she said it was because his physical symptoms were scaring him.] *Eventually, I got to my feet and headed for the house with intentions of calling 911. By the time I got to the house, I was angry. I needed to vent that anger. In the past, splitting wood has done this. I went out to the wood pile, and I started splitting heads. I was screaming profanities, and I kept swinging blow after blow. I went through all the FLEC members, lawyers, FBI agents until my wife came home. And after seeing her reaction to the message of making another arrest, I found my machete in the barn, covered in cobwebs, rusty. Went out and cut down an oak tree. And again, my wife said she could hear me screaming profanities. I vented my anger on that oak tree 'til it fell."*

When Barbara pulled into the driveway that afternoon around 4:30 p.m., she saw Brent over by the woodpile, and he was throwing the ax.

"And I knew," she said. "I knew he'd been in touch with a lawyer or someone because it wasn't good."

She asked him what happened, but Brent could not talk; he just shook his head. She asked if someone had died. He led her into the living room and said he was only going to do this once. And he played the taped message from Yvonne for Barbara and her mother.

"For me it was like someone had kicked me right in the stomach," Barbara said about listening to the message. "I don't know how many times I've said over the last couple of years, 'I never know what I'm going to come home to' or the thought has crossed my mind, 'when are they going to call again or when is the next call going to come?'

"As much as you hope it's not going to, it was there," she continued. "Hearing her voice, I was pretty much in hysterics. I said a lot of words I never said in front of my mother before."

Barbara watched from the kitchen window as Brent went after the tree with the machete.

"It scared the crap out of me," she said. "I stepped out onto the steps [of the porch], and I could hear him past where we park the cars, and I could hear him, but I couldn't understand the words."

Finally, she talked him into a walk down their road. When they returned, they called me. At 5:30 p.m. Yvonne called again, leaving a pager number.

Brent and Barbara had no intention of calling Yvonne Bryant back. Brent refers to her as the "government's advocate." They finally decided to call the victim advocate at the Victim Services & Rape Crisis Center in Gainesville.

"She knew right away when she heard," Barbara said. "She asked us if she could be a liaison."

Brent also asked the victim advocate to find out what would happen if he simply refused to testify. She made some calls and the answer "was enough to scare the crap out of us," Brent said.

"If you have a medical or illness that will not allow you to go to a trial, they will certainly take that into consideration," Brent said about the investigation into his question. "However, if you flat out say you don't want to cooperate, they will send federal marshals to your house to physically take you off of your property for questioning wherever they want to take you."

This could not have been worse news for Brent. His feelings of anxiety concerning the government amplified at this time. He felt as if he had become hostage once again.

"OK, so you've been taken hostage initially," he said. "So excuse me, now the government's going to come and do the same thing?"

The Government's Advocate

They asked the victim advocate in Gainesville to e-mail Yvonne to tell her they did not want to talk to her. Since Yvonne was supposedly trained as a victims advocate, they assumed she would understand what a trigger hearing her voice had been for both of them.

Donna Miller is a victim advocate in St. Augustine, Florida. She has worked with the State Attorney's Office for the past decade. She believes that the victims advocate plays a very specific, important role in the healing process, and the triggers heighten the sense and exhaust rationale, Miller said.

"Each time they hear, smell, see something that is a trigger, an acute spike is maintained, and it is difficult to find a new normal," Miller concluded.

The victim advocate in Gainesville did e-mail Yvonne on July 6, telling her the Swans had received her messages, and they would be in touch when they could. She wrote, ". . . but have been reacting to such emotional and physical extremes that they feel unable to respond at the moment."

The intensity of Yvonne's messages after receiving the warning of their state of mind only confirmed Brent's suspicions that Yvonne did not care about them, but only worked for the government. In the tapes of her messages left for the Swans, her words are often slurred, and her speech, hesitant and nervous. The voice on these tapes does anything but offer comfort or calm to a mind troubled with the symptoms of PTSD. In fact, the voice itself triggered severe reactions in Brent.

Minutes after the e-mail was sent from Gainesville to Yvonne, she called the Swans on Wednesday, July 6, and left the following message:

> *"This is Yvonne Bryant. I just wanted to let you know I did call. I got an e-mail from, and uh, in Alachua, and she did e-mail, and she explained to me what's going on. I want to touch now, I want [you] to hear it from us before you heard it in the news that he was arrested in another country [slurring here]. Bembe was arrested in another country, and uh, feel free to call her or if you want to call me, I can explain more but no trial or nothing [sic] like that is happening, you know, and if it happens, it'll be way, way in the future because he was arrested in another country, and there's extradition issues so please feel free to give me a call. I do not want to stress you out. I wanted you to have information, and I know sometimes when you don't have information, you imagine a lot of things. Feel free to call me [gives her phone number here]. If you feel more comfortable calling [the woman in Gainesville] that's fine. She can e-mail me."*

The next day, the Gainesville woman sent another e-mail to Yvonne with questions from the Swans. The questions concerned the current situation and past questions never answered about Tchibassa. They wanted to know where Bembe's arrest was made and by whom and if the United States would push for extradition.

They also wanted questions answered about Tchibassa's appeal. Brent also wanted to know if his property could be returned. And a final question, "Jennifer [Levy] mentioned at one point to the Swans that only two FLEC members were left on the indictment, which leaves one unaccounted for. Is this member dead or permanently detained somewhere?"

Instead of replying through e-mail as requested, Yvonne once again called the Swans on Friday, July 8.

> "Hi, Mr. and Mrs. Swan, this is Yvonne Bryant. I'm calling to answer some of your questions. However, I need to talk to you in person. I can't, we can either talk in person or we can write letters. I can't go through an intermediary like [the woman in Gainesville] so feel free to give me a call. I'd love to answer all your questions. Um. She did e-mail me the questions, and I have some answers for you [big sigh is heard on the tape as she says this]. I can answer a few of them on your voice mail, but we need to, physically, we need to talk or you can call me or I can call back. We can do that. I don't feel comfortable going through [the woman in Gainesville], and I've sent her an e-mail with that because this is confidential information. I'm at [phone number]. It's five fifteen on Friday evening, July 8. Um, you had some questions you wanted to know, and I sent you a letter also. And the letter should answer some of your questions. [Antonio Bento Bembe] was arrested in the Netherlands from your questions. It was Bembe. The Dutch Law Enforcement made the arrest. He was arrested on our charges pursuant to a Dutch arrest warrant, called a provisional arrest warrant. Will we be pursuing him to be uh, uh, to be extradited to this country? And the answer is yes. Please feel free to give me a call, and I'm going to redirect you to me because our office is handling this case. Thank you and have a good weekend, and I'll be here."

Angola and the Oil Connection

Since the mid-1990s, Angola's importance to Chevron and the United States has steadily been on the rise. New discoveries of deep oil fields offshore of Cabinda brought more attention to the area and a deeper need for tighter ties with the nation plagued by civil unrest. When President George W. Bush began forming his coalition of the willing in 2002, Angola became one of the countries successfully courted to support Bush's invasion of Iraq.

A report in *Insight on the News*, published April 29, 2002, sheds some light on the complicated relationship between the Angolan government and outside forces. UNITA—formerly a strong force opposing the Angolan government of MPLA—lost its clout on February 21, 2002, when its leader Jonas Savimbi was killed. *Insight* reported that sources told them Angola's president Jose Eduardo dos Santos ordered the murder of Savimbi "six days before dos Santos's face-to-face meeting in Washington with President George W. Bush, a meeting supposedly intended to encourage reconciliation between the warring factions."

After meeting with dos Santos and the presidents of Mozambique and Botswana, Bush made the following statement: "Today I met with three presidents who can help bring peace and prosperity to southern Africa. The three presidents also discussed the tragic wars in Angola and the Democratic Republic of the Congo. We agreed that peace is within reach of both countries. I urged President dos Santos to move quickly toward achieving a cease-fire in Angola. And we agree that all parties have an obligation to seize this moment to end the war and develop Angola's vast wealth to the benefit of the Angolan people."

Within days, according to *Insight*, Savimbi's second-in-command, Antonio Dembo, was killed by the Angolan Armed Forces (FAA) in Angola. Sanctions brought against UNITA by the U.S. presidencies of Bill Clinton and George W. Bush and the lack of any response to the killings by the U.S. government may have led dos Santos to believe the United States approved of the destruction of UNITA's leadership structure.

It is clear that Chevron and the United States both have an interest in maintaining the status quo within Angola where *Insight* suggests much of the $3.5 billion oil revenues never make it into the coffers of the constantly broke Angolan government. The *Economist* magazine reported in January of 2000, "The bulk of the money bypasses the budget, disappearing straight into the hands of the presidency."

Insight quotes former U.S. Ambassador Paul Hare, now executive director of the U.S.-Angolan Chamber of Commerce, as saying in October of 2001, "It appears the new American administration wants to pursue a policy of active engagement with the Angolan government. The emphasis will be on the practical results and not rhetorical statements. The reasons for this approach are several fold. Angola's present and potential energy resources are becoming more important every day. The oil is plentiful and accessible, and is also the type of crude which the United States needs."

Condoleezza Rice was appointed national security advisor in January of 2001. The same day of her appointment, Rice had to resign as a member of Chevron's board of directors. After several suggestions of conflict of interest, Chevron changed the name of the tanker called the "Condoleezza Rice" in April of 2001. However, Chuck Lewis of the Center for Public Integrity, a think tank in Washington, does not think the tanker renaming is the most important issue. He told *Insight*, "These multibillion-dollar oil interests are active all over the world. So how in the world do you recuse yourself from the interests of a company like Chevron? . . . I don't see any way at all honestly that she can serve as national-security advisor and fully, 100 percent, take herself out of matters that may pertain to Chevron. I think it would virtually be impossible for her to function, in all honesty."

With the threat by UNITA to Angola's current government settled, FLEC loomed as the next threat to the balance created between Angola, Chevron, and the United States. FLEC was taking their case to the international field holding meetings in France and the Netherlands in 2004 and 2005. Despite the denouncing of the sentencing of Tchibassa by the Cabinda-based Web site, the leaders of FLEC, including Antonio Bento Bembe, said little publicly about the arrest. Most likely Bembe knew that an indictment—just like the one used to issue the warrant for Tchibassa's arrest—existed for him.

Bembe's provisional warrant that was used to arrest him in the Netherlands was signed by Condoleezza Rice.

CHAPTER 18

Why Now?

Ibinda.com (Translation from Portuguese to English provided by Internet)

HAIA (June 28, 2005)—The secretary-generality of the Front of Release of the Enclave of Cabinda (FLEC), Blessed Bembe, is withheld in Holland since the passed [sic] Friday, running the risk of being extradited for the United States of America (U.S.A.) had confirmed to the Ibinda.com sources of the movement.

The detention of Blessed Antonio Bembe, that was in Holland with the knowledge of the Dutch authorities, occurred Friday in Haia, of where it [he] was transferred to Roterdao in the beginning of this week.

The operation was efectuada [conducted] by the Interpol, with the participation of the FBI, the order of U.S.A . . .

Blessed Bembe . . . was in Holland to participate in the annual meeting of the UNPO (Organization of the Nations and Peoples Not Represented).

Source of the FLEC, in declaration to the Ibinda, that the secretary-generality of the FLEC was in Haia in "mission of peace," having as objectivo the resolution the conflict in the enclave.

The Case of Antonio Bento Bembe

Subsequent information about Bembe's arrest in the Netherlands did not come to the Swans through the U.S. Justice Department after the last call from Yvonne Bryant in July of 2005. Neither did the Justice Department issue a press release.

The Swans did Internet searches to find out what they could about the possible extradition of Antonio Bembe to the United States to stand trial. Most of what they found came from the Ibinda.com news service out of Portugal or on the Unrepresented Nations and Peoples Organization Web site, both of which presented sympathetic versions leaning toward Bembe and FLEC.

Despite an indictment with his name on it in the United States, Bembe had traveled several times to the Netherlands on an extended visa in 2004 and 2005. News of his travels made it to various publications. Of most interest was the trip he made during the first half of 2004, when the presidents of the two remaining factions of FLEC—N'Zita Henriques Tiago of FLEC-FAC and Bembe of FLEC-Renovada—met and agreed to merge into one group simply called FLEC.

According to a news report on the Netherlands television program *Netwerk* on October 4, 2005, Bembe was arrested on June 28, 2005, at the checkpoint for The Hague outside of the Peace Palace. Making the arrest were two police officers, one of whom was identified by Marino Busdachin, secretary-general of UNPO and witness to the arrest, as an American FBI agent. The *Angola News Digest* reported on July 7 that FLEC reached the conclusion that the arrest was "a kidnapping organized by the FBI aimed at satisfying the demands of the MPLA's Angolan Government."

Ibinda.com states on June 28, 2005, that Bembe was "in Holland with the knowledge of the Dutch authorities" as the president of the Cabinda Forum for Dialogue and as one "[who] always appealed to the negotiations with Angola [for] the end of hostilities in Cabinda."

The Association of the Treaty of Simulanbuco out of Lisbon, Portugal, stated on Ibinda.com on July 2, 2005, a request for the "International Community, especially to Holland and the European Union" to respect the Geneva Convention as well as humanist and Christian principles, in an effort to show support for the release of Bembe.

Brent Swan's name does not appear in any of the reports. One account mentions Bembe as sharing in the abduction of American citizen in 1990.

FLEC declared its support of Bembe publicly and urged the Dutch government to not allow extradition of Bembe to either the United States or Angola, while also asking European nations "to use their political and diplomatic influence to expedite the start of negotiations" between the Forum and the Angolan government, according to a report published online at CountryWatch on July 6, 2005.

While being confined in Holland, Bembe sent a message to Ibinda.com on July 15, 2005, regarding the peace negotiations.

The message states, "Blessed I, son of Cabinda, President of the Forum of the Cabindas to negotiate with the Government of Angola for the peace in Cabinda, this imprisoned moment [sic]. I appeal to all Cabindans [united and conjointly]. We will have to be successful. I am not deceased, I am alive and I will live. The peace is irreversible. Courage to all. God will be connosco [with us]."

FLEC issued a statement in the same release calling Bembe's incarceration as the "intentional detention of the peace."

Where Is the Justice?

Even though Brent recorded his accounts on the events of the day he received the call from Yvonne, he could not listen to it after he made it. During the summer of 2005, both Barbara and Brent worried about each other's personal well-being. When Barbara remembered the day she came home from work after the call in June of 2005 and found Brent chopping down trees, she would only talk about it when Brent was not in the room. Brent also worried about his wife's emotional state and decided he did not want Barbara to know much about Bembe's arrest and subsequent extradition hearings. He said she was not handling things very well.

"I'm not giving Barbara any more information than I have to," Brent said. "I haven't told her that I have decided to help put Bento [Bembe] behind bars."

He did call victim advocate in Gainesville and told her about his decision, but he worried about Barbara's ability to handle the news that Brent would not fight being a witness, despite their psychiatrist's letter to the U.S. Justice Department indicating that testifying could cause further trauma to the already fragile emotions of Brent.

"Barbara has lost another three weeks of work with just the information he had been arrested," he said. "She doesn't understand how I feel that they need punishing."

Barbara and Brent spent the remainder of 2005 afraid to answer their phone and unwilling to speak to the journalists who attempted to contact them from the Netherlands. I fielded all the calls and relayed the messages to Brent. One of the journalists from *Netwerk* television told me that Bembe's lawyer suggested the reporter contact Brent Swan because he would be sympathetic to the cause of peace for Cabinda and Antonio Bembe's plight.

Sympathy was not on Brent's mind.

"Bembe's a terrorist, and there is an indictment," Brent said. "And he needs to come to the United States and face a trial just like any other terrorist."

On September 9, 2005, the Web site of the U.S.-Angola Chamber of Commerce published a press release announcing Bembe's arrest after an article appeared in the Dutch newspaper *NRC-Handelsblad*. The release states that Bembe was in the Netherlands at the "invitation of the Dutch ministry of foreign affairs." It further states the arrest came as a result of "an official request from the U.S. authorities who said he was involved in the kidnapping of an employee of U.S. oil company Chevron in 1990 in Cabinda."

UNPO called Bembe the "African peace negotiator." Brent remembers him as the kidnapper who brought letters to and from the embassy in Kinshasa, Zaire. When Brent saw Bembe's picture in the news stories found on the Internet, he immediately recognized him as "the secretary for FLEC."

"He did a lot of running back and forth," Brent remembered. "He brought a lot of letters into me and took a lot of letters out.

"He was the one who loved bloodshed," he continued. "He heard there was some fighting going on in Cabinda City one day, and he was all excited about it."

At question in the Dutch courts was the jurisdiction of the United States and the actions of Dutch foreign affairs and justice ministries. On September 13, 2005, Bembe's case was discussed in The Hague Court, but no decision was reached, according to UNPO, "As the Court found there were too many questions remained [sic] ambiguous and unanswered."

The court wanted some questions answered regarding the role played by the Dutch Ministry of Foreign Affairs and the authority of the Ministry of Justice. UNPO stated on its Web site on September 14, 2005, "The issue of jurisdiction is put forward as a decisive matter, relating whether there is indeed legal grounds for the extradition since the alleged crime was not committed on Dutch soil, nor is the person arrested of U.S. citizenship. Another fear concerns the sentence that Bembe could be issued if extradited to the U.S."

An initial hearing was held on October 4, 2005, with the Dutch courts still at odds with the response of the Ministry of Foreign Affairs to the role they played in Bembe's visit to the Netherlands. The court also questioned the inconsistencies in the police report. UNPO stated on October 4, 2005, that Judge van Rossum released Bembe until the next hearing, scheduled for early November.

A later report from UNPO claimed Bembe disappeared soon after the October hearing and before the November hearing. The report states, "Police in Holland said this week they had been searching for the prominent campaigner for the independence of Cabinda after he failed to report to them under his bail conditions."

As a result, the court dismissed the "U.S. demand for extradition because the man is presumably no longer within Dutch jurisdiction."

The Swans learned of his escape and the failed extradition request from an Internet search.

Gone Camping

Sometime in February of 2006, Brent left his home in Chiefland. He packed his truck and told Barbara he needed to go into the woods to "yell at the niggers."

Brent Swan is a kind and gentle man who speaks softly. He is sensitive to others around him and for years enjoyed working with the African people of Cabinda. However, one of the symptoms of his PTSD has been a hatred toward those of dark skin color. The word "nigger" is not one he ever used in his life. When he says it now, the contrast between his soft demeanor and his harsh words clash, and the conflict and pain within this man become evident. One time during the summer, Barbara found herself reacting out of fear upon seeing a group of black men when they were out on the river. It surprised her to feel this way, but she knew she was only reacting to the atmosphere of fear that had been created since the last call from Washington.

One day in the summer of 2005, they went for a walk down their secluded country road. Brent's paranoia began asserting itself as they walked, and he cautioned Barbara that they were probably being watched by satellite. They both shot the satellite, the bird. When Brent mentioned the satellite again as they returned to their home, Barbara pulled down her pants in the middle of the road and shot a moon toward the sky where in a few hours the new moon made its appearance known.

Brent said it was difficult to pick up the phone and call someone, and there were so many calls they wanted and needed to make. During 2005, they often wrote letters to elected officials at both the state and federal level, asking for victim assistance. Very few answered the letters. One response came from Senator Mel Martinez on May 24, 2005. The Florida senator informed the Swans, "As for your request for victim/witness assistance, according to the United States Department of Justice, you and your wife have been provided with extensive, personal care since the apprehension of Artur Tchibassa, both as required by law and in recognition of the difficulties you have faced as victims of violent crime."

Barbara and Brent wrote back asking clarification for the "extensive, personal care" mentioned in the letter because all they had received was a referral to a psychiatrist and help to pay the insurance deductible during 2003.

Senator Bill Nelson of Florida wrote the Swans on September 19, 2005, and enclosed a letter from the U.S. Department of Justice, signed by John C. Richter, acting assistant attorney general. His account of the Swans' ordeal and treatment differs greatly from what the Swans experienced and remembered. He also refers to the "extensive, personal care" since the apprehension of Tchibassa. In addition, Richter provides a little background explanation of why it took so long to arrest Tchibassa.

"Investigating, disrupting and prosecuting those responsible for committing terrorist activities are the highest priorities of the Department of Justice. The Department of Justice and the FBI fully investigated this case as soon as Mr. Swan was released from captivity, and as a result of this investigation, an indictment was returned in 1991, charging Arthur Tchibassa and others with hostage taking and conspiracy. The indictment was sealed by the U.S. District Court for the District of Columbia at the request of the government, to help law enforcement authorities develop and pursue apprehension plans in order to effectuate the arrest of Tchibassa in 2002. As I am sure you can appreciate, apprehending a suspect overseas is not a simple task and keeping an indictment sealed allows the Government to pursue the suspect without tipping him off."

The letter acknowledges that the delay in prosecution could possibly mean the victim/witness suffers "emotional turmoil twice—once at the conclusion of their ordeal and a second time, when they must relive that ordeal during the prosecution of the persons responsible for the crimes."

However, Richter states that at the time of Brent's kidnapping, help for victims at both state and federal levels was minimal. He states, "Immediately after Mr. Swan's hostage taking, there may not have been full recognition of his needs as a victim of violent crimes, and thus Mr. and Mrs. Swan may well have felt that their needs were not being addressed."

He further states that at the time of Tchibassa's arrest, recognition of the needs of victims of violent crime had expanded so thoroughly that "Swans received extraordinary care and assistance from the victim-witness assistance unit in the U.S. Attorney's Office in Washington DC." Perhaps that is why Brent refers to Yvonne Bryant as the "government's advocate."

The letter further states that this "victim-witness advocate" continues to "be a resource for the Swans."

The Swans do not view Yvonne Bryant as a "resource," except as a vehicle to drive the Swans right back into full-blown symptoms of PTSD with just the sound of her voice. The letter indicates that Bryant has once "again reached out to the Swans" as a result of Bembe's arrest in the Netherlands.

Richter's concluding statement on the matter scares the Swans the most.

"This care will continue in the wake of the second arrest in this case, which is expected to result in a second trial in the United States."

With elected officials unwilling or unable to do anything to help, the Swans called the United Civil Liberties Union and were told to call someone else because they could not help. They called a lawyer in Washington who told them he had no idea who they should call. They attempted to call and fax the National Organization for Victims Assistance, but they have never had a response.

The Swans want someone to help them financially, legally, and emotionally; but everywhere they turn, they hit walls. The state of Florida says this is a federal issue; the feds say he was a resident of Florida. They are told the statute of limitations has expired on receiving any compensation since it has been so many years since the kidnapping. No one understands that the trauma suffered by the U.S. government has been just as painful as the actual kidnapping itself. As a result, neither can function enough to hold down full-time jobs.

Two days before Brent decided to go into the woods in February of 2006, he had finished reading a draft of *Two Moons in Africa,* which caused the memories to come flooding back along with flashbacks.

He no longer trusted his psychiatrist. After finding out that Bembe had escaped, Brent told the doctor that he knew where Bembe was. Immediately, the doctor sat up and quickly asked Brent, "Where is he?"

Brent felt decidedly uneasy with the response and suspected the doctor was in contact with the U.S. Justice Department. Brent reasoned he had been recommended by Yvonne Bryant. Both Barbara and Brent stopped going to their sessions on a regular basis. Besides the bills kept mounting, and there was no compensation forthcoming.

Brent began remembering little details. When he started doing interviews for the book, he remembered he had actually unlocked the door for his kidnappers that very first morning when the grenade launcher came crashing down on the window. It astounded him that he had actually assisted these men.

Early in 2006, he remembered how the soldiers sanitized the needles for their malaria shots by boiling them in water and reusing and redipping them into the medicine. He became so concerned about the unsanitary way they used the needles; he went to have an AIDS test even though he had not been injected with the needles. Barbara said Brent had become obsessed around this same time with keeping the counters in the kitchen clean, complaining when even a little crumb could be found. Somehow, Barbara felt the two were connected.

The day he went into the woods, he made a bed in the back of his pickup truck and packed his camping dishes and a box of cereal. He did not pack the camp stove. He took every last bit of medication with him from tranquilizers to sleeping pills to blood pressure medicine. He took all of his socks and a few shorts. He drove off after Barbara left for work on a Friday morning. He had some cash, a credit card, and a phone card.

Barbara knew their life was going to change in some significant way as a result of Brent's retreat. She could not determine whether the change would be positive or not. He had never taken off by himself.

—

Brent returned home on Sunday while Barbara was working. Her mother told her he just came in and said hello and grabbed a box and left again. Barbara took a personal day on Monday because she had been very stressed at work the day before.

When Brent came to the house on Sunday, he entered through the back of the property, which upset Barbara. She wanted him to come in the front and not sneak back that way. She went to the hardware store and bought a lock for the back gate so he couldn't drive in.

During the week of Brent's disappearance, Barbara would have periods of anger at her husband. At those times, she removed his Cabinda artifacts from the walls and packed away his clothes. She removed his personal items from the bed stand. While she was at work on Friday, Brent came by the house and went into the bedroom. When Barbara came home, there was a note from Brent on the washing machine. He told her he was going further away and would be in touch when he returned. The following Monday, Brent went to the doctor to get the result of his AIDS test, which came back negative. He came back to Chiefland and his home with a determination to find some help.

Barbara again suffered from medical problems during the spring of 2006, which resulted in the removal of her gallbladder in June. Brent spent a lot of time thinking about how the lives of victims of violent crimes should be treated and how the criminals should be punished.

And they finally found a psychologist—whose office is a three-hour drive from their home—who understands both of their needs and their traumas. Both are willing to drive there to visit this man because he is the only one who listens and knows that trauma such as this does not disappear with the arrest, conviction, and sentencing of the perpetrator. The trauma has left a permanent scar, and no amount of steel prison bars can erase the damage done from days and months of wondering whether a trip to the latrine might be the last act completed before the guns open fire and bring a welcome finish to the life of a hostage.

The ripples from terrorism spread into waves, washing over its victims in an endless cycle of repetition, as daily routines become cause for alarm. Time does not heal in all cases.

Two Moons in Africa represents a lifetime of moons for the Swans.

The End?

—

From Brent
May 11, 2006

As Two Moons in Africa comes closer to publication, the more I wish we could write:
The End.

I never really thought about it, how fitting and powerful just two little words could be. How many times when you finish reading a story and you get to "The End" you lay the book down, completely satisfied that the story had complete closure.

Two Moons in Africa didn't end with two cycles of the moon; it was only the beginning—once a hostage, always a hostage. I was released from FLEC into the hands of the FBI, whose favorite quote is, "We will never forget." Even if they could put the indictment aside on the three others, I will always be a hostage.

I can see where things could have been different. Justice must be swift. If the Justice Department is going to pursue an arrest, then they should do it. Why seal an indictment against four members of the group, none of whom were directly involved in the hostage taking? Why wait for it to be convenient for the U.S. government eleven years later and then only arrest one of them?

And why does our Justice Department have to treat the victims the way that they do? It needs some major changes. Any judge or district attorney can seize and detain any citizen for questioning at any time for any reason they deem fit. Sure doesn't make me feel like a free citizen of the United States.

Why do judges ask the question "Do you swear to tell the truth, the whole truth, and nothing but the truth?" Try answering with a "No." You will be taken hostage and detained with the excuse that you are obstructing justice. What about the exercise of freedom of speech?

Our system of justice needs changing. Trials should not be a live theatrical performance put on for the jury. Punishment guidelines should be expanded, providing opportunity for the victim's input. The victim should have some say in the punishment. In all cases, the victim should be able to walk away feeling that justice was served. Complete closure for the victim should be the ultimate goal in all crimes.

Victims should have more rights than the criminals. Only when that happens, will there be justice, and until that happens, there will be no end.

Barbara and Brent today in their home in Chiefland.

Epilogue

I finished writing the complete manuscript—all eighteen chapters—of *Two Moons in Africa* on Sunday, June 25, 2006. I called Barbara and Brent almost immediately after I typed "The End." Their response did not match my elation at having finished the book. They told me later, for them, there is no end; the story is not complete. *Two Moons in Africa* continues. When I said I finished *Two Moons in Africa*, they could not fathom what that meant for me as a writer, just as I had failed to grasp what those words implied to them.

Three days later, we met at a library in Gainesville. When I pulled into the parking lot, I noticed both of them standing next to their car, smoking cigarettes. In all the time we had spent together, I never saw them smoking. Both their shoulders were hunched over, and they made short jerky movements with their hands as they smoked. I immediately noticed tension filled the air, rather than the smoke from their cigarettes.

We walked over to a bench outside the entrance of the library, and I presented the "finished" book. My hope that the completed manuscript would bring them joy or resolution or both was quickly dashed as Barbara and Brent seemed reluctant to take the manuscript from me.

I brought two copies: one for them and one to mail to the copyright office. I also brought the application for copyright, and we filled it out with all three of our names sharing the copyright designation. While they mailed the manuscript to Washington the next day on June 29, I mailed a couple of manuscripts to publishers and submitted two copies to a contest.

Then we waited. I posted information on the book to my Web site and did interviews throughout 2006. I also promoted the book during book talks and signings for my novel *Tortoise Stew*, published in April 2006.

Nothing much happened until August 2, 2006, when I received a message through my Web site from a Charles Beaudoin, who said he helped get Brent released from captivity. I replied to the message that I would like to talk to him and gave him my telephone number. Charles called me the next day.

He told me he retired from the FBI in 2004 and was now head of security for a major corporation and living on Long Island. He said he never received closure on Brent's case because he was sent home from Angola three weeks after Brent's kidnapping.

Even though he was not there when Brent was released, he told me he had become emotionally attached to the case. He is from New Hampshire so when Brent's first letter came with mention of the New Hampshire license plate, Charles immediately told the others working the case what it meant.

He told me there had been a weird dynamic working for the FBI because they had to pretend they weren't working on the case when in actuality they were. When he returned to the States, he received a letter from William Sessions, head of the FBI at the time, thanking him for his work with "Brent Alvin Swan." The letter hangs in his office to this day. He said that letter was the last individual letter the FBI wrote an agent because of fear of revealing too much about individual agents.

Charles said he still thought about the case and did occasional Internet searches looking for Brent. The most recent search resulted in finding information on *Two Moons in Africa* on my Web site. He indicated he wanted to help tell the story, but first wanted to call a friend still at the FBI to ask about protocol. I wasn't sure what to think. The Swans felt the FBI had done nothing to help with his release and only cared what Chevron did in negotiating with terrorists. At first, I thought I might have to go back and change parts of the book, especially if Charles granted me an interview.

Nearly three weeks passed before I heard from him again.

In the meantime, things happened that made me understand Brent's feeling of always being watched. Taken in isolation these events might be merely a coincidence, but pulled together with the sequence of events that occurred, coincidence is not the right word.

—

Soon after the call with Charles, I received the manuscript and application for copyright in the mail. The copyright office mailed it back with a letter stating the fees for copyright had been raised from $30 to $45 on July 1, 2006, even though the manuscript had a postmark of June 29 on it. The Swans' check was not returned with this package.

Barbara and Brent spent the next several weeks calling the copyright office trying to find out what happened to the check, which had not been cashed. They heard several different versions of what could possibly have happened, but they were told repeatedly the manuscript was not filed. While they still tried to figure out how to resolve the issue, in late August, I received a letter from a publisher asking me to give his company a chance at publishing the manuscript. The letter stated he learned of the book when he noticed the book had been filed for copyright.

On August 25, Charles left a voice message. It seems—"coincidently"—another former FBI agent had called him the week before. Gary Nosener had been the head FBI agent negotiating Brent's release, according to both Charles and Gary Nosener. He said Gary was surprised a book had been written about Brent. Gary also left me a voice mail that same day saying he was eager to speak with me about the book. I called the Swans right away.

Barbara answered the phone, but she was not prepared to hear what I had to tell her. She had just received word that her mother, who lived with the Swans in Florida, had been accepted into an assisted-living facility in New Hampshire. Brent and Barbara had to leave the next day to take her there. They were frantically packing. The news that FBI agents—former or not—wanted to talk to me upset Barbara.

"I have no intention of having anything to do with them or helping them find closure on the case," she said.

Since I also was leaving for Michigan in the next week, I told Barbara I would call the ex-FBI men and see what they had to say, but I would make no commitments. Barbara and I made tentative plans to talk when we both returned to Florida in mid-September.

I called Charles first. He seemed eager to talk to me and help with the book. He said he wanted to see the story told right and provide information on how the FBI assisted with the case. Charles said Gary Nosener was the "best negotiator in the FBI." Charles and I talked about meeting with Gary in Washington DC on my return from Michigan. I told him I would call Gary Nosener next. Charles mentioned he hoped he could talk to Brent. In both conversations with Charles, I mentioned Brent and Barbara suffered from the symptoms of PTSD. I told him Brent most likely would refuse to talk with him.

Next I called Gary Nosener, who told me Brent's case was only the second time the FBI had ever negotiated a hostage release in a foreign country. He said it was a "new territory." I told him Brent had no recollections of the FBI's involvement. I told him about Brent's difficulty with coping especially since the trial of Tchibassa and then the subsequent arrest of Bembe. I knew Gary Nosener would never be a part of this book when he made light of the PTSD as if he couldn't understand why Brent would have problems so long after the case. I mentioned the victims advocate, and he said, "The victim advocates know nothing about the case. They're just there to help."

Gary Nosener said he was present the night Brent was released in Kinshasa, and he flew back to Atlanta with Brent. He remembered that Brent didn't want to leave Africa and was concerned about his job with PHI. Gary Nosener claimed in this phone conversation with me in 2006—sixteen years after the kidnapping—that the FBI was there every second working on his release.

I wrote in my notes after the phone conversation ended, "I found Gary Nosener very defensive and only concerned with the FBI's portrayal."

I told Gary it was Brent's story, not the FBI's. I told him if I needed anything, I would call him. I have never heard back from either of them.

When I returned from Michigan around September 15, 2006, a self-addressed, stamped envelope I sent to Potomac Books in Dulles, Virginia, along with the proposal and query for *Two Moons in Africa* was returned to me with nothing inside the envelope. The return postage for return of the proposal amounted to over $4. The envelope was stamped "empty contents." The original package sent to the publisher also contained a letter of recommendation from Kevin McCarthy, a professor at the University of Florida in Gainesville. Kevin wrote me an e-mail on September 16 telling me his letter had been sent back to him from the Jacksonville Post Office with a note stating the packet had been found in "empty equipment." Kevin was confused, but no more so than I and the Swans.

The copyright was eventually filed, but the original check was never found. The Swans went back to living their lives, never completely whole, never healed. The completed manuscript sat in a file cabinet drawer in my office as the three of us lost our enthusiasm for pursuing publication. The Swans and I occasionally corresponded as we all went through family deaths—Barbara's mother and two of my brothers. Health challenges continued to plague Barbara.

Despite the judge's order for Tchibassa "to make restitution of $303,954 to the hostage as recompense for the cost of the consequences of his captivity," the Swans had only received $1,058 by 2009, five years after the sentencing.

In 2009, I started a blog. In one of my entries, I wrote about the disappointment of knowing a completed manuscript sat unpublished. I mentioned it probably disappointed the Swans more. Within a week of publishing the blog, I received an e-mail from Brent. "Let me know when you have some time to talk." He had read the entry and decided it was time to do something.

When we spoke later the same day, he told me he was ready to publish the book. And he meant it. Within the week, he and Barbara had signed a contract with Xlibris and now those pages sitting in a file cabinet drawer have been dusted off and given life.

Here's to this book giving life back to the Swans as well.

Patricia Camburn Behnke
May 2009
Tallahassee, Florida

SELECT BIBLIOGRAPHY

The following works have been of use in the writing of this book, although it is not an exhaustive record of all sources consulted.

Articles

"Angola's Cabinda has more onshore than offshore oil." *Afrol News* (1 February 2005). http://www.afrol.com/articles/15453

"Cabinda: Politics—Let the People Decide." International Spotlight: Angola. *Washington Post*, 2003.

Eviatar, Daphne. "Africa's oil tycoons." *The Nation*, 12 April 2004, 11.

Lucier, James P. "Chevron Oil and the Savimbi problem." *Insight on the News*, 29 April 2002, 15–19.

Massing, Michael. "Upside down in Angola: Chevron socialists versus Reaganite guerrillas." *The New Republic*, 3 March 1986, 16+.

Nudell, Mayer and Norman Antokol. "The democratic dilemma." *Security Management*, March 1991, 26+.

"Swimming in Oil." International Spotlight: Angola. *Washington Post*, 2003.

Books

Mair, Karl. *Angola: Promises and Lies.* Rivonia, Great Britain: William Waterman Publications, 1996.

Simon, Jeffrey D. *The Terrorist Trap: America's Experience with Terrorism.* Indiana University Press, 1994.

Brochures and Scholarly Papers

"Background Notes: Angola." Bureau of African Affairs, August 2005.

"Background Notes: Angola." United States Department of State, Bureau of Public Affairs, June 1987.

Bender, Jerry. "The Front for the Liberation of the Cabinda Enclave (FLEC)," July 1990.

Collelo, Thomas. "Angola." Library of Congress Studies, 9 September 1990 (data as of February 1989).

"Crisis Abroad—What the State Department Does." U.S. Department of State, Bureau of Consular Affairs, 1986.

McCormick, Shawn. "Angola in Transition: The Cabinda Factor." CSIS Africa Notes. Center for Strategic and International Studies, 1991.

Porto, Joao Games. "Cabinda Notes on a soon-to-be-forgotten war." Institute for Security Studies ISS Paper 77, August 2003.

Wells, Jeremy (Flinders University). "Cabinda and Somaliland—A Comparative Study for Statehood and Independence." African Studies Association of Australasia and the Pacific 2003 Conference Proceedings—Africa on a Global Stage.

Index

N

Nelson, Bill, 240
Netwerk, 236, 238
New Hampshire, 28, 41–42, 60,
    62, 65, 68, 108, 128, 209, 218,
    248–49
New York Times, The, 26, 49, 112
Nhumba, Alfredo, 60, 111
Nosener, Gary, 249–50
NOVA (National Organization for
    Victim Assistance), 134, 201
NRC-Handelsblad, 238
Nzulu, Mauricio, 148, 161

O

Oberhelman, Richard A., 156
Organization of African Unity, 169

P

Patarini, John, 194, 199
Peace Palace, 236
Petroleum Helicopters Inc. (PHI),
    21–22, 24, 29–31, 39, 41–42,
    46, 56–57, 61, 63, 67, 71–72,
    75, 80–83, 85–86, 88, 93, 95,
    109, 122, 126, 129–31, 136,
    141, 143–44, 146–48, 152–55,
    158–59, 162–63, 165–66, 171,
    173, 179–81, 189, 199, 208, 216,
    250
porcupine, 50, 62, 78, 117
Portland Press Herald, 57
Portuguese protectorate, 95, 219
post-traumatic stress disorder
    (PTSD), 13, 16, 147, 157–58,
    168, 182–84, 188, 194, 213, 231,
    239, 241, 250

R

Reagan, Ronald, 43, 69, 171, 203
Red Cross, 92, 95, 144
revictimization, 183, 196
Rice, Condoleezza, 234
Rodrigues, Francisco, 60–61, 106,
    111, 115, 129, 148
Russia, 30, 175

S

Sala, Joe, 167–68
Scott, Gerald, 73, 76–78, 80, 86, 92,
    94, 104, 113–15, 127, 224
Sessions, William, 248
Simon, Jeffrey D., 150
    *Terrorist Trap: America's Experience
    with Terrorism, The*, 150
Snell, Jennifer, 183–84, 193, 199, 218
Snow, Olympia, 84
Sonangol, 30
Soviets, 20, 34, 44, 69, 97, 112, 141,
    178
State Department, 29, 57–58, 65,
    67–70, 81–83, 86, 90, 134, 148,
    170
Stockholm syndrome, 83, 121
Swan, Denise, 27, 29, 41, 71, 85–86,
    90, 94, 145, 147, 152–53, 155,
    208
Swan, Hugh, 21, 29, 41, 71, 73, 85,
    90, 94, 108, 122, 124, 132, 145,
    147, 152, 155
Swan, Melanie, 28–29, 56–57,
    66–69, 81, 83–84, 90–92, 94–96,
    107, 121–25, 131–39, 145–47,
    153, 155–56
Swan, Ross, 11, 57, 90, 137, 153,
    155, 182, 186-87
Symbionese Liberation Army, 82